The Difficult Dialogue

Dedication

"The strongest thing in Ireland is nationalism, I suppose it's the strongest thing in the world; there's millions of men have died for nationalism in various countries, in England, in Russia, in Germany, America, countless millions of people have died, but very few have died for socialism. My experience is that throughout the world men will die for their country but are not prepared to die for an 'ism'."
Liam, veteran Belfast Republican.

The Difficult Dialogue

Marxism and Nationalism

Ronaldo Munck

Zed Books Ltd

The Difficult Dialogue was first published by Zed Books Ltd.,
57 Caledonian Road, London N1 9BU, and 171 First Avenue,
Atlantic Highlands, New Jersey 07716, USA, in 1986.
Edition for India published by Oxford University Press,
Delhi, in 1986.

Cover designed by Andrew Corbett.
Printed in the United Kingdom at The Bath Press, Avon.

British Library Cataloguing in Publication Data

Munck, Ronaldo
  The difficult dialogue: Marxism and
  nationalism.
  1. Nationalism — Developing countries
  2. Nationalism and socialism
  I. Title
  320.5'4'091724   JF60

  ISBN 0-86232-493-9
  ISBN 0-86232-494-7 Pbk

Contents

Acknowledgements

To Robert for his unerringly critical eye, to Lesley for typing instead of painting, and to the comrades who taught me what counts.

Introduction

The national is a phenomenon which colours our every act: the way we speak, eat, think and behave. Nationalism is a form of politics which is also all-pervasive: it motivated Britain's recapture of the Falkland-Malvinas islands, and it motivates the guerrilla fighters of the IRA. Yet Marxism — an ideology which claims to plot a course for the liberation of humankind — has had singular difficulty in understanding nationalism. This book traces the various encounters and conflicts between Marxism and nationalism. We hope it will lay the basis for renewed theoretical debate and a clearer — as against misinformed — political practice.

Historically, the formation of nations, or rather nation-states, was a product of the world-wide expansion of capitalism. Marxist writing has tended to focus on the economic phenomenon of capital accumulation and has neglected the accompanying physical and political consolidation of territory. Its analysis has concentrated exclusively on economics as the sole determinant of social classes, and these classes as the sole engine of human history.

Marxists have been frustrated by the chameleon qualities of nationalism; it takes many different forms, is supported by many different social groups and has very different political effects. It is the driving force behind revolutionary advances in Central America and the cause of socialist dissension in South-east Asia. It has underlain many victories for socialism — from Vietnam to Cuba — and many other retreats from socialism — from the USSR to Algeria. Yet diversity alone cannot explain the difficulty which Marxists have had in understanding nationalism. To be blunt, nationalism has often been in competition with Marxism. Socialist movements have stolen the clothes of nationalism when it suited them, or denounced it when it did not. There is also an element of wilful ignorance in much of the Marxist discourse on nationalism, bred from the arrogance of those who think they know the only true path to salvation. Today, in the era of the crisis of Marxism, we must take a more considered and balanced view of nationalism.

That nationalism is of vital importance today should be self-evident: a cursory survey of world politics is sufficient to alert us to its continued importance. For some, the era of the multinational corporations has banished the nation-state to the dustbin of history. For the working class, nationalism is considered an outmoded ideology of the 19th Century; yet curiously, this is usually a criticism directed by socialists living in a powerful state to those in a small oppressed nation. Taking the argument one step further, we could say that nationalism matters because people die for it, as the quotation at the start of this book argues. This *can* be discounted as the effect of 'false consciousness': misguided proletarians going to die for a cause which is not their own. Yet it would be a curious form of idealism which would allow a Marxist to dismiss a concept for which people are prepared to die. If people are prepared to die 'for their country', then this must be a phenomenon worth investigating. Marxism cannot simply hide behind the banners of rationalism and reject all other causes as simple superstition or irrationalism.

Essentially, Marxism has no theory of nationalism. Referring to the limited attention given to the concepts of the nation-state and nationalism, Tom Bottomore argues that

> Marxists have contributed little in the way of analysis or research into these phenomena, and have indeed tended to ignore or dismiss them as being of minor significance.[1]

Marx and Engels left an incomplete and contradictory legacy on the issue of the national; but Lenin's sustained attention to the right of nations to self-determination cannot be dismissed so lightly. But as with the theory of imperialism, Lenin's contribution has since been frozen into a 'Marxist-Leninist' orthodoxy which contributes little to our understanding of a changing world. Other writers are even more decisive than Bottomore in condemning the record of Marxism on nationalism. According to Nicos Poulantzas,

> we have to recognise that there is no Marxist theory of the nation; and despite the passionate debates that have taken place within the workers' movement, it would be far too evasive to say that Marxism has underestimated the reality of the nation.[2]

There is now a growing tendency to accept that Marxism simply cannot allow for the phenomenon of nationalism. In a similar way, the women's movement has gradually come to the conclusion that Marxism has not only neglected the 'women's question', but that its theories, concepts and practice do not equip it to even begin to understand the issues raised by modern feminism. Arguably, nationalism is another irreducible phenomenon beyond the grasp of Marxism as we know it; we certainly cannot afford to reject this conclusion out of hand. Regis Debray, for example writes that

> Marxists always complain of their inadequate theoretical understanding of the nation. But this 'inadequate theory' is not accidental: the nation resists conceptualization because Marxism has no concept of nature. It has only concepts of what we do not determine — that is, not of what we produce, but of that which produces us.[3]

These questions should guide our analysis of Marxism and nationalism but they should not prejudge our findings. We must look to see how far Bottomore is right, and carefully outline the contribution of Marxism to our understanding of nationalism.

In Chapter 1 we examine the separate and joint contributions of Marx and Engels on nationalism. Much of this analysis centres on the rather questionable distinctions between historic and non-historic nations or, as Marx preferred to say, revolutionary and non-revolutionary nations. Some of Marx's and Engels' more controversial judgements, such as support for the French conquest of Algeria and the USA's invasion of Mexico, are examined in this context. A misplaced faith in the progressive and civilizing role of capitalism in what is now known as the Third World, did not, however, prevent Marx and Engels from developing a principled position on Polish and Irish nationalism.

It could be argued that their positions on Ireland, encapsulated in the phrase "a people which oppresses another, cannot itself be free", represented a decisive break with their earlier work. A few tentative notes by Marx on Russia towards the end of his life indicate that his break with a mechanical evolutionism could have proceeded further. Our conclusion is that although Marx and Engels left a contradictory legacy on the national question, it is one which repays a careful reconsideration today. In this context it is well to remember that Marx and Engels were, above all else, internationalists; we therefore need to reconsider the meaning of their famous statement that 'the working men have no country'.

In Chapter 2 we examine the successors of Marx and Engels in the Second International founded in 1889. As a group, these socialists departed from the principles established by Marx in analysing nationalism. This change of view went with the rise of imperialism and the ambiguous attitude of the Second International towards it. The 'revisionism' of Eduard Bernstein was unequivocally in favour of imperialism and consequently paid little attention to the nationalism of the oppressed. Karl Kautsky took his stand on Marxist 'orthodoxy' and became the established authority on the national question. Kautsky believed that colonialism belonged to the era of mercantilism and was the policy of the old aristocratic state; with the development of industrial capitalism it would assume a less violent, more progressive role. The development of capitalism did not, however, lead to a lessening of national exploitation and Kautsky was ill-equipped to cope with the rise of the colonial revolution. In the imperialist heartlands, inter-imperialist rivalries led eventually to the First World War and the virtual collapse of the Second International into its national components. Perhaps one of the most interesting theories of nationalism developed during this period was that of Otto Bauer. In his survey of Marxism, Kolakowski described Bauer's study of *The Nationality Question and Social Democracy* (1907) as the "best treatise on nationality problems to be found in Marxist literature and one of the most significant products of Marxist theory in general".[4] Though criticized by Lenin for advocating merely a policy of 'cultural autonomy' for the oppressed nations, this work is seminal. The diverse contributions to Ber Borochov and James Connolly are also considered in this chapter.

In Chapter 3 we take up the sustained polemic against nationalism by Rosa

Luxemburg and the 'radical left' (*Linksradikale*) writers Joseph Strasser and Anton Pannekoek. These writers ignored the difference between imperialist and revolutionary wars, between the nationalism of the oppressor and oppressed nations. They equated the 'defence of the fatherland' approach of the chauvinists with the principle of self-determination. They operated on the assumption that the development of capitalism was making nationalism obsolete and that henceforth only the class antagonism between bourgeoisie and proletariat would count. From political positions diametrically opposed to those of the 'revisionists' at home, they came to surprisingly similar negative conclusions on the right of oppressed nations to self-determination. Bukharin for a time supported this line within the Bolshevik party, arguing in 1915 that though they would not support a big power's suppression of a revolt in an oppressed nation, neither would they mobilize the forces of the proletariat on the right of nations to self-determination. This does not mean that Luxemburg and her co-thinkers have nothing to contribute to our understanding of nationalism. Luxemburg began from the correct premise that conditions in Poland had changed considerably since the period when Marx and Engels had supported national independence for that country. Her position on Polish nationalism was to an extent shared by Lenin; but the latter was correct in criticizing her for elevating the Polish case to a theoretical principle.

From the 'opportunism' of the social democrats and the 'ultra-leftism' of the *Linksradikale* opposition, we pass in Chapter 4 to Lenin's fundamental and highly influential views on the right of nations to self-determination. His approach was historical and concrete, rejecting any timeless or abstract theory of nationalism. He stressed contradictions — between the oppressed and oppressor nations, between bourgeois and revolutionary nationalism. His analysis of nationalism was always put in terms of the strategic interests of the working class and thus he always emphasized the relation between nationalism and democracy. Lenin's realism emerges in his support for the 1916 Easter Rising in Ireland against the 'purists' in his own party: "to imagine that social revolution is *conceivable* without revolts by small nations in the colonies and in Europe . . . is to *repudiate social revolution*".[5] In the real class struggle, the national question and many other 'impurities' inevitably play an important role. Lenin's dynamic approach is ignored in Stalin's famous essay *Marxism and the National Question* (1913) where he provides his abstract definition of what a nation is. The principles enunciated in this work became the established orthodoxy on the national question within the international communist movement, and are still quoted favourably today by those totally opposed to everything else Stalin stood for. As well as exploring the relationship between Lenin and Stalin on this issue, we will examine one of Lenin's last political battles, to oppose Stalin's 'Great Russian chauvinism'. As with Marx and Engels, Lenin's legacy on the national question is an incomplete but rich one.

Leninism was internationalized through the Third (or Communist) International; we examine its policy in Chapter 5. It would be quite artificial to draw a rigid boundary between the national and colonial questions; but we confine ourselves here to the issue of nationalism and do not go into the question of imperialism and colonialism in any great detail. The Second Congress of the International in 1920 saw a major debate on the potential of nationalism between Lenin and the Indian delegate M.N. Roy. Our focus here is on the shifting analysis of the relationship between nationalism and socialism from this Congress onwards. According to Bill Warren, the Seventh Congress in 1928 marked a decisive shift and

> the blurring of the distinction between bourgeois-democratic and socialist revolution in Third World countries . . . the loss of any distinction whatever between anti-imperialist and anti-capitalist or socialist struggle . . . .[6]

Though they would not agree with Warren's analysis of imperialism as progressive, the communist parties of the Third World began a process of adaptation towards bourgeois nationalism. We examine the evolution of Comintern policy on Latin America and its relation to the unfolding Chinese revolution. We find Lenin's uncertainties and contradictions being replaced by the frozen hand of 'Marxist-Leninist' orthodoxy. When revolutions did occur, as in China, it was *against* the theories and directives of the Comintern. In time, the once proud Communist International became, more or less, an instrument of Soviet foreign policy. A different form of nationalism from that of the oppressed was here taking its revenge, as it had earlier with the Second International.

With the collapse of the Third International in 1943, our attention shifts in Chapter 6 to the colonial revolutions in the Third World after the Second World War. The new revolutionary wave from Algeria, through Cuba to Vietnam, inevitably brought up the question of nationalism and its relation to socialism. In Africa, it was Amilcar Cabral who went furthest in theorizing on the nature of the national revolutions in that continent. He saw imperialist domination, rather than the class struggle, as the motor of history. The concept of patriotism, which entails a commitment to social change as well as anti-imperialism, was a central theme in his work and practice. This brings home to us the difficulty Marxism has in dealing with concepts such as patriotism and freedom, which appear abstract but which motivate practical revolutionaries. Turning next to Latin America we take Ernesto 'Che' Guevara as the epitome of the revolutionary hero in that continent. The slogan of almost all the 'Guevarist' organizations has been a variant of *Patria o Muerte* (Fatherland or Death), graphically illustrating the central importance of nationalism. Guevara also inspired a radical revision of the orthodox communist appreciation of the 'national bourgeoisie', which we shall critically examine. It was finally Maoism which went furthest in developing what became known as 'Third Worldism'. This posited a struggle between the 'proletarian' or revolutionary nations and the imperialist heartlands. This takes us back to the historic/non-historic nation distinction drawn by Engels and is just as faulty, both theoretically and historically.

The way the states of 'actually existing socialism' have coped with nationalism is examined in Chapter 7. In the *Communist Manifesto*, Marx and Engels had somewhat optimistically commented that

National differences and antagonisms between peoples are daily more and more vanishing . . . The supremacy of the proletariat will cause them to vanish still further.[7]

Engels had declared earlier, at the 1845 Festival of Nations in London to celebrate the establishment of the French Republic, that

The great mass of proletarians are, by their very nature, free from national prejudices . . . Only the proletarians can destroy nationality, only the awakening proletariat can bring about fraternisation between the different nations.[8]

In practice, the socialist revolutions of this century have found it much harder to cope with what is still considered the national 'problem'. The Union of Soviet Socialist Republics was a laboratory for Marxist theories of minority nationalities and Soviet accomplishments are considerable, in spite of the well-known 'problem cases'. Yugoslavia, too, is a country of many nations and the socialist state has forged a unity out of previously warring nationalities. It is interesting that Yugoslav theoretician Edvard Kardelj has developed a theory of nationalism which does not assume that it will die as socialism is born. The most poignant proof of this is the recent round of wars in Indo-China between the nominally internationalist states of China, Vietnam and Kampuchea. These events have raised fundamental questions as to the nature of the post-revolutionary societies and shown the persistence of national phenomena even after the proletarian revolution.

In Chapter 8 we examine some of the contemporary debates in Marxist works on nationalism. Amongst the writers considered will be Tom Nairn for whom

The puzzle of Marxism's 'failure' over nationalism is simple: the problem is so central, so large, and intimately related to other issues that it could not be focused on properly before. History is now helping us move towards a solution.[9]

The interpretation Nairn puts forward links nationalism with economic development: it accompanies human society's passage to modernity as it were. We also examine the relationship between nationalism and development in the work of Ernest Gellner.

A second area on which recent work has focused is the relationship between nation and state. According to some writers, it is correct to talk only about the nation-state, which should be the fundamental category of Marxist analysis. As Breuilly argues, "the modern state both shapes nationalist politics and provides that politics with its major objective, namely possession of the state".[10] In short, the development of the state is central to the formation of nationalism and the two cannot — as often happens — be divorced. The changes which occur when nationalist movements become governments can also be related to the question of state power. Another problem raised by Nairn, along with such diverse writers as Poulantzas, Laclau and Davis, is the tendency to 'reduce' national to class phenomena. Earlier Marxists had been inclined to see national struggles as masks for the 'real' underlying class struggle, or a simple ideological diversion. There is a wide-ranging debate over the relationship between the national and class dimensions, which cannot satisfactorily be dealt with by allowing the first a 'relative autonomy' and leaving it at that.

Finally, by way of conclusion, we turn in Chapter 9 to some of the general problems and issues which arise from our analysis of the relationship between Marxism and nationalism. We first examine the various schematic models which have prevented a full understanding of the national. These include the model of the French Revolution as paradigm of the bourgeois revolution, and the continuing tendency to see the economy as the determinant of all social processes. This leads us into the second area, expressed in the well-worn phrase 'placing politics in command'. Under that rubric we advance a preliminary theory of nationalism based on the analyses of the more perceptive Marxist writers such as Bauer, Borochov and Gramsci. To conclude this chapter we turn to the antithesis of nationalism: internationalism. We consider the prospects for internationalism by looking at the historical experience of the Marxist movements and the transformations of the world economy in recent decades.

Our methodology could appear to be a history of ideas. We certainly do not provide a full structural/historical analysis of nationalism; the very breadth of the subject makes this impossible. However, there are problems with the history-of-ideas approach to which Foucault, amongst others, has alerted us.[11] Its themes are genesis, continuity and totalization; it credits the discourse that it analyses with coherence. Foucault directs us instead to the study of discontinuity and ruptures. Above all, for Foucault, "contradictions are neither appearances to be overcome, nor secret principles to be uncovered . . . ."[12] It should be made clear, too, that we do not use Marxism as an infallible scientific guide to nationalism, a grid through which to read off a simple ideological phenomena. Our concern is simply the relation between the two.

The organizing concepts and definitions used in this study are the following:

People: ethnic group, a socio-cultural unit or community.

Nationality: a community which is also defined historically and by its action in the political field.

Nation: originally derived from the Latin *natio* (breed or race), later understood as the type of political society established by a nationality.

Nation-state: the symbiosis established between a nation and a given state in the era of the bourgeois revolution.

Nationalism: the political movement whereby a given nationality strives to accomplish its nationhood or free itself from domination by another.

National question: denotes the Marxist problematic covering all the above phenomena and their resolution under socialism.

The chapters which follow trace the evolution of the 'national question' in the Marxist discourse, focusing in particular on the relation between national and class struggles, and their relation to the 'question of imperialism', understood in the broadest sense of domination by one nation of another.

Notes

1. Tom Bottomore, 'Sociology' in D. McLellan (ed.) *Marx: The First 100 Years* (Fontana, London, 1983) p.140.

2. Nicos Poulantzas, *State, Power, Socialism* (New Left Books, London, 1980) p.93.

3. Regis Debray, 'Marxism and the National Question', *New Left Review*, No. 105, September/October 1977, p.30.

4. Leszek Kolakowski, *Main Currents of Marxism*, Vol.II (Oxford University Press, 1978) p.255.

5. V.I. Lenin, *Collected Works*, Vol. 22 (Progress Publishers, Moscow, 1964) p.354.

6. Bill Warren, *Imperialism: Pioneer of Capitalism* (New Left Books, London, 1980) p.109.

7. Karl Marx and Frederick Engels, *Collected Works 1845-48*, Vol.6 (Lawrence and Wishart, London, 1976) p.503.

8. Ibid., p.6.

9. Tom Nairn, 'The Modern Janus', *New Left Review*, No. 96, November/December 1975, p.25.

10. John Breuilly, *Nationalism and the State* (Manchester University Press, 1982) p.352.

11. See Michel Foucault, *The Archaeology of Knowledge* (Tavistock, London, 1972).

12. Ibid., p.151.

1. Marx and Engels

Though the founders of Marxism produced only disparate and largely journalistic writings on nationalism, they were always very conscious of it. They were well aware of the impact on politics caused by the division of the world into national states. They never produced a theoretical analysis, because class issues took priority within the explanatory framework of historical materialism. There was no 'scientific revolution' in this area comparable to that brought about by Marx in the critique of political economy. Instead, Engels, who took up the 'specialist areas' of less interest to Marx, such as military matters, revived the Hegelian distinction between 'historic' and 'non-historic' nations. We look below at why these categories were developed and how they prevented the elaboration of a 'Marxist' theory of nationalism.

As is well known, Marx and Engels took a great interest in Ireland, particularly after the mid-1860s, and came to recognize the legitimate aspirations of the revolutionary nationalist movement in that country. In spite of this breakthrough, Marx and Engels left a contradictory legacy on the national question. The stirring internationalist declarations of the *Communist Manifesto* are as relevant today as on the day on which they were written. On the other hand, their writings on India and the 'Third World' generally show a tendency towards Eurocentrism. This chapter then, begins with the revolutions of 1848 and the distinction between the 'progressive' and the 'non-historic' nations. Ireland, and very late in Marx's life, Russia, provide the opportunity for a break in this schema. In the final section we are left to unravel a very tangled legacy.

Non-historic nations

Marx and Engels were fervent supporters of German unification; but this does not make them simple German nationalists. For them, national unification was the principal task of the German revolution; the first of *The Demands of the Communist Party in Germany* was that "the whole of Germany shall be declared a single and indivisible republic".[1] But Engels had earlier stated clearly that "the liberation of Germany cannot . . . take place without the liberation of Poland from German oppression".[2] In 1848 he restated that

9

"Germany will liberate herself to the extent to which she sets free neighbouring nations".[3] Marx too had said in relation to Poland that "the victory of the proletariat over the bourgeoisie is at the same time, the signal of liberation for all oppressed nations".[4] Marx and Engels were equally sympathetic to the ongoing process of national unification in Italy:

> The defeat of the Italians [in 1849] is bitter. No people, apart from the Poles, has been so shamefully oppressed by the superior power of its neighbours, no people has so often and so courageously tried to throw off the yoke oppressing it.[5]

Engels had previously said that the German people

> greet with undivided applause every step forward by the Italian people, and, we hope they will not be missing from the battlefield at the right moment to put an end to Austrian magnificence once and for all.[6]

Here we get a hint that support for nationalist demands was not unconditional, nor was it granted in its own right; rather, it was tied to the big power politics of the period and in particular to the domination of the Austro-Hungarian and Russian empires. We shall see shortly that the founders of Marxism were not above national stereotyping either.

In 1847 Engels wrote of the Swiss people:

> They busied themselves in all piety and propriety with milking the cows, with cheese-making, chastity and yodelling . . . They were poor but pure in heart, stupid but pious and well-pleasing to the Lord, brutal but broad-shouldered and had little brain but plenty of brawn.[7]

This was bad enough, but Engels went on to say that

> It is necessary, urgently necessary, that this last bastion of brutal, primitive Germanism, of barbarism, bigotry, patriarchal simplicity and moral purity, of immobility, of loyalty unto death to the highest bidder, should at last be destroyed.[8]

Two years later, Engels used an article on the Swiss press to return to this theme, writing of its

> most servile bowing and scraping to the repellent narrow-mindedness of a small nation, which in addition to its smallness is split and immeasurably puffed up — a nation of antediluvian Alpine herdsmen, hidebound peasants and disgusting philistines.[9]

The charge of anti-Semitism is not really proven against Marx and Engels, although the latter did write in 1848:

> We observe the victory of the bourgeois over the Austrian imperial monarchy with real satisfaction. We only wish that it may be the really vile, really dirty, really Jewish bourgeois who buy up this venerable empire. Such a repulsive, flogging, paternal, lousy government deserves to be under the heel of a really lousy, unkempt, stinking adversary.[10]

Do all these statements mean that Marx and Engels were prey to racist and chauvinist sentiments? Perhaps; but over and above that they indicate a concept of nations which accepts privilege for the large and centralized over the small and scattered.

For Marx and Engels, neither a common language and traditions nor geographical and historical homogeneity constituted a nation. Rather, a certain level of economic and social development was required, with a priority given to larger units. This principle explains their strenuous opposition to the ceding of the Schleswig and Holstein territories to Denmark in 1848. Engels wrote that

> Whereas in Italy, Posen and Prague the Germans *were fighting against the revolution*, in Schleswig-Holstein they *were supporting it*. The Danish war is the first *revolutionary war* waged by Germany. We therefore *advocated* a resolute conduct of the Danish war from the very beginning . . . . [11]

In short, Germany was 'revolutionary and progressive' compared to the Scandinavian nations because of its higher level of capitalist development. He went on to say that

> By the same right under which France took over Flanders, Lorraine and Alsace . . . by that same right Germany takes over Schleswig: it is the right of civilisation against barbarism, of progress as against stability. [12]

The right of nations to self-determination is here replaced by 'the right of civilisation against barbarism' which was of course later the justification for imperialism. There is undoubtedly an evolutionary strain in Marxism which explains this position which, however, runs counter to the revolutionary essence of Marxism. It must be noted that the international politics of Marx and Engels were determined by the needs of the international proletariat as they saw them. Even while they supported the 'revolutionary war' against Denmark they declared that "this does not denote the slightest kinship with the sea-girt bourgeois beer-garden enthusiasm". [13]

The year 1848 was one of revolution in Europe, and allowed Marx and Engels to become practical revolutionaries. [14] The new ideas of liberalism, democracy, socialism and nationalism burst onto the revolutionary scene simultaneously. The February revolution in Paris detonated a popular uprising in Vienna in March which then spread to Berlin, Prague and Budapest. The great Habsburg Empire seemed on the point of disintegration as the Italians and Hungarians pressed their claims for national independence. This was truly an international revolution, embracing the central and peripheral nations of Europe. Yet within a year it had been defeated and the counter-revolutionary forces were restored. The revolution lasted longest in Italy and in Hungary where the crucial issue of national liberation required the continued mobilization of the masses by otherwise lukewarm moderates. [15] Elsewhere, Slav national aspirations clashed with the 'revolutionary' nations such as the Germans and the Magyars (Hungarians) and the Czech left regarded the Habsburg Empire as a protection against absorption into a national Germany.

In 1848 socialism and the working class played a key role; but they failed to integrate with the democratic aspirations of the national movements. The 1848 revolutions failed *mainly* because the democratic, liberal and socialist forces did not maintain unity. But the split between these elements — including followers of Marx — and the nationalists also played an important negative role.

The intervention of Marx and Engels in the revolutions of 1848 can be traced in the pages of *Neue Rheinische Zeitung*, of which Marx was editor. With the overthrow of absolutism, the formation of strong national states was necessary; the 'great historic nations' of Germany, Poland, Hungary and Italy fulfilled the criteria for viable national states. These peoples had *gained* this right through their previous struggles for unity and independence; there was no absolute right to self-determination. Other, smaller, less dynamic nationalities were deemed 'non-historic' and undeserving of working-class support. Engels wrote of

> These relics of a nation mercilessly trampled under foot in the course of history, as Hegel says, these *residual fragments of peoples* always become fanatical standard-bearers of counter-revolution and remain so until their complete extirpation or loss of their general character, just as their whole existence in general is itself a protest against a great historical revolution. Such, in Scotland are the Gaels, the supporters of the Stuarts from 1640 to 1715.
>
> Such, in France, are the Bretons, the supporters of the Bourbons from 1792 to 1800.
>
> Such, in Spain, are the Basques, the supporters of Don Carlos.
>
> Such, in Austria, are the pan-Slavist *Southern Slavs*, who are nothing but the *residual fragments of peoples* .... [16]

These Southern Slavs — the Czechs, Slovaks, Serbs and Croats — were according to Engels "peoples which have never had a history of their own ... [who] are not viable and will never be able to achieve any kind of independence".[17] This mistaken analysis was to have dire political consequences. As Cummings argues:

> It was not because they were reactionary 'by nature' that the Austrian Slavs tended to remain aloof from the revolutionary movements of 1848: rather did this tendency stem from a belief that neither the Hungarians nor the liberal 'Germans' offered a more attractive alternative.[18]

The Hungarian revolutionary leader Kossuth was quite intolerant of the national minorities, and the 'German' liberals in Austria were little better. That these small nationalities did not turn towards them was not therefore surprising. German opposition towards Czech independence, shared by the *Neue Rheinische Zeitung*, drove Czech nationalism to look towards Russia; Hungarian repression of Croat nationalism, also backed by Marx's paper, led to the Croat army invading revolutionary Vienna in support of the Habsburg monarchy. Thus, unresolved 'national questions' helped to defeat the democratic revolutions of 1848.

The writings of Marx and Engels from this period set down an incorrect framework for future analysis of the national questions. The counter-revolutionary alliances formed by the Scottish and, for that matter, the Irish peoples during the 19th Century were not the result of some national characteristic but of the concrete social, economic and political circumstances of the time. The Basques did ally with Don Carlos, but only to defend their democratic *fueros*, or autonomy rights, against Spanish absolutism. In short, the whole concept of 'national viability' is metaphysical and explains very little. It can lead to statements such as that by Engels who called for the Germans and Hungarians to unite "all these small, stunted and impotent little nations into a single big state", admitting casually that

> Of course, matters of this kind cannot be accomplished without many a tender national blossom being forcibly broken. But in history nothing is achieved without violence and implacable ruthlessness .... [19]

If omelettes cannot be made without breaking eggs, nor can revolutions. The question is what criteria should be used in deciding which eggs/nations/classes should be broken. Marx and Engels were correct in 1848 in saying that oppression and emancipation are historical concepts and not timeless abstractions. Not every nationalist movement is progressive. They went on to argue that the sole fact of national oppression did not make it incumbent on the democratic movement to support the oppressed nationality. To which Rosdolsky responded ironically:

> As though hostility towards national oppression (through which democracy is denied to a given group) did not pertain to the very essence of democracy itself and only applied when special conditions were met![20]

That the founders of Marxism had to borrow their theories directly from Hegel to explain nationalism is proof in itself of their backwardness on this topic. No national group can be condemned to the 'counter-revolutionary' dustbin of history, nor can any democratic force call for their annihilation "by the most determined use of terror", as Engels did.[21] Historical conditioning explains some of these errors but by no means all of them and the editors of the Marx and Engels *Collected Works* are somewhat disingenuous to declare simply that

> This point of view was not final. Later on, substantial corrections were made which took into account the liberation struggles of the oppressed peoples in Europe and in the colonial countries against national enslavement.[22]

The unfortunate categories of historic and non-historic nations were also to frame the writings of Marx and Engels on what is now called the Third World. After the war between Mexico and the United States in 1845-7 which resulted in the annexation of large areas of Mexico, Engels argued that it was in the interests of 'civilization':

> Or is it perhaps unfortunate that splendid California has been taken away from the lazy Mexicans who could not do anything with it? That the energetic Yankees by rapid exploitation of the Californian gold mines ... for the first time really open the Pacific Ocean to civilisation ... ?[23]

For Engels, the development of capitalism took precedence over 'independence' and 'justice' and other 'moral principles'. In 1861, however, Marx could write that

> The contemplated invasion of Mexico by England, France and Spain, is, in my opinion, one of the most monstrous enterprises ever chronicled in the annals of international history.[24]

Though an advance on the earlier position, Marx's articles were bland enough to be used in the British parliament by the opponents of Palmerston's foreign policy. Marx's longstanding hostility towards Napoleon III may have been a factor motivating him to write them.

In 1858 Marx wrote an article on Simon Bolivar, a military leader of the independence struggle and promoter of Latin American unity, for *The New American Encyclopaedia*.[25] Though by this stage Marx had moved on from his earlier position on the national question he still shared Hegel's pessimistic view of Latin America's prospects. His portrayal of Bolivar was unflattering, to say the least, stressing his penchant for pomp and ceremony and his growing personality cult, which prompted Marx to compare him with Napoleon III. Later commentaries such as that by the editors of the Marx and Engels *Collected Works* stress that "his attitude to Bolivar was to a certain extent determined by the fact that the sources he used exaggerated Bolivar's striving for power", admitting that in reality

> Bolivar played an outstanding role in Latin America's struggle for independence . . . [and helped] to establish republican forms of government, and to carry out progressive bourgeois reforms.[26]

It must be said that his sources did however contain material on the role of the various social classes in the independence wars, and Marx hardly carried out a 'Marxist' analysis of this. In fact, Marx could not really 'see' a class struggle in Latin America at all, because he accepted Hegel's judgement of the continent's arbitrary, absurd and irrational character. The Latin American nation did not seem to be a product of an insurgent nationalism but the *ex post facto* construct of the state. Latin American history was reduced to a pale reflection of Europe's — its internal dynamic was beyond Marx's grasp. However, as Arico notes, this is not only the result of Marx's Eurocentrism, but also of the real uniqueness of the continent's history: neither centre nor periphery, the product of a 'passive' revolution in Gramsci's sense and the basically statist character of its national formations.[27] Perhaps not surprisingly, Marx, therefore, saw Bolivar as a pale 'Third World' version of Bonaparte.

Engels also wrote several times on Algeria, showing a certain evolution in his thinking on nationalism and colonialism. In 1848, Engels wrote that "the conquest of Algeria [by France] is an important and fortunate fact for the progress of civilization".[28] While "we may regret that the liberty of the Bedouins of the desert has been destroyed, we must not forget that these same Bedouins were a nation of robbers . . . . "[29] Modern bourgeois civilization was, in short, preferable to the barbarian state of society before conquest. By 1858 Engels had moved towards a much more negative evaluation of French rule:

The Arab and Kabyle tribes, to whom independence is precious and hatred of foreign domination a principle dearer than life itself, have been crushed and broken by the terrible razzias in which dwellings and property are burnt and destroyed, standing crops cut down, and the miserable wretches who remain massacred or subjected to all the horrors of lust and brutality.[30]

Furthermore, Engels stressed the continued resistance against French rule arguing that "their supremacy is perfectly illusory, except on the coast and near the towns. The tribes will assert their independence and detestation of the French regime"[31]. At around the same time, Engels wrote on Burma, exposing the motives behind Britain's annexation of the country, and also on Afghanistan where he detailed the 1840-1 rising of this "brave, hardy and independent race" which succeeded in driving the British invader from their country. Clearly a shift in the Marxist appreciation of nationalism had taken place after 1848.

The Irish break

Changing historical circumstances led Marx and Engels to revise their attitudes on various aspects of the 'nationality problem'. During the Crimean War of 1853-6 they supported the independence demands of the Slav peoples in the Balkans oppressed by the Turkish Empire. When the Russo-Turkish war broke out in 1877 Marx went even further when he sensed that a revolution would follow a Russian defeat:

The crisis is *a new turning point* in European history. Russia . . . has long been standing on the threshold of an upheaval; all the elements of it are prepared . . . This time the revolution begins in the East, hitherto the unbroken bulwark and reserve army of counter-revolution.[32]

He went on to say that "compared with the crises in the East, the *French crisis* is quite a secondary event". As it happens these expectations were not borne out, as the Turkish side won the war; but they show a quite different Marx from the one who thought that France was the revolutionary nation *par excellence* and that nothing worthwhile could come from the barbaric East. To fully understand this shift and all its implications we need to turn our attention to Ireland; here, during the 1860s, Marx and Engels came to revise their attitudes towards the national question.

The 'Irish turn' is clearly indicated by Marx in a letter to Engels in 1867: "Previously I thought Ireland's separation from England impossible. Now I think it inevitable, although after separation there may come *federation*".[33] In spite of the caveat about ultimate federation, Marx and Engels now stood squarely behind the Irish movement for national independence. Their stance was summed up in the simple yet eloquent phrase: "Any nation that oppresses another forges its own chains".[34] That this was not just a position dictated by their foreign policy is made clear by the intervention by Engels at the General Council of the First International when the English representatives proposed bringing the Irish sections under the British Federal Council:

> In a case like that of the Irish, true Internationalism must necessarily be based upon a distinctly national organisation; the Irish, as well as other oppressed nationalities, could enter the Association only as equals with the members of the conquering nation, and under protest against the conquest. The Irish sections, therefore, not only were justified, but even under the necessity to state in the preamble to their rules that the first and most pressing duty, as Irishmen, was to establish their own national independence.[35]

For the workers of a dominant nation to call on those of a dominated nation to 'sink their differences' in a spirit of proletarian internationalism was seen by Engels as a smokescreen for continued domination.

This more sympathetic attitude towards nationalism was expressed forcefully in a letter from Engels to Kautsky in 1882:

> I therefore hold the view that *two* nations in Europe have not only the right but even the duty to be nationalistic before they become internationalistic: the Irish and Poles. They are most internationalistic when they are genuinely nationalistic.[36]

But, is that last sentence just a turn of phrase, or were Marx and Engels now distinguishing between the nationalism of the oppressed and the nationalism of the oppressor? We shall turn to their analysis of Ireland to demonstrate their considerable insight into the dynamic of nationalism and class. At this point we can see how, in relation to Poland, Marx and Engels were beginning to recognize that national demands could also be working-class demands. In 1875, at a meeting to commemorate the Polish uprising of 1863, Marx declared that the programme of the International Working Men's Association (First International) "expresses the reunification of Poland as a working-class political aim".[37] In fact, the First International had been formed at a meeting called in London in 1864 in solidarity with the Polish rebels. Why should the international workers' movement have a special interest in Poland?

> First of all, of course, sympathy for a subjugated people which, with its incessant and heroic struggle against its oppressors, has proven its historic right to national autonomy and self-determination.[38]

Marx went on to mention more pragmatic facts, such as the effect of Polish reunification on the countries which had occupied it by force since 1785: Russia, Prussia and Austria. Essentially though, Marx saw the class struggle in Poland as a prior condition for a resolution of the national question.

To what extent did the renewed Marxist interest in Ireland during the 1860s lead to an adequate analysis of the social and national revolution in that country? There was a glimmer of what today would be called the 'dependency' theory when Engels wrote: "Every time Ireland was about to develop industrially, she was crushed and reconverted into a purely agricultural land".[39] Ireland's domination by Britain led to its role as agricultural and labour reserve for the latter's Industrial Revolution. The land question was crucial but as Marx wrote "it is not merely a simple economic question but at the same time a *national* question, since the landlords there . . . [are] . . . its mortally hated oppressor".[40] Marx had a clear grasp of the relation between these two — land and national questions — and the class struggle:

> In Ireland *the land question* has hitherto been the *exclusive form* of the social question, because it is a question of existence, of *life and death*, for the immense majority of the Irish people, and because it is at the same time inseparable from the *national* question.[41]

If Marx saw how integrated the national and class dimensions of the Irish struggle were, he was also clear about the remedy:

> What the Irish need is:
> 1) Self-government and independence from England.
> 2) An agrarian revolution . . .
> 3) *Protective tariffs against England.*[42]

The Act of Union with Britain had "destroyed all industrial life in Ireland" which was why Marx considered protectionism necessary to encourage national industry. This contrasts with the surprising free-trade optimism which Marx and Engels had earlier shown, and which is in part explained by their hostility towards nationalism.

What were the social forces which would implement this programme of national independence, agrarian reform and industrialization? According to Engels, "From after the establishment of the Union (1800) began the *liberal-national* opposition of the *urban bourgeoisie* . . . . "[43] These "need the peasants; they therefore had to find slogans to attract the peasants". On the other hand "in the *social* field the Land League pursues more revolutionary aims [but] it acts rather tamely in *political* respects and demands only Home Rule".[44] The older resistance of the agrarian societies such as the Ribbonmen was judged by Engels as "*local, isolated*, and can never become a general form of political struggle".[45] As to the more contemporaneous Fenians, Marx wrote that they were "characterised by a socialistic tendency (in a negative sense, directed against the appropriation of the soil) and by being a lower orders movement".[46] In conclusion as Marx wrote in 1870: "the moment the *forced union* between the two countries ends, a social revolution will immediately break out in Ireland, though in outmoded forms".[47] This was because of the still outstanding agrarian tasks of the bourgeois-democratic revolution. Marx and Engels were involved in the practical tasks of solidarity with the Irish national revolution in Britain. But when the Fenians set off an explosion at London's Clerkenwell Prison in 1867 in a bid to free imprisoned comrades, Marx wrote to Engels that this

> was a very stupid thing. The London masses, who have shown great sympathy for Ireland, will be made wild by it and driven into the arms of the government party. One cannot expect the London proletarians to allow themselves to be blown up in honour of the Fenian emissaries. There is always a kind of fatality about such secret, melodramatic sort of conspiracy.[48]

Disapproval of the Irish rebels' methods extended to Ireland as well, as testified by Engels' comment in 1882 that

> The 'heroic dead' in Phoenix Park [the killing of British Chief Secretary Lord Cavendish and his Under Secretary in Dublin] appears if not as pure stupidity, then at least as pure Bakuninist, bragging, purposeless *propagande pour le fait*.[49]

It is sometimes suggested that Marx and Engels were only interested in Ireland because of its impact on the *English* class struggle and not in its own right. Marx was certainly deeply concerned about the divisions within the English labour movement:

> Every industrial and commercial centre in England now possesses a working class *divided* into two *hostile* camps, English proletarians and Irish proletarians. The ordinary English worker hates the Irish worker as a competitor who lowers his standard of life. In relation to the Irish worker he feels himself a member of the ruling nation . . . .[50]

He believed that the English working class could "never do anything decisive" in its own country until it broke with the policy of its ruling class on Ireland. For them "the national emancipation of Ireland is no question of abstract justice or humanitarian sentiment, but *the first condition of their own social emancipation*".[51] Marx believed that the English aristocracy maintained its social domination at home through its domination of the Irish nation. As he wrote to his daughter Laura in 1870, "to accelerate the social revolution in Europe, you mush push on the catastrophe of official England. To do so, you must attack her in Ireland. That's her weakest point. Ireland lost, the British Empire is gone and the class war in England till now somnolent and chronic, will assume acute forms".[52] These are his thoughts when he tells his daughter that in his support of the Irish struggle he was "not only acted upon by feelings of humanity. There is something besides".[53] In short, Ireland was analysed in terms of the European and British revolution, but it is well to remember that Marx says he was motivated not *only* by humanity.

Finally, what was the overall significance of the 'Irish turn' we have analysed in the context of the Marx-Engels attitude on the national question? For Georges Haupt,

> Though the Irish problem leads to a definition of the principled position on the relation between dominant and oppressed nations and allows the national movement to be assigned new functions, the refusal to generalize, to integrate the national dynamic without reservations within the theory of revolution remains manifest.[54]

In other words, this was not a turning point but an adaptation to a new situation, which necessitated a strategic alliance between the national movement and the workers' movement, without blurring the lines between them. Jose Arico articulates another position, arguing that Ireland represents

> a real turning point in Marx's thought which opens up a new perspective in the

analysis of the difficult problem of the relations between class struggle and national struggle, that real *punctum dolens* [sore point] in the whole history of the socialist movement.[55]

The Eurocentric Marx of the *Communist Manifesto* who praised the objectively progressive effects of capitalist expansion is subjected to deeply contradictory influences when studying Ireland. Though the turning point is decisive the break is still not complete, and the national movement is supported mainly in so far as national divisions disrupt the labour movement of the dominant country. But from now on there is not a monolithic Marx and, although his sanguine hopes for the Irish revolution did not materialize, he deepened his break with evolutionism in his later analysis of Russia. Perhaps the most enduring aspect of Marx's writing on Ireland is the three point programme cited above ("what Ireland needs") which would still apply to most Third World dependent nations.

Marx had written in *Capital* that "the country that is more developed industrially only shows, to the less developed, the image of its own future".[56] In this evolutionist image, one country will simply 'follow the leader' in a succession of mechanical stages. This unilinear conception was modified when Marx turned his attention to Russia in the 1870s. The suppression of the Paris Commune in 1871 and the collapse of the First International the following year left him more prepared to see a revolutionary potential in the East. Referring to the applicability of *Capital* to Russia, Marx condemned those who

metamorphose my historical sketch into an historico-philosophic theory of the general path which every people is fated to tread, whatever the historical circumstances in which it finds itself . . . .[57]

In the French edition of *Capital* (1875), Marx rewrote the passage on primitive accumulation to refer only to Western Europe. By implication, national particularities in the East could dictate another form of revolutionary development. The crucial issue in the debate between Russian revolutionaries was over the possible role of the village commune (*mir*); specifically, whether its communal nature would allow a direct transition to socialism, thus 'skipping' the capitalist stage. To resolve the dispute Marx's advice was sought.

Marx wrote to one of his Russian correspondents, Vera Zasulich, that the 'historical inevitability' of primitive accumulation as described in *Capital* was *expressly* limited to Western Europe.[58] Though *Capital* did not in his view assign reasons for or against the commune, after considerable research he had decided that "this community is the mainspring of Russia's social regeneration".[59] Less cryptic was an earlier letter which concluded:

If Russia continues to pursue the path she has followed since 1861 [i.e. towards capitalism], she will lose the finest chance ever offered by history to a people and undergo all the fatal vicissitudes of the capitalist regime.[60]

This seems quite conclusive: there is no iron law of development stages applicable to all nations equally. Engels developed this analysis when he wrote to Vera Zasulich after Marx's death in 1883. He saw in Russia a society

> where every stage of social development is represented, from the primitive commune to modern large-scale industry and high finance, and where all these contradictions are violently held in check by an unexampled despotism . . . .[61]

H e thought that revolution could break out 'any day' and given the tremendous contradictions that existed that "this [was] one of the exceptional cases where it [was] possible for a handful of people to *make* a revolution",[62] although they would find it hard to maintain power. In this remarkable analysis we have something very similar to Trotsky's theory of combined and uneven development. There is also an uncanny hint of Lenin's great worry that the Russian revolution would be easier to make than consolidate. As Shanin has quite correctly noted,

> The issue of the Russian peasant commune was used by Marx . . . as a major way to approach a set of fundamental problems, new to his generation, but which would be nowadays easily recognised as those of 'developing societies' — be it 'modernisation', 'dependency' or the 'combined and uneven' spread of global capitalism and its specifically 'peripheral' expression.[63]

The 'Irish turn' was being consolidated as Marx, in the last decade of his life, moved into as yet uncharted territory. Rejecting his earlier vision of an irresistible march of 'progress', he could perhaps better conceive of nationalism as the product of uneven capitalist development. It would seem that Engels was less prepared to go down this road and that he maintained a much more evolutionist vision of historical materialism. He did, however, have an angry exchange of letters in 1882 with Karl Kautsky, the 'Pope of socialism' in the new Second International, over the latter's indulgent attitude towards colonialism. Kautsky had suggested that the ownership of India by the English proletariat would be beneficial to both, because the latter would prevent it from falling into despotism and lead it to socialism. Engels replied that the Indian revolution "would not pass off without all sorts of destruction" but "a proletariat in process of self-emancipation cannot conduct any colonial wars".[64] He concluded:

> One thing alone is certain: the victorious proletariat can force no blessings of any kind upon any foreign nation without undermining its own victory by so doing.[65]

Engels was here perfectly consistent with his phrase of 1847 directed against Prussian involvement in the partition of Poland: "A nation cannot become free and at the same time continue to oppress other nations".[66]

A contradictory legacy

Nationalism was not a central interest for Marx and Engels; rather it was marginal and peripheral to their main concerns. The concepts of nation, nationality and nationalism were employed according to their current usage by Marx and Engels and were not the subject of a 'theoretical revolution'. According to Bloom, Marx believed "that nation was a complex product and function of environmental, economic, historical, and other influences", from which followed the conclusion that "nationality was an objective condition, not a subjective preference".[67] As to nationalism, this was a very fluid concept in the Marxist discourse: exaltation of the 'fatherland', worship of the state or simply attachment to one's homeland. Above all, the category of class was accorded absolute primacy in understanding the evolution of capitalist society. The nation was seen as transient and its development dependent on the level of economic and social progress achieved. More precisely, the internal structure of a nation was seen to depend on the level of development of the productive forces and the social division of labour. The modern nation-state was seen as a product of the rise of the bourgeoisie and, as we shall see, fated to disappear when this class was overthrown. Hobsbawm sums up well the attitude of Marx and Engels on the national question:

> They may be criticised for underestimating the political force of nationalism in their century, and for failing to provide an adequate analysis of this phenomenon, but not for political or theoretical inconsistency. They were not in favour of nations as such, and still less in favour of self-determination for any or all nationalities as such.[68]

In their general analysis of the national question, Marx and Engels turned to Hegel's distinction between the 'historic' and the 'historyless' peoples. There was an element of metaphor in this and Marx perferred the more political categories of 'revolutionary' and 'non-revolutionary' nations. Still, these categories, which were employed by Engels right up to his death in 1895, cannot be said to form the basis of a Marxist analysis of the national question. Essentially, these categories reflect a form of Social Darwinism — a survival of the fittest peoples with the losers being condemned to oblivion. Certainly, Engels later revised his 1848 condemnation of the Slavs and agreed that they could redeem themselves if they entered the flow of history. But the whole principle underlying this is a metaphysical one and is far from meeting Marx's and Engels' own insistence on a *class* perspective. Haupt and Weil argue, however, that we should grasp the precise political sense in which these categories were used by Marx and Engels, stressing that the ambiguous notion of 'historyless peoples' was only used in a limited sense and always in association with the well defined concepts of national oppression and emancipation.[69] This points to the great advance made by Marx and Engels over their liberal and democratic contemporaries: to found a historically determined concept of national oppression. Certainly, human sympathy was not a *political* criterion on which to base the support of the labour movement for the small nations seeking political independence.

Before the 1848 revolutions, Marx and Engels shared the general democratic sympathy towards the small nations of Europe. Faced with the full complexity of nationalism in 1848 they moved towards a more realist assessment based on the international conjuncture. It even meant that they revised firmly held opinions, for example on Poland, where earlier they had fervently supported the movement for national unification. In 1851, Engels wrote to Marx that

> The Poles are *une nation foutue* . . . [their] . . . sole contribution to history has been to indulge in foolish pranks at once valiant and provocative. Nor can a single moment be cited when Poland, even if only in comparison with Russia, has successfully represented progress or done anything of historical significance.[70]

As we saw above, this verdict was reversed in later years when the international situation had changed once again. The point is not that of inconsistency but that Engels could have such an unstable point of reference from which to draw conclusions based on fluctuating relations between the European nation states, and the dubious distinctions between progress and backwardness, viable and non-viable peoples. The priority of class analysis led Engels to rather peremptory statements, such as "among all the pan-Slavists, nationality, i.e. an imaginary common Slav nationality, *takes precedence over the revolution*".[71] Marx and Engels condemned Pan-Slavism much too rapidly (Bakunin held a more sympathetic position on this); and anyway, who is to judge whether an 'imaginary nationality' is more or less important than 'the revolution'? The messianic faith in the 'international revolution' reached its peak in 1848 when Germans, Poles and Magyars were identified as the only revolutionary 'bearers of progress' amongst the Austrian nations and nationalities:

> The chief mission of all the other great and small nationalities and peoples is to perish in the universal revolutionary storm. They are therefore now counter-revolutionary.[72]

This could hardly help to mobilize the oppressed nationalities behind the democratic camp.

To leave things at this would be incorrect because Marx and Engels did develop their thinking on the national question after 1848. Ireland in the 1860s and Russia in the 1870s led to a qualitative break with the earlier outlook. Now an explicit recognition of the distinction between oppressed and oppressor nations coexisted uneasily with the earlier historic/non-historic division. The evolutionism which saw England as the future of India, even while England was exploiting India, was now threatened, if not displaced, by a recognition of a multiplicity of paths to social transformation. The national question was still not an object of enquiry in its own right; Marx did not really recognize the 'relative autonomy' of the national domain. Davis stretches the facts when he writes of Marx and Engels "taking the part of oppressed nationalities *as such*, not merely when their political actions had a revolutionary character".[73] But Ireland led Marx to recognize the real weight of the nationalist movement and the need for labour to articulate its progressive aspects. The Polish case demonstrated, according to Marx, how democracy was the only way to achieve national independence. The Cracow rising of 1846 shared the unity of the national and democratic causes. In short, Ireland and Poland led Marx and Engels to recognize the interdependence between the national and the social in the bourgeois-democratic revolution. In these countries the basic democratic task — agrarian reform — was impossible without national independence. National demands were still not seen as democratic in their own right; but their fulfilment was now seen as a prerequisite for social democracy. The social revolution could only advance once the national question was settled.

Where Marx's thought evolved most was in relation to 'progress', once unambiguously hitched to the capitalist bandwagon. It is well known how in his 1850s articles on India, Marx was lavish in his praise of British accomplishments.[74] The British army, the electric telegraph, the free press and steam were all part of a progressive transformation of a traditional society. Even so, Marx was quite dialectical, recognizing that the destructive role of British imperialism was proceeding faster than its regenerating side. The Indian people would not reap the fruit of capitalist modernization until they overthrew the English yoke. Around the same time Marx became very interested in Spain, particularly in how the national liberation movement there combined the spirit of political and social regeneration with the spirit of reaction:

> All the wars of independence waged against France bear in common the stamp of regeneration, mixed up with reaction; but nowhere to such a degree as in Spain.[75]

Far from reducing national particularities to their economic base, Marx shows in these writings a marked sensitivity to the effects of uneven and combined development in Spanish society. Marx is here operating not with an overall schema but with a flexible methodology which recognizes the role of tradition, culture, institutions and even religious elements. In short, Marx's writings on Spain show him capable of a "concrete analysis of a concrete situation", which fully accepts the importance of the national question and understands why it may combine reactionary and progressive elements.

Let us now turn to the issue of Marx and internationalism. Is it true, as some authors maintain, that behind their internationalist rhetoric Marx and Engels displayed the unmistakable traits of German chauvinism? On the contrary, the internationalism of the *Communist Manifesto* was never repudiated by Marx and Engels. For millions of people the *Manifesto is* Marxism, so its perspective on the national question is in a sense more important that the dispersed post-1848 writings we have considered in the pages above.

The internationalist phrases of the *Manifesto* are so familiar that their true significance sometimes eludes us:

> National differences and antagonism between peoples are daily more and more vanishing, owing to the development of the bourgeoisie, to freedom of commerce, to the world market, to uniformity in the mode of production and in the conditions of life corresponding thereto.[76]
>
> In the national struggles of the proletarians of the different countries, they point out and bring to the front the common interests of the whole proletariat, independently of all nationality.[77]

Marx and Engels are first of all saying that national differences tend to disappear as the universalizing effects of capitalism take effect. The bourgeoisie, with its exploitation of the world market, is said to give production a cosmopolitan character, and this "has drawn from under the feet of industry the national ground on which it stood".[78] Production has been internationalized; but even today's transnational corporations have not done away with the nation-state. Capitalism has *not* spread uniformly throughout the globe: the development of imperialism is only hinted at by Marx. The other side of the *Manifesto* is its sanguine hopes for international proletarian solidarity. Clearly, "national one-sidedness and narrow mindedness" have not disappeared. Engels' comment at the 1845 Festival of Nations in London that "the great mass of proletarians are, by their very nature, free from national prejudices and their whole disposition and movement is essentially humanitarian, anti-nationalist",[79] seems hopelessly naive.

The *Manifesto* is of course a call to arms, and that is how it must be assessed. The key phrases in the *Manifesto* on the national strategy of the proletariat are as follows:

> The Communists are further reproached with desiring to abolish countries and nationality.
> The working men have no country. We cannot take from them what they have not got. Since the proletariat must first of all acquire political supremacy, must rise to be the leading class of the nation, must constitute itself *the* nation, it is, so far, itself national, though not in the bourgeois sense of the word.[80]

Many interpretations have been built around this section of the *Manifesto*, often focusing on the simple sentence that workers "have no country". Does that mean they have no interest in the nation? Is it that they do not have a stake in the nation at present but *will* after the revolution? The context should clarify this. Marx and Engels do not wish to abolish countries. Nationality is not something that can be taken away from workers because they are outcasts in their own society. But workers must become the 'leading class' ('national class' in the first German edition) in a particular nation-state, so that they become 'national'; but not in the bourgeois or chauvinist sense. Once in power the proletariat can work to diminish national antagonisms. This interpretation is supported by another statement in the *Manifesto*:

> Though not in substance, yet in form, the struggle of the proletariat with the bourgeoisie is at first a national struggle. The proletariat of each country must, of course, first of all settle matters with its own bourgeoisie.[81]

Workers of any country must "of course" settle things with their own bourgeoisie (not international capitalism), which means that the *form* of the struggle is a national one; workers will achieve power only with a *national* strategy.

The question of the 'national class' in the Marxist system is an important one. As societies are divided into classes, the 'national interest' must be represented by one of them. The most progressive class in society would be truly 'national' in so far as it was able to take the whole society forward, even while it was promoting its own interests. Following Bloom,

> The dominance of a ruling class had national justification so long, and only so long, as it promoted economic progress. In brief, the national class was that class which led the nation, the individual society, along the line of progress.[82]

In *The Class Struggles in France* Marx wrote that

> In general, the development of the industrial proletariat is conditioned by the development of the industrial bourgeoisie. Only under the role of the bourgeoisie does it begin to exist on a broad national basis, which elevates its revolution to a national one . . . .[83]

The tragedy of 1848 was that the struggle of the industrial wage-labourer against the industrial bourgeoisie was but "a partial phenomenon" and thus the working class "was not able to provide the national substance of a revolution".[84] It was the bourgeoisie which had represented the whole of modern society against the old order in the great French revolution of 1789; in 1848 the proletariat was not developed enough to perform this role. Writing on the Paris Commune of 1871 Marx said that

> This was the first revolution in which the working class was openly acknowledged as the only class capable of social initiative, even by the great bulk of the Paris middle class . . . .[85]

More specifically Marx wrote,

> If the Commune was thus the true representative of all the healthy elements of French society, and therefore the truly national government, it was, at the same time, as a working men's government, as the bold champion of the emancipation of labour, emphatically international.[86]

As the Prussian army annexed Alsace and Lorraine to Germany and moved to crush the Commune alongside the French reactionaries, "the Commune annexed to France the working people all over the world". Marx sees no contradiction between this bold internationalism and the Commune as "truly national government". Historical development had still not reached the stage when the proletariat could not only seize power but maintain it. It was 1917 before the Bolsheviks led another "national class" to victory.

Commentators differ on the Marxist vision of the post revolutionary status of nations and nationalism. For Bertell Ollman

> the divisions we are accustomed to seeing in the human species along the lines of nation, race, religion, geographical section (town dwellers and country dwellers), occupation and class have all ceased to exist

in the communist society Marx foresaw.[87] Solomon Bloom, the cautious and meticulous author of an early study of Marxism and nationalism, says less optimistically that

What the authors [of the *Manifesto*] foresaw was not the complete disappearance of all national distinctions whatever but specifically the abolition of sharp economic and social differences, economic isolation, invidious distinctions, political rivalries, wars, and exploitation of one nation by another.[88]

This in itself is a tall order but one which is more realistic than Ollman's version where we all end up speaking Esperanto, and racism, sexism and religious differences disappear. The *Manifesto* is of course an enigmatic document open to differing interpretations. Though it may be absurd to posit the 'abolition' of existing ethnic and linguistic communities, Marx and Engels did clearly recognize that the seizure of power by the proletariat within the boundaries of given national states was only the first step. In fact, this, as Rosdolsky reminds us

> *will be only a transitional stage on the way to the classless and stateless society of the future*, since the construction of such a society *is possible only on the international scale!*[89]

That is why "WORKING MEN OF ALL COUNTRIES, UNITE!", the famous phrase which closes the *Communist Manifesto*, is more than rhetoric.

Notes

1. K. Marx, *The Revolutions of 1848. Political Writings*, Vol. 1 (Penguin Books, Harmondsworth, 1973) p.101.
2. K. Marx and F. Engels, *Collected Works*, Vol. 6 (Lawrence and Wishart, London, 1976) p.389.
3. K. Marx and F. Engels, *Collected Works*, Vol. 7 (Lawrence and Wishart, London, 1976) p.166.
4. K. Marx and F. Engels, *Collected Works*, Vol. 6, p.388.
5. K. Marx and F. Engels, *Collected Works*, Vol. 9 (Lawrence and Wishart, London, 1977) p.170.
6. K. Marx and F. Engels, *Collected Works*, Vol. 6, p.555.
7. Ibid., p.369.
8. Ibid., p.373.
9. K. Marx and F. Engels, *Collected Works*, Vol. 8 (Lawrence and Wishart, London, 1977) pp.246-7.
10. K. Marx and F. Engels, *Collected Works*, Vol. 6, p.535.
11. K. Marx and F. Engels, *Collected Works*, Vol. 7, p.421.
12. Ibid., p.423.
13. Ibid., p.421.
14. For an overview of Marx's and Engels' politics in 1848 see A. Gilbert, *Marx's Politics: Communists and Citizens* (Martin Robertson, Oxford, 1981).
15. This and the next sentence draws on E. Hobsbawm, *The Age of Capital 1848-1875* (Abacus, London, 1977) p.30.
16. K. Marx and F. Engels, *Collected Works*, Vol. 8, p.234.

17. Ibid., p.367.

18. I. Cummings, *Marx, Engels and National Movements* (Croom Helm, London, 1980) p.41.

19. K. Marx and F. Engels, *Collected Works*, Vol. 8, p.370.

20. R. Rosdolsky, *Friedrich Engels y el Problema de los Pueblos "sin Historia"* (Siglo XXI, Mexico, 1980) pp.22-3.

21. K. Marx and F. Engels, *Collected Works*, Vol. 8, p.378.

22. Ibid., p.xxvi.

23. Ibid., p.365.

24. S. Avineri (ed.), *Karl Marx on Colonialism and Modernization* (Anchor Books, New York, 1969) p.425.

25. 'Bolivar y Ponte' in K. Marx and F. Engels, *Collected Works*, Vol. 18 (Lawrence and Wishart, London, 1982).

26. Ibid., pp.584-5.

27. J. Arico, *Marx y America Latina* (Alianza Editorial Mexicana, Mexico, 1982) p.140.

28. S. Avineri (ed.), *Karl Marx on Colonialism and Modernization*, p.47.

29. Ibid.

30. K. Marx and F. Engels, *Collected Works*, Vol. 18, p.67.

31. Ibid., p.69.

32. K. Marx and F. Engels, *Selected Correspondence* (Progress Publishers, Moscow, 1965) p.308.

33. K. Marx and F. Engels, *Ireland and the Irish Question* (Progress Publishers, Moscow, 1971) p.143.

34. Ibid., p.163.

35. Ibid., p.303.

36. Ibid., p.332.

37. K. Marx, *The First International and After: Political Writings*, Vol. 3 (Penguin Books, London, 1974) pp.380-1.

38. Ibid., p.391.

39. K. Marx and F. Engels, *Ireland and the Irish Question*, p.132.

40. Ibid., p.281.

41. Ibid., p.293.

42. Ibid., p.148.

43. Ibid., p.334.

44. Ibid.

45. Ibid.

46. Ibid., p.147.

47. Ibid., p.162.

48. Ibid., p.149.

49. Ibid., p.336.

50. Ibid., p.293.

51. Ibid., p.294.

52. Ibid., p.290.

53. Ibid.

54. G. Haupt, 'Les marxistes face à la question nationale: l'histoire du problème', in G. Haupt, M. Lowy and C. Weill (eds.), *Les Marxistes et la Question Nationale 1848-1914* (Maspero, Paris, 1974) p.19.

55. J. Arico, *Marx y America Latina*, p.65.

56. K. Marx, *Capital*, Vol. 1 (Penguin Books, London, 1976) p.91.

57. K. Marx and F. Engels, *Selected Correspondence*, p.313.

58. Ibid., p.339.

59. Ibid., p.340.

60. Ibid., p.312.

61. Ibid., p.385.

62. Ibid., p.389.

63. T. Shanin (ed.), *Late Marx and the Russian Road* (Routledge and Kegan Paul, London, 1983) p.16.

64. K. Marx and F. Engels, *Selected Correspondence*, p.351.

65. Ibid.

66. K. Marx and F. Engels, *Collected Works*, Vol. 6, p.389.

67. S. Bloom, *The World of Nations: A Study of the National Implications in the Work of Karl Marx* (AMS Press, New York, 1967) p.22.

68. E. Hobsbawm, 'Marx, Engels and Politics', in E. Hobsbawm (ed.), *The History of Marxism,* Vol. 1 (Harvester Press, Brighton, 1982), pp.248-9.

69. G. Haupt and C. Weill, 'L'eredita di Marx ed Engels e la questione nazionale', *Studi Storici*, XV, 2, 1974, p.295.

70. K. Marx and F. Engels, *Collected Works*, Vol. 38 (Lawrence and Wishart, London, 1982) p.363.

71. K. Marx and F. Engels, *Collected Works*, Vol. 8, p.577.

72. Ibid., p.230.

73. H.B. Davis, *Nationalism and Socialism: Marxist and Labor Theories of Nationalism to 1917* (Monthly Review Press, New York, 1973) p.30.

74. 'The Future Results of British Rule in India', in S. Avineri (ed.), *Karl Marx on Colonialism and Modernization*, pp.132-9.

75. K. Marx and F. Engels, *Collected Works*, Vol. 13 (Lawrence and Wishart, London, 1980) p.403. On Marx's Spanish writings see M. Lowy, 'Marx y la revolución española, 1854-1856' in *Dialectica y Revolucion* (Siglo XXI, Mexico, 1975).

76. K. Marx and F. Engels, *Collected Works*, Vol. 6, p.503.

77. Ibid., p.497.

78. Ibid., p.488.

79. Ibid., p.6.

80. Ibid., pp.502-3.

81. Ibid., p.495.

82. S. Bloom, *The World of Nations*, p.59.

83. K. Marx, *Surveys From Exile: Political Writings*, Vol. 2 (Penguin Books, London, 1973) p.45.

84. Ibid., p.46.

85. K. Marx, *The First International and After*, p.214.

86. Ibid., p.216.

87. B. Ollman, 'Marx's Vision of Communism: A Reconstruction', *Critique*, No. 8, Summer 1977, p.22.

88. S. Bloom, *The World of Nations*, p.26.

89. R. Rosdolsky, ' "Worker and Fatherland": A Note on a Passage in The Communist Manifesto', *Science and Society*, Vol. XXIX, No. 3, p.335.

2. The Second International

When the Second or Socialist International was formed in 1889, Engels recognized the need for powerful national organizations; but he could hardly have foreseen that within twenty years these would turn their back on the basic principles of internationalism. Though this chapter will focus on the collapse of the Second International in the holocaust of the First World War, we cannot read its earlier history as a simple prelude to this chauvinist volte face. In the first section we therefore examine Karl Kautsky's elaboration of the orthodox post-Marx and Engels theory of nationalism. We also turn our attention to the Second International's policy on the colonial expansion of the Western European nations. The tendency towards the 'revisionism' of Marxist principles had its effect here, where the new phenomenon of imperialism was viewed rather optimistically. Then we turn to the collapse of the International into its component national sections in 1914, which can be counterposed to Lenin's clear internationalist stance which called on workers to turn the inter-imperialist war into a civil war. Finally, we turn to Otto Bauer's seminal contribution towards a Marxist *theory* of nationalism, also assessing the criticisms of his work made by Kautsky, Lenin and Stalin. Two other, quite diverse, working-class leaders who confronted nationalism are assessed: the socialist-Zionist Ber Borochov and the socialist-republican, James Connolly. All three writers, Bauer, Borochov and Connolly, have been sadly neglected by the international labour movement. Their contributions are in many ways probably more interesting today than Kautsky's orthodoxy.

Kautsky's orthodoxy

Karl Kautsky was the undisputed 'expert' on the national question within the Second International. While Engels was still alive, Kautsky maintained a lively correspondence with him, which often touched on the question of nationalism. During a visit to London in 1887, Kautsky became very interested in the Irish question, which helped him to deepen his understanding of nationalism. That year he published *The Modern Nationality* in *Die Neue Zeit*, which reopened the question of the small nationalities within the modern capitalist nation-states.[1] Kautsky argued that the classical form of the modern state was the national state, even though this was a tendency rarely realized completely. Just as capitalism coexisted with remnants of previous modes of production, so the nation-state embraced other fragments of nations. At this stage, Kautsky still subscribed to Engels' arguments on the inability of small national groups to survive in a world of large national units. Kautsky wrote that

> The most important factor, which influences in the most decisive manner the formation of nations is that which represents the absolutely necessary medium to establish relations: the language.[2]

Without a common language there was no communication and hence social production was impossible. The case of Ireland showed for Kautsky "how closely linked the economic welfare of a people was to their national independence, and the organization of the nation in its own independent state . . . ."[3] Finally, Kautsky believed that while the development of capitalism threw the capitalist of one nation into competition with that of another, there were no contradictions between the workers of different countries.

In 1896, Kautsky was called upon, during the preparations for the Fourth Congress of the International in London, to arbitrate between the Polish Socialist Party (PPS) and the Social-Democratic Party of Poland led by Rosa Luxemburg. For the PPS, the class struggle was subordinate to the struggle for Polish national independence. Socialists, they argued, should be at the head of the nationalist movement. For Rosa Luxemburg, the national question was not a priority for the working class and detracted from the specific tasks of a socialist movement (see Chapter 3). Kautsky drafted a compromise motion which reaffirmed the right of nations to self-determination but, as Haupt points out, "it sought more to close a debate which was judged inopportune, than a conscious effort to clarify positions of principle".[4] Kautsky was again called on by the international socialist movement after the Russian revolution of 1905. The rise of the nationalities in the vast Russian Empire led the movement to re-evaluate its premises and its policies, hitherto based largely on analysis of the multinational Austrian state and the Balkans question. In *The National Question in Russia* (1905), Kautsky argued that the struggle of the nationalities for independence from the autocratic Russian regime should be allied to the democratic and proletarian movement.[5] Only on this basis could national equality be assured within a 'United States of Russia' based on territorial autonomy. Kautsky did not believe that independence for the nationalities was a solution to the 'national problem'. In fact he argued later in 1917 that:

> Not the differentiation, but the assimilation of national groups, not the access to national culture, but access to European culture which becomes ever more of equal significance with world culture is the aim of socialist development.[6]

The first and most systematic attempt to provide the socialist movement with a national policy was the Brünn Programme of 1899, largely inspired by Kautsky. Growing national tensions within the Austrian Empire had forced the Austrian social democrats to face the issue of nationalism against the better judgement of their leader Victor Adler who considered the question explosive. Kautsky proposed the democratic transformation of the Austrian state along the lines of the federal structure of the socialist movement, which in its 1897 Congress had divided into six national parties. The Brünn resolution advocated a restructuring of Austria along the boundaries of language divisions, against a minority who called for extra-territorial cultural autonomy (that is, peoples could group together across national boundaries). Its main points are worth quoting in full because it was often to be misrepresented, not least by Stalin:

> Because national conflicts in Austria are obstructing all political progress and the cultural development of the nationalities, because these conflicts result primarily from the backwardness of our public institutions and because the prolongation of these conflicts is one of the methods by which the ruling classes insure their domination and prevent measures in the true interests of the people, the congress declares that:
>
> The final settlement of the nationality and language question in Austria in the spirit of equality and reason is primarily a cultural demand, and therefore is one of the vital interests of the proletariat.
>
> This is possible only under a truly democratic regime based on universal, equal and direct elections, a regime in which all feudal privileges in the state and the principalities will have been abrogated. Only under such a regime will the working classes, the elements which really support the state and society, be able to express their demands.
>
> The nurturing and development of the national peculiarities of all peoples in Austria are possible only on the basis of equal rights and the removal of oppression. Therefore, state-bureaucratic centralism and the feudal privileges of the principalities must be opposed.
>
> Only under such conditions will it be possible to create harmony among the nationalities in Austria in place of the quarrelling that takes place now, namely, through the recognition of the following guiding principles:
>
> 1. Austria is to be transformed into a democratic federation of nationalities [Nationalitätenbundesstaat].
>
> 2. The historic Crown lands are to be replaced by nationally homogeneous self-ruling bodies, whose legislation and administration shall be in the hands of national chambers, elected on the basis of universal, equal, and direct franchise.
>
> 3. All self-governing regions of one and the same nation are to form together a nationally distinct union, which shall take care of this union's affairs autonomously.
>
> 4. A special law should be adopted by the parliament to safeguard the rights of national minorities.
>
> 5. We do not recognize any national privilege; therefore we reject the demand for a state language. Whether a common language is needed, a federal parliament can decide.
>
> The party congress, as the organ of international social democracy in Austria, expresses its conviction that on the basis of these guiding principles, understanding among peoples is possible.
>
> It solemnly declares that it recognizes the right of each nationality to national existence and national development.
>
> Peoples can advance their culture only in close solidarity with one another, not in petty quarrels; particularly the working class of all nations must, in the interest of the individual nationalities and in the general interest, maintain

international cooperation and fraternity in its struggle and must conduct its political and economic struggle in closely united ranks.[7]

The debate at the Brünn Congress clearly revealed the conceptions of nationalism current within the social-democrat ranks. Seliger introduced the debate by saying that it was ironic that those who were accused of being nationally neutral should be resolving the national problem. He stressed that "above all, the question of the nationalities should not be seen as a question of power, but as a cultural question".[8] Delegate Daszynski disputed this view, arguing that "there is no national question without an economic base".[9] The Ruthenian socialists pledged their support but reminded the congress that part of their people lived outside Austria in the Russian-dominated Ukraine:

> We are convinced that the international power of the proletariat will only be developed when each nation can decide its history. We know that social and political liberation also presuppose national liberation.[10]

Most delegates emphasized that national disputes had to be resolved as a precondition for the advance of the labour movement. A minority argued on the contrary that "our activity is taken up too much by the national question" and that they had often recruited workers precisely because they did *not* raise the national question.[11] The problem posed by the relationship between national and social struggles was best articulated by the Polish delegation: Polish socialists would act within Austrian workers' organizations but they would also "act incessantly within the whole Polish people to eliminate the grave national injustice exercised against the Polish people".[12] The proletariat could not ignore brutal national oppression and the partition of their country. Mere cultural autonomy could not suffice.

Kautsky went on to develop his ideas on the national question in *The national tasks of socialists amongst the Balkan Slavs* (1909) and *The self determination of nations* (1917).[13] With regard to the Austro-Slav groups, Kautsky had always disagreed with Engels' characterization of them as non-historic nations. He argued that these national groups had in practice disproved their description as mere unions of nations (*Völkerabfälle*) destined for extermination. Kautsky wrote:

> Today, when those people have achieved such great power and significance, to refer to them in the old Marxian terms of 1848/1849 does appear most unfortunate.[14]

Even if the verdicts of 1848 *had* been correct, this would not have called into question socialist support for national self-determination during the First World War. But the right of national independence was relative and not absolute for Kautsky, and depended on the wider national community. In 1909 he wrote that "we are not anti-national any more than we are hostile or even indifferent to personality. But the welfare of our nationality is not the ultimate criterion of our action".[15] Kautsky in practice only advocated that Austria should continue on a federal basis. Nationalism should not preclude the unification of the Balkan peoples in a federal state. A Democratic Balkan Federation would be free at once from the local dynasties and the dominance of the big powers. Thus the stage would be set for the development of the workers' class struggle. As Kautsky put it in 1917, "it is the partisans of imperialism within the social democrats who refuse to support the revindication of peoples' self-determination".[16] Only socialism would assure the free and diverse development of each nation, as it would for each individual personality.

How can we sum up Kautsky's contribution to a Marxist theory of nationalism? Haupt has argued that Kautsky's approach was more intuitive than analytical. He certainly did confront the empirical manifestations of the national question as they became more evident at the end of the 19th Century. He distinguished more clearly between nation and nationality, words which entered the Marxist vocabulary along with that of ethnic group. Yet the 'national question' was still largely considered only in relation to the problems presented by the multi-national empires. Until 1905 at least, internationalism was a slogan only, based on the cosmopolitan outlook of the liberal democratic bourgeoisie. This somewhat utopian universalism could easily go hand in hand with national sentiment of the 1848 variety. Furthermore, Kautsky's Eurocentric approach — based on the particular development of nation, language and state in one geographical area — left him ill prepared to perceive different forms of the national question outside Europe. Nationalism as a concept was not an issue for Marxism; the issue was a multitude of individual national struggles. Kautsky's inability to provide a definition is made clear in 1908:

> The nation must be considered as a social structure difficult to perceive, as a product of social development, as one of the most powerful factors in social evolution . . . Nationality is a social relation which is modified continuously and which under different circumstances has a very different meaning; it is a Proteus which slides through our fingers when we try to seize it . . . .[17]

As conclusive definitions these thoughts are rather vague and do not amount to a Marxist theory of nationalism.

While the European social democrats focused on the 'problem' of nationalism within their own countries, they also needed to come to terms with the foreign policy of their own nation-states. This was the age of imperialism, when the countries of Europe expanded their empires in what is now called the Third World. What attitude would supporters of social democracy take towards this overseas expansion and the subsequent nationalist revolts in the Third World? Where Marx and Engels had been ambiguous in their attitudes, the Second International developed a much more clearly 'social-imperialist' line.

In 1896, Eduard Bernstein, the main mover of 'revisionism' in the German Social Democratic Party, wrote an article on the party's response to the 'Turkish disturbances'. For the first time, a Marxist of international authority came out in favour of colonialism. Bernstein wrote that although the party had a natural tendency to extend its sympathy to any emancipatory movement, "not all struggles of the oppressed peoples against those who dominate them are equally emancipatory struggles".[18] More specifically, though we will oppose certain methods through which the savages [sic] are subdued, we will not question nor oppose their being subdued and the rights of civilization upheld.[19]

The freedom of 'some insignificant nationality' outside Europe could hardly be compared to the development of the highly civilized peoples of Europe. Not surprisingly, Bernstein argued that the famous slogan about the workers having no fatherland had to be 'modified'. As fully enfranchised citizens the workers could share in the nation's destiny and henceforth "internationalism [would] not prevent the safeguarding of national interests".[20]

This tendency towards 'social-imperialism', as the revolutionary tendency dubbed it, came to the fore more openly at the Amsterdam Congress of the International in 1904. In a debate on the colonial question, the Dutch social democrat Van Kol presented a report which argued that

the new needs which will make themselves felt after the victory of the working class and its economic emancipation will make the possession of colonies necessary, even under the future socialist system of government.[21]

The letter from Engels to Kautsky (see Chapter 1) in which he poured scorn on this idea, had long since been forgotten. Instead, these socialists were refusing to "abandon half the globe to the caprice of peoples still in their infancy" and advocated a "socialist colonial policy" all "in the interest of all humanity".[22] Only the English delegate Hyndman denounced "the ignominity of modern capitalism in the colonies" and, referring to his own country's role in India, called upon the Congress "to denounce before the civilized world, the statesmen and the nation guilty of this infamy".[23] But Hyndman later became a confirmed social-imperialist.

At the Stuttgart Congress of 1907, Van Kol's report was debated more thoroughly. Eduard David from Germany called on the socialist congress to accept the principle of colonialism arguing that "Europe needs colonies. It does not even have enough of them. Without colonies, we should be comparable, from an economic standpoint, to China".[24] Bernstein entered the debate to state that there were always two categories of people — the rulers and the ruled. A Polish delegate came in:

David has recognised the right of one nation to put another nation in tutelage. What such tutelage is worth we Poles know, we who have had as tutors the Tsar of Russia and the Prussian government.[25]

Kautsky made a balanced and forceful plea for a return to Marxist orthodoxy only to be rebuffed by Van Kol for his 'bookish theory'. Van Kol made merry about Kautsky's naive proposal to gain the confidence of primitive peoples: "We must, on the contrary, have arms in hand in order eventually to defend ourselves, even if Kautsky calls this imperialism".[26]

That Kautsky stood by Marxist orthodoxy does not mean that his vision of imperialism and the colonial revolution was without contradictions. Imperialism for Kautsky was not inherent in the development of capitalism: rather it was the policy of the old democratic state of mercantilism. Industrial (or Manchester) capitalism did not require colonies; in fact industrialists, because they need buyers, became philanthropists in the colonies and were opposed to slavery. The preachers of the virtue of free trade also wish for peace, according to this perspective. These arguments were advanced in Kautsky's *Old and New Colonial Policy* published in *Die Nieue Zeit* in 1897-8.[27] In his *Socialism and Colonial Policy* of 1907 he developed these points in a polemic against Van Kol's pro-colonialist position. Here he distinguished between the old style exploitation colonies and the new immigration colonies such as the United States which

> emerged precisely as a result of efforts to avoid class domination. They do not consist of the exploitation and domination of the natives; rather they rest on the work of the immigrants themselves, and thus these colonizers do not establish any new form of class formation with regard to them.[28]

Here again, Kautsky is torn between 'good' colonialism and 'bad'.

Kautsky always tried to reconcile the revolutionary principles of Marxism with the reformist practice of German social democracy.[29] This 'centrism' led him to oppose the open pro-imperialism of the 'revisionists'; but in the end these views were accommodated, because they were more in line with the party's practice. As Davis writes

> The centrists were shocked to see what inroads had been made on the working class by the propaganda of jingoistic nationalism. But instead of maintaining their anti-imperialist position, they gave ground to the nationalists and damped down the criticism of imperialist expansion.[30]

The increased vote for the party in the 1912 elections seemed to prove the productiveness, if not correctness, of verbal internationalism and practical nationalism. The whole concept of a peaceful phase of capitalist expansion — ultra-imperialism — advanced by Kautsky was utopian. He could therefore hardly be expected to understand the growing role of the colonial revolution. By 1911 the other great figure of Marxist orthodoxy, August Bebel, could call for "complete equality" between German and French exploitation of Morocco.[31] That year, the Agadir incident in Morocco led to a clash between France and Germany. The German 'internationalists' could only call for equal rights for 'their' bourgeoisie in the exploitation of a Third World nation. This was a far cry from the position developed by Marx and Engels on Ireland and their belief that a nation which enslaves another forges its own chains.

World war and collapse

It would be wrong to see the collapse of internationalist principles in 1914 as inevitable, as though it had been inscribed in the logic of the Second International's development since its foundation. In fact, between 1911 and 1913 the International was engaged in a quite successful pacifist struggle. In

October 1912, a quarter of a million workers mobilized in Berlin alone against the war; in November the extraordinary Basle Congress of the International declared 'war on war' in ringing tones. The turning point came in 1913 after a new eruption of the Balkans crisis. It now seemed that the threat of war had faded and the International entered into a mood of false optimism. Kautsky actually claimed in July 1914 that the International had never been as strong or as united.[32] This was after the assassinations in Sarajevo in June 1914 which set in motion the events that led to the First World War. When the ruling body of the International — the International Socialist Bureau — held its last meeting at the end of July 1914 it thought that the war between Austria and Serbia could be contained and that a European conflagration was unlikely. The German Social Democratic Party, the largest and most coherent of the international socialist movement, urged the government not to enter the war and promised that it would not vote for war credits. Yet, at the historic parliamentary session of 4 August 1914, the once proud German internationalists threw their weight behind the cause of 'national defence' and its representatives voted unanimously for the war credits which the government demanded. French socialists rallied behind their government; those in Belgium and England rapidly followed suit.

To excuse this *dèbacle* Karl Kautsky could only say that "the International is an instrument for peace, not for war".[33] He found it quite natural that

In every national state the working class must also devote its entire energy to keeping intact the independence and the integrity of the national territory.[34]

He thought that the International would simply regroup after the storm had blown over, because after all

The difference between the German and French Socialists is to be found in their standards of judgement, not in their fundamental point of view, but merely in the difference of their interpretation of the present situation, which in its turn, is conditioned by the difference in their geographical position.[35]

So the collapse of the international socialist movement was not a question of principles (or lack of them) but simply the product of a geographical accident. The obvious question to ask is whether the ebbing of the anti-militarist movement amongst the European working class simply swept the socialists along or whether the tactics of the social democrats had helped to demobilize the movement. Haupt argues that we should probably reverse Kautsky's statement of the problem (nationalist currents paralyzing the socialist and trade union movements) and begin by "regarding the datum 'wave of nationalism' not as the cause but as the consequence of the breakdown of the socialist parties".[36] Consistent anti-war propaganda — however unpopular in the short term — could realistically have altered the course of the world war.

Once the war had started the governments of the Entente posed as the liberators of the oppressed nationalities ("gallant little Belgium") and the champions of democracy. Lenin came out squarely against this notion, arguing that "in the present war the national element is represented *only* by Serbia's war against Austria" but this "is not, and cannot be, of *any* serious significance in the general European war".[37] For 99% of the peoples of Europe the war was an imperialist war and therefore the national liberation aspect which concerned the other 1% was secondary. Rosdolsky argues correctly that

> Lenin's analysis appears to be inadequate: he still apparently underestimated the tremendous elemental force of the *national movements in Austro-Hungary*.[38]

This abstention on the national question allowed the powers of the Entente to impose their solution to the nationalities question in Central and Southern Europe. The position of Austro-German social democracy was even less sympathetic to the Slav peoples rebelling against Austrian imperialism. A leading article in *Arbeiter-Zeitung* in August 1914 declared:

> And now for the sake of semi-barbaric Serbia, a war of destruction has to be let loose between the noblest civilized nations of the continent. This is madness . . . a continent must go up in flames, the fruits of civilization must be trampled in filth and blood, so that some ruler in the Balkans, *whose name no civilised person can even pronounce*, the tsar of all the Russians can proclaim himself the undisputed protector and master of his borders.[39]

Lenin's strength during World War I was his clear analysis of the causes of the war and the proletarian policy which flowed from it.[40] The war was an imperialist war and the socialist movement had not responded in an internationalist spirit but rather succumbed to 'social nationalism' (Lenin later preferred the term 'social chauvinism'). This meant an alliance between the socialists and the bourgeoisie in defence of the fatherland. For Lenin the real duty of all socialists during the war was clear:

> Develop the workers' revolutionary consciousness, rally them in the international revolutionary struggle . . . and do everything possible to turn the imperialist war between the peoples into a civil war of the oppressed classes against the oppressors, a war for the expropriation of the class of capitalists . . . and the realisation of socialism.[41]

In short, socialists should strive for the defeat of their 'own' country — revolutionary defeatism. This was genuine internationalism and every other line was simply a variant of national-liberalism. Lenin at times simply blamed nationalism *per se* for the world war and the collapse of the International; at other points he referred to 'chauvinism', especially once he had clearly drawn the line between oppressed and oppressor nations. His clear recognition of the importance of nationalism was made clear in an article of 1914 when he argued that

> One cannot be 'national' in an imperialist war otherwise than by being a socialist politician, i.e. by recognising the right of oppressed nations to liberation, to secession from the Great Powers that oppress them.[42]

It was opportunism on the question of imperialism that had led the Second

International to forget this Marxist position and fall into 'social chauvinism'.

There were various socialist conferences during the war to try to salvage an internationalist movement. In 1915, the anti-war socialists met in Zimmerwald and rejected Lenin's resolution as dangerous nonsense, adopting instead a manifesto following Trotsky's draft. Revolutionary defeatism was replaced by pacifist and liberal sentiments:

> This struggle is the struggle for freedom, for the reconciliation of peoples for socialism. It is necessary to take up this struggle for peace, for a peace without annexations or war indemnities.[43]

Nor would the conference call for a new Third International, as Lenin urged. The conference did not even call on the German delegates to refuse war credits in parliament or withdraw from ministries. A second conference in Kienthal in 1916 again saw Lenin in the minority, but with slightly more support for his position. This time the final resolution not only called for an immediate peace settlement without annexations but also called for all socialist representatives to refuse to grant war credits.[44] Though it did not call for a Third International, it roundly criticized the International Socialist Bureau for its betrayal of international principles and its granting of a political truce to the bourgeoisie in the cause of the 'defence of the fatherland'. The so-called Zimmerwald left carried out a vigorous propaganda campaign against the war which found considerable sympathy amongst a war-weary proletariat. The Russian Revolution of March 1917 accelerated the realignment within the socialist movement and helped release a tremendous popular yearning for peace.

Leon Trotsky developed an analysis of the First World War which in part differed from Lenin's. For him

> The present war is at bottom a revolt of the forces of production against the political form of nation and state. It means the collapse of the national state as an independent economic unit.[45]

He believed that the war would lead to the breakdown of the existing national economic centres and their being subsumed by a world economy. As the national state collapsed so too did the contemporary national socialist parties which

> had become ingrained in the national states with all the different branches of their organisations, with all their activities and with their psychology.[46]

Trotsky may have foreseen the tremendous development of internationalized production; but it was premature to see this leading to the demise of the nation-state. Nor did the need for a new socialist international preclude the development of strong *national* parties, notwithstanding the evolution of German social democracy. In his opposition to the war Trotsky lagged considerably behind Lenin:

> 'Immediate cessation of the War' is the watchword under which the Social Democracy can reassemble its scattered ranks, both within the national parties,

and in the whole International . . . Real national self-defence now consists in the struggle for peace.[47]

Pacifist slogans, and ambiguous calls for "real national self-defence" were no match for Lenin's absolutely clear call to turn the imperialist war into a civil war.

Otto Bauer's contribution

Otto Bauer was part of that movement known as Austro-Marxism, which describes those theorists active in the Austrian socialist movement at the turn of the century. They belonged to the 'Marxist centre' led by Kautsky, and after the First World War they tried to find a third course between bankrupt social democracy and the new communism. The context of Bauer's work was the threat posed to the unity of the working class by national tensions within the Austro-Hungarian Empire. The Brünn Congress of 1899 resolved this conflict by allowing each national party to present the cultural demands of its own nation, while the economic struggle was waged at the state level. As one critic notes, this established a principle

> according to which internationalism allowed the workers of each nation to be nationalists, as long as they granted the same right to the workers of other nations.[48]

Otto Bauer and Karl Renner went beyond the Brünn resolutions in arguing that the principle of national-cultural autonomy was based on the principle of personality rather than the territorial determinations accepted at that Congress. All the various nationalities of the state would administer their own cultural affairs regardless of territory thus ensuring the integrity of the multi-national Austrian state. Not surprisingly, the Austrian social democrats were referred to as the 'KUK' (*Kaiser-lich und König-lich* — imperial and royal) Social Democrats following the official designation of the Austrian crown. In spite of this clear reformist tendency, Bauer's remains a significant contribution to the Marxist theory of nationalism.

According to Bauer's definition in *The Nationality Question and Social Democracy* (1907) "The nation is the totality of men bound together through a common destiny into a community of character".[49] This is a methodological pointer which directs Bauer to a painstaking investigation into the historical conformation of modern nations. A nation is seen as a 'community of fate', whose character results from its history; this in turn reflects the conditions under which people laboured to survive, and divided the products of this labour. Bauer began to develop a theory of social forms, following the distinction between community (*Gemeinschaft*) and society (*Gesellschaft*) drawn by Tönnies; but he never fully elaborated this. Kautsky was quick to attack Bauer's theory. In *Nationality and Internationality* (1908) he argued that "Bauer has not taken into account sufficiently the importance of language both for the nation and the state".[50] For Kautsky, language was the most important factor in the historic development of the nation. Bauer replied in his *Observations on the Question of Nationalities* (1908) that he did not deny that the nation was a community of language, but that he sought to find the 'community of culture' which lay behind the generation, transformation and limits of language.[51] By this stage it should be clear that Bauer was working within the framework of historical materialism but with a remarkable lack of the economic reductionism so typical of Second International Marxism. At last the 'relative autonomy' of the national question was being recognized within Marxist discourse.

Bauer's second major contribution was to break decisively with the Marx-Engels position of 1848 on the 'non-historic' nations. He agreed with Engels that there were peoples in Central Europe who could be called non-historic, but disagreed on their future possibilities. For him

> The nations without history are revolutionary, they also struggle for constitutional rights and for their independence, for peasant emancipation; the revolution of 1848 is also their revolution . . . .[52]

They also had a future; indeed Bauer wrote extensively on "the awakening of the nations without history", which he saw as one of the major revolutionary changes at the turn of the century. It was the progressive features of capitalist development which had re-awakened the national self-consciousness of the non-historic nations. Kautsky argued that it was doubtful that the autonomy of nations could be achieved before the proletariat seized power and in his reply Bauer agreed. Where Bauer could *not* agree was on Kautsky's accusation that he "enormously exaggerated the national factor".[53] He thought there was an element of 'naive cosmopolitanism' in the workers and socialists of the more powerful nations. They could hardly understand the nationalism of the workers in the 'awakening nations':

> The working class section of the *nations without history* in Austria was nationalist: the state which enslaved them was German; the court which protected the property owners and threw the dispossessed in jail was also German; each death sentence was written in German, and German was used to issue the orders to the armies which were sent to crush each strike by the hungry and defenceless workers.[54]

The third major element we shall focus on is Bauer's statement that "nationalist hatred is a transformed class hatred".[55] The growing competition between German and Czech workers revealed for Bauer a clear connection between national and class differences. Bauer concluded that capitalism did not produce an anational class proletariat, but on the contrary a *nationally* class conscious proletariat. National exclusiveness was not something which the orthodox Marxists would readily recognize. For Kautsky it was simply a question of Bauer not understanding that the proletariat was predominantly international rather than national in orientation. Kautsky saw the proletariat as aspiring towards an international rather than national culture, especially as international trade was leading to a world-wide language. To these abstractions

Bauer counterposed a more realistic appraisal of the intermeshing of class and national struggles. Bauer, too, sought the international unity of the proletariat but believed that

> We can only defeat bourgeois nationalism ... when we discover the national substance of the international class struggle ... We must defeat nationalism on its own ground.[56]

This could mean national opportunism; but it also recognizes that socialists cannot choose at random the terrain on which they fight. Bauer viewed the Second International in a more realistic way than Kautsky, arguing that even in peace time it was not an effective instrument when the vested interests of the big states were at stake. It was unfortunate that Bauer's political role was not prominent enough to affect the issue before the First World War; after the war he became the leader of the left-wing Austrian Social Democrats.

Lenin carried out a sustained polemic against the Austro-Marxist nationalities policy, arguing that

> 'Cultural-national autonomy' implies precisely the most refined and, therefore, the most harmful nationalism, it implies the corruption of the workers by means of the slogan of national culture ... In short, this programme undoubtedly contradicts the internationalism of the proletariat and is in accordance only with the ideals of the nationalist petty bourgeoisie.[57]

Lenin was undoubtedly right to stress the adaptation of the Austrian social democrats to the various nationalities, but was the simple slogan of 'internationalism' sufficient as an alternative? Bauer, in fact, moved after 1909 to reject his earlier hope that the nationality problem could be solved under capitalism. After 1917 he also fully accepted the 'Leninist' theory of the right of nations to self-determination. A more cogent criticism made by Lenin is on Bauer's tendency towards psychologism — his emphasis on personality and national character. Stalin took this criticism further, arguing that Bauer's definition of the nation divorced psychology from territory and economic conditions. Stalin's criticism is, however, weakened by his own definition of nation as "a historically evolved, stable community of language, territory, economic life, and psychological make-up manifested in a community of culture",[58] which borrows heavily from Bauer as well as Kautsky. We shall return to Lenin and Stalin in Chapter 4; here we can conclude that Bauer's concept of the nation was framed by the historical circumstances in which he worked. Its weaknesses cannot detract from the great advances he made over his predecessors.

Karl Renner's work on nationalism is often referred to as though it simply complements Bauer's; in fact, it is quite distinctive even though his political recommendations were similar. He criticized the Brünn programme for, in his mind, not resolving the fundamental contradiction between historic rights and national rights. His own juridical approach to the nationality problem in the Austrian state attributed a major role to the state as a regulating body. He wrote that

> Aside from Austria-Hungary the great states of Europe are nation states: consequently with them nation and state coincide, and for that very reason the national idea, in the last generation, has been totally inspired by the needs of statehood and the economic requirements of the state.[59]

Renner put forward a detailed legal blueprint to reorganize the multi-national Austria into a supra-national state, which could even be a model for the socialist future. His accommodation to nationalism went much further than Bauer's: the nation was virtually seen as a 'natural' pre-ordained phenomenon. Not surprisingly, when the First World War broke out in 1914, Renner became the leader of the 'social patriotic' faction of his party, and after the war he became the first chancellor of the new Austrian Republic. Nevertheless, his early works *State and Nation* (1899) and *The struggle of the Austrian nationalities for the state* (1902),[60] written before he became a Reichsrat deputy in 1907, are an important contribution to the more specialized question of the constitutional and legal regulation of the nationalities.

Ber Borochov

Borochov was born in the Ukraine in 1881 and joined the Social Democratic Party in 1900, although he did not remain long in the movement. In 1907 he went to Europe where he became a leading figure in the Poale Zion (Labour Zionist) movement. In 1917 he returned to Russia as an enthusiastic supporter of the Bolshevik revolution, becoming a delegate to the Constituent Convention of the Russian Republic. He died in 1917; Poale Zion went on to join the Communist International in 1920. Borochov's major study *The National Question and the Class Struggle* dates from 1905, at which time it had considerable influence amongst Ukranian socialists; it later slipped into obscurity.

Borochov begins his analysis of nationalism by distinguishing between the relations of production and the 'conditions' of production. The first depend on the level of development of the forces of production, and are in that sense humanly controlled. The *conditions* of production, on the other hand, include the sum total of conditions under which production takes place: they are geographic, anthropological and historical.[61] The process of the development of productive forces can take various forms according to the differing conditions of production. At first the natural, non-social conditions of production predominate, but as society develops the social and historical environment gain in importance. Borochov then argues that

> In this conception of the 'conditions of production' we have a sound basis for the development of a purely materialistic theory of *national question*. For in it is contained the theory and the basis of national struggles.[62]

Whereas social conflicts developed from the clash between the developing forces of production and the existing relations of production, national conflicts are seen to result from the clash between the developing forces of production of a nation and the conditions of production under which it lives. A national struggle, paraphrasing Marx, comes about when the existing conditions of production are no longer compatible with the fullest development of production.

Borochov's theory of nationalism is explicitly materialist:

> The national struggle is waged not for the preservation of cultural values but for the struggle of material possessions, even though it is very often conducted under the banner of spiritual slogans.[63]

Nationalism or national consciousness emerges from life under the same conditions of production (when these are harmonious) in the same way that relations of production shape the formation of social classes. Nationalism seeks to control the material possessions of the nation; the assets of the social body lying in its control of the conditions of production. Social classes may share the same conditions of production but their role in the social relations of production will be different. So there will be a diversity of national interests, and types of nationalism. As Borochov puts it: "Each class has a different interest in the national wealth and therefore possesses a different type of 'nationalism' ".[64] It may be aggressive or defensive, conservative or progressive and it may be directed internally or externally.

Borochov recognizes a contradiction between class consciousness and national consciousness: each is liable to weaken the other. When the conditions of production are 'abnormal' — e.g. when part of the national territory is lacking — national consciousness is heightened and that of class weakened. National propaganda under 'normal' conditions will seek to make people believe that their interests are more harmonious than they really are. In this case it is detrimental to the whole nation because it masks the different social interests contained without it. Borochov argues in fact that

> It is always harmful to obscure the class or national consciousness of a given group, irrespective of whether this is a result of class or national demagogy.[65]

This perspective sees class and national contradictions as equally important, and the progressive resolution just as vital. Not surprisingly, Borochov recognizes that there is a "nationalism of the proletariat" in the sense that workers have a stake in the national wealth. This is distinguished from the attitude of the ruling classes which Borochov calls 'nationalistic' rather than truly national. It is for that reason he wrote in *Nationalism and the World War* (1916) that

> It is absurd to contend that nationalism alone is responsible for the present World War. It is a grave injustice to burden the national impulse with the sole responsibility for this bloodshed . . . .[66]

He recognized, of course, the role of 'reactionary chauvinism' in causing the imperialist war. But he rejected the idea that "it is the sacred task of all radicals to vilify all nationalism and to strive for the abolition of all nations".[67]

Borochov has provided us with a valuable attempt at a materialist theory of the national question, the source of which is located in the conflict between socio-economic formations and is manifest in international competition. It is the development of capitalism, with its expansionist tendencies, which brings nationalism to the forefront. The nationalism which springs from this need to expand the market is inevitably aggressive and consciously bellicose. The other meaning of nationalism was that held by

> all oppressed strata at the time of the French Revolution [who] were imbued with the feeling of a common nationality which was being oppressed by the 'upper strata'.[68]

This nationalism which was part of the internal struggle of the oppressed classes must therefore be distinguished from that manifest in the external politics of the ruling classes. In fact, Borochov argues, "Genuine nationalism in no way obscures class-consciousness. It manifests itself only among the progressive elements of oppressed nations".[69] Genuine nationalism seeks only to provide the nation with normal conditions of production so that the proletariat may pursue its class struggle. The instinct of self-preservation in nations is shared by the socialist working class and national differences will remain once those based on class have been overcome. Borochov wrote, though, during World War I that

> Only international Socialism based upon a realistic approach to nationalism can liberate sick humanity in this capitalistic era, and cure this society of the social and national conflict.[70]

This conclusion we can share, in spite of Borochov's more debatable attempt to fuse socialism and nationalism.

James Connolly

James Connolly, though revered in Ireland by the nationalist and socialist movements, is less well known internationally. This contemporary of the Second International elaborated his position on the relationship between nationalism and socialism largely in isolation from the international socialist movement. His work is almost exclusively centred on Ireland and for that reason it has not been generalized.

Connolly's major statement on the relation between nationalism and socialism was uttered on the eve of the Easter Rising of 1916: "The cause of labour is the cause of Ireland, the cause of Ireland is the cause of labour. They cannot be dissevered".[71] In practice, the labour and nationalist movements went their separate ways after the victory against the British occupation in 1912-20. Connolly was, of course, making a programmatic statement: the workers should seek a free Irish nation; the Irish nation should become the guardian of the interests of the people of Ireland. It was Connolly who took the advance guard of the Irish labour movement — the Irish Citizen Army formed during the great Dublin lockout of 1913 — into the revolutionary nationalist or republican rising of 1916. This does not mean, however, that he simply 'capitulated' to nationalism as his socialist contemporaries, and many since, have believed. In fact, he deliberately advised workers to "hold onto their rifles" after the rising, so as to confront their erstwhile allies from the nationalist movement if need be.

Connolly's attitude towards nationalism was consistent, from his earliest writings until his execution by a British firing squad in 1916. Nationalism was for him "not merely a morbid idealizing of the past" but an answer to the economic and political needs of Ireland at the turn of the century. But if the workers had an interest in national independence this in itself would not be sufficient:

> If you remove the English army tomorrow and hoist the green flag over Dublin Castle, unless you set about the organization of the Socialist Republic your efforts would be in vain . . . Nationalism without Socialism . . . is only recreancy.[72]

His vision of Ireland under a bourgeois nationalism has an uncanny resemblance to the present 26 county state known as the 'Republic of Ireland':

> After Ireland is free, says the patriot who won't touch Socialism, we will protect all classes, and if you won't pay your rent you will be evicted same as now. But the evicting party, under the command of the sheriff, will wear green uniforms and the Harp without the Crown, and the warrant turning you out on the roadside will be stamped with the arms of the Irish Republic.[73]

For Connolly this was an end not worth fighting for. For his Irish Socialist Republican Party, "national independence [is] the indispensable groundwork of industrial emancipation", but the party of the working class was "equally resolved to have done with the leadership of a class whose social charter is derived from oppression".[74] Connolly never submitted to a subordinate alliance with the 'national' bourgeoisie.

If Connolly was opposed to bourgeois nationalism he had a more subtle appreciation of the petty-bourgeois-led Republican movement. Shortly after Sinn Féin (Ourselves) was formed in 1908, Connolly wrote an article on its relation to socialism.[75] With the self-reliance aspect of Sinn Féin he was in full agreement, and even argued that it should be applied to the labour movement, in so far as the emancipation of the workers depended on themselves alone. But Connolly also remembered that much of the prior nationalist struggle in Ireland

> was not a fight for freedom, it was a fight to decide whether the English governing class, or the Irish governing classes should have the biggest share of the plunder of the Irish worker.[76]

He squarely rejected the economics of the early Sinn Féin based on the doctrines of Frederick List; its call for "the restoration of the native Parliament" of 1782; and its admiration for 'the Hungary system', i.e. the dual monarchy with Austria. The industrial working class of the North-east could not be won over by simply offering them the green flag of Irish nationalism. Nevertheless, while Connolly could understand why socialists would wish to refuse to have anything to do with nationalism, it was inconsistent to be "opposed to oppression at all times" but also "opposed to national revolt for national independence".[77] Connolly therefore called for an alliance between the socialist element in Sinn Féin and

> Socialists who realise that a socialist movement must rest upon and draw its inspiration from the historical and actual conditions of the country in which it functions and not merely lose themselves in an abstract 'internationalism' (which has no relation to the real internationalism of the Socialist movement).[78]

Connolly was, however, an uncompromising internationalist and his support for the Easter Rising of 1916 was motivated as much by international considerations as Irish ones. Like Lenin, he was horrified by the collapse of the international socialist movement in August 1914. For him "the Socialist of another country is a fellow-patriot, as the capitalist of my own country is a natural enemy".[79] He also followed Lenin, without knowing it, in his uncompromising call that "the signal of war ought also to have been the signal for rebellion".[80] A civil war would have been infinitely preferable to the imperialist slaughter — at least workers would not have died in vain. Of course Connolly was not taken in by British claims to be fighting Germany on behalf of small nationalities. What Connolly called for was that

> The working class in Europe, rather than slaughter each other for the benefit of kings and financiers, [should] proceed tomorrow to erect barricades all over Europe, to break up bridges and destroy the transport service that war might be abolished . . . .[81]

The immediate task in Ireland, pending this Europe-wide rising, was to ensure that the people of Ireland did not starve, as England requisitioned food supplies and conscripted soldiers:

> Starting thus, Ireland may yet set torch to a European conflagration that will not burn out until the last throne and the last capitalist bond and debenture will be shrivelled on the funeral pyre of the last war-lord.[82]

The tragedy was, as Lenin wrote, that Ireland rose in 1916 before October 1917 ushered in the new era of proletarian revolution.

Notes

1. Cited from the translation in E. Bernstein, E. Belfort, E. Box, K. Kautsky and K. Renner, *La Segunda Internacional y el Problema Nacional y Colonial (Primera Parte)* (Siglo XXI, Mexico, 1978).

2. Ibid., p.125.

3. Ibid., p.130.

4. G. Haupt, 'Les marxistes face à la question nationale: l'histoire du problème', in G. Haupt, M. Lowy and C. Weil (eds.), *Les Marxistes et la Question Nationale 1848-1914* (Maspero, Paris 1974) p.40.

5. Ibid., p.112.

6. Cited in C. Herod, *The Nation in the History of Marxian Thought* (Martinus Nijhoff, The Hague, 1976) p.77.

7. The Brünn resolution is discussed in C. Kogan, 'The Social Democrats and the Conflict of Nationalities in the Habsburg Monarchy', *Journal of Modern History*, No. 3, 1949.

8. E. Bernstein *et al.*, *La Segunda Internacional y el Problema Nacional y Colonial*, p.187.

9. Ibid., p.195.

10. Ibid., p.198.

11. Ibid., p.208.

12. Ibid., p.216.

13. Cited in C. Herod, *The Nation in the History of Marxian Thought*, p.71.

14. G. Haupt, 'Les marxistes face à la question nationale', p.147.

15. Ibid., p.149.

16. Ibid., p.24.

17. E. Bernstein *et al.*, *La Segunda Internacional y el Problema Nacional y Colonial*, p.122.

18. Ibid., p.48.

19. Ibid., p.49.

20. Ibid., p.21.

21. H. Carrère d'Encausse and S. Schram (eds.), *Marxism and Asia* (Allen Lane The Penguin Press, London, 1969) p.125.

22. Ibid., p.126.

23. Ibid., p.127.

24. Ibid.

25. Ibid., p.131.

26. Ibid., p.133.

27. In E. Bernstein *et al.*, *La Segunda Internacional y el Problema Nacional y Colonial*, pp.74-107.

28. R. Calwer, K. Kautsky, O. Bauer, J. Strasser and A. Pannekoek, *La Segunda Internacional y el Problema Nacional y Colonial (Segunda Parte)* (Siglo XXI, Mexico, 1978) pp.62-3.

29. For an excellent overview of Kautsky's political development (or degeneration) see M. Salvadori, *Karl Kautsky and the Socialist Revolution 1880-1938* (New Left Books, London, 1979).

30. H.B. Davis, *Nationalism and Socialism: Marxist and Labor Theories of Nationalism to 1917* (Monthly Review Press, New York, 1973) p.98.

31. E. Bernstein *et al.*, *La Segunda Internacional y el Problema Nacional y Colonial*, p.24.

32. Cited in G. Haupt, *Socialism and the Great War: The Collapse of the Second International* (The Clarendon Press, Oxford, 1972) p.134.

33. Cited in G. Novack, D. Frankel and F. Feldman, *The First Three Internationals* (Pathfinder Press, New York, 1974) p.74.

34. Cited in L. Trotsky, *The War and the International* (Wesley Press, Wellawatte, 1971) p.49.

35. Ibid., p.48.

36. G. Haupt, *Socialism and the Great War*, pp.236-7.

37. V.I. Lenin, *Collected Works*, Vol. 21 (Progress Publishers, Moscow, 1964) p.235.

38. R. Rosdolsky, 'Imperialist War and the Question of Peace' (Part I), *Revolutionary Communist*, No. 8, 1978, p.38.

39. R. Rosdolsky, 'Imperialist War and the Question of Peace' (Part II), *Revolutionary Communist*, No. 9, 1979, p.47.

40. See in particular V.I. Lenin, *Collected Works*, Vol. 21.

41. Ibid., p.348.

42. Ibid., p.274.

43. H. Gruber (ed.), *International Communism in the Era of Lenin* (Anchor Books, New York, 1972) p.56.

44. Ibid., p.68.

45. L. Trotsky, *The War and the International*, p.vii.

46. Ibid., p.xii.

47. Ibid., p.74.

48. R. Löew, 'The Politics of Austro-Marxism', *New Left Review*, No. 118, 1979, p.21.

49. O. Bauer, *La Cuestión de las Nacionalidades y la Socialdemocracia* (Siglo XXI, Mexico, 1979) p.142. Fragments of this book are available in T. Bottomore and P. Goode (eds.), *Austro-Marxism* (Clarendon Press, Oxford, 1978).

50. R. Calwer *et al., La Segunda Internacional y el Problema Nacional y Colonial (Segunda Parte)*, p.149.

51. Ibid., p.176.

52. O. Bauer, *La Cuestión de las Nacionalidades y la Socialdemocracia*, pp.266-7.

53. R. Calwer *et al., La Segunda Internacional y el Problema Nacional y Colonial (Segunda Parte)* , p.166.

54. O. Bauer, *La Cuestión de las Nacionalidades y la Socialdemocracia*, p.296.

55. Ibid., p.259.

56. R. Calwer *et al., La Segunda Internacional y el Problema Nacional y Colonial (Segunda Parte)*, p.184.

57. V.I. Lenin, *Collected Works*, Vol. 19 (Progress Publishers, Moscow, 1964) p.541.

58. J. Stalin, *Marxism and the National Question* (Foreign Languages Publishing House, Moscow, 1945) p.11.

59. T. Bottomore and P. Goode (eds.), *Austro-Marxism*, p.123.

60. Translated in E. Bernstein *et al., La Segunda Internacional y el Problema Nacional y Colonial (Primera Parte)*; for an overview of Bauer and Renner see A. Agnelli, *Questione Nazionale e Socialismo: Contributo allo studio del pensiero de K. Renner e O. Bauer* (Il Mulino, Bologna, 1969).

61. B. Borochov, *Nationalism and the Class Struggle: A Marxian Approach to the Jewish Problem* (Greenwood Press, Westport, 1973), (originally published 1937) pp.137-8.

62. Ibid.

63. Ibid., p.141.

64. Ibid., p.144.

65. Ibid., p.149.

66. Ibid., p.109.

67. Ibid.

68. Ibid., p.161.

69. Ibid., p.164.

70. Ibid., p.113.

71. P. Beresford Ellis (ed.), *James Connolly: Selected Writings* (Penguin Books, Harmondsworth, 1973) p.145.

72. Ibid., p.124.

73. Ibid., p.136.

74. Ibid., p.130.

75. J. Connolly, 'Sinn-Féin and Socialism', Cork Workers Club, *Historical Reprints*, No. 19, 1977. For an overview of Connolly's relationship with Irish nationalism see R. Faligot, *James Connolly et la mouvement rèvolutionnaire irlandaise* (Maspero, Paris, 1978).

76. Ibid., p.10.

77. Ibid., p.13.

78. Ibid., p.12.

79. P. Beresford Ellis (ed.), *James Connolly*, p.242.

80. Ibid., p.253.

81. Ibid., p.237.

82. Ibid., p.238.

3. Rosa Luxemburg and the 'Leftists'

Rosa Luxemburg's name is rightly synonomous with uncompromising internationalism in the socialist movement. There is, however, a general over-simplification of her position on nationalism, which is far more complex than most commentaries allow. Writing at the turn of the century, at the same time as Kautsky, she provided a much more creative application of the Marxist method. In short, Luxemburg's approach to the national question cannot be discovered just from her famous argument with Lenin. We therefore examine below all her major writings on the question before turning to criticisms of them. Luxemburg influenced the thinking of the 'radical left' current, expressed in the writings of Joseph Strasser and Anton Pannekoek. There was even a tendency within the Bolshevik party itself which adopted 'Luxemburgist' positions on the national question much to Lenin's disquiet. Finally, we look at those Marxists today who are squarely opposed to nationalism, examining in particular a series of debates on Ireland Lenin debated with Radek, when the latter dismissed the Easter Rising of 1916 as a 'putsch'. The socialist playwright Sean O'Casey regretted Connolly's participation in the same events and described it (see Chapter 2) as a capitulation to bourgeois nationalism. Today, a current of 'Socialists against nationalism' has carried out a comprehensive revision of traditional 'Connollyite' attitudes on the relation between nationalism and socialism.

Luxemburg and Poland

Rosa Luxemburg's discussion of the national question in her native Poland must be seen against the background of the orthodox position established by the founders of Marxism, who supported the aims of national independence and reunification in that country. Quite correctly, Luxemburg refused simply to repeat the formulations of Marx and Engels, trying instead to apply their method to a new historical situation. What may have been a correct position in one historical situation was not necessarily so in a new era. Russia was no longer the bulwark of European reaction in the 1890s that it had been in the 1840s; there were no major social classes in Poland itself which supported the aims of national independence. For Polish Social Democracy, its tasks lay not in the seeking of sanctions for earlier nationalist slogans in Marx's obsolete views on Poland: instead, the *method* and underlying principles of the Marxist doctrine had to be applied to the conditions of Polish society.[1]

Luxemburg went further than this on occasion, arguing that the very manner in which Marx and Engels had derived their earlier positions was not 'Marxist':

> By failing to analyze Poland and Russia as class societies bearing economic and political contradictions in their bosoms, by viewing them not from the point of view of historical development but as if they were in a fixed, absolute condition as homogeneous, undifferentiated units, this view ran counter to the very essence of Marxism.[2]

Marx and Engels had effectively developed a foreign policy for the labour movement which operated on the same basis as that of the liberal bourgeoisie (see Chapter 1).

In her doctoral thesis, *The Industrial Development of Poland* (1898), Luxemburg addressed herself to those issues tackled by Lenin in *The Development of Capitalism in Russia*. She presented abundant statistical evidence of Poland's steady growth and concluded that the future of Poland's continued economic development lay within the Russian Empire. While industrialization would strengthen the bourgeoisie it would also create a growing proletariat. It was only by a continuation of this tendency that a proletariat capable of seizing power and building socialism could be formed. To preach the separation of Poland from Russia would interrupt this process. Her argument, as summarized by Herod, was that

> just as continued economic activity between Russian and Polish business interests tended to blur national lines at the social, economic and political level — so too would come about a similar community of interest between the developing Polish and Russian proletariats.[3]

Quite consistently then, she took the SDKP (Social Democratic Party of Poland and Lithuania, after 1899) into the Russian Social Democratic Party as an autonomous party in 1906. There she dropped the argument against the Bolsheviks' doctrine of self-determination which her supporters had attacked at their 1903 party congress. By 1912, the centralist Lenin had ended this *de jure* participation of Polish socialists in the Russian revolutionary movement. He wrote:

> No Russian Marxist has ever thought of blaming the Polish Social Democrats for being opposed to the secession of Poland. These Social Democrats err only when, like Rosa Luxemburg, they try to deny the necessity of including the recognition of self-determination in the programme of the *Russian* Marxists.[4]

The debate on Poland entered the international socialist movement at the 1896 London Congress of the Second International (see Chapter 2). There, Luxemburg attacked the nationalism of the Polish Socialist Party, and the resolution presented to the congress calling for the independence of Poland. The support for self-determination meant for Luxemburg that "the nationalist position is to be smuggled in under the international banner".[5] She argued that the resolution was silent on the question of *how* the proletariat would liberate Poland. If the resolution on Poland were adopted

> the door would be opened wide to national struggles and nationalist organizations. Rather than a working class organized in accordance with political realities, there would be an espousal of organization along national lines . . . .[6]

But nationalism *was* a "political reality". Rosa Luxemburg, however, could only see "a series of fruitless national struggles" weakening the coherent political struggle of the proletariat. Luxemburg's hostility towards Polish nationalism did not preclude her support for other oppressed nations — when the Greeks on the island of Crete revolted against the Turkish Empire in 1896 she supported the demands for national liberation by those peoples (Greeks, Serbians, Bulgarians, Armenians) oppressed by Turkey. Whereas Marx supported Polish reunification and supported the Turks against Russia, Luxemburg rejected Polish nationalism and supported the rights of those peoples oppressed by the Turkish Empire. As we shall shortly see, this was only an apparent contradiction.

After the Russian revolution of 1905, the national question became more central to the international socialist movement. In a foreword to an anthology on *The Polish Question and the Socialist Movement*, Luxemburg laid out her position in considerable detail. She developed her critique of those who wished "to revive and renovate the dormant legacy of Marx's 1848 position [on Poland]".[7] It was not a question of condemning nationalism — "Of course there never had been any doubts about the sympathy and compassion for oppressed nations!"[8] These sentiments flowed naturally from the socialist world view. It was rather that the working class was the only agency fitted to carry out these tasks of national liberation. Luxemburg argued that the proletariat should strive for "the broadest democratization of the partition countries, to which national autonomy is a self-evident corollary".[9] Since the 1905 revolution in Russia, the only element that remained of Polish nationalism was its reactionary side, while its revolutionary side (armed insurrection) had vanished. It therefore became "anti-nationalist" (despite its outward trappings) and it was up to the workers to maintain the Polish national cultural heritage. Luxemburg was quite explicit that "the cause of nationalism is not alien to the working class — nor can it be".[10] It was not through separatism that Polish national identity could be best served, but through the struggle to overcome despotism in alliance with the Russian proletariat. In fact, it was "the untarnished class movement of the Polish proletariat", produced by the development of capitalism, which would make the best "contribution to *national patriotism* in the best and truest sense of the word".[11] In practice, Luxemburg considered the preservation of an "untarnished" labour movement more important than Polish "national identity".

Luxemburg's most systematic discussion of nationalism possibly occurred in a series of articles on *The National Question and Autonomy*, published between 1908 and 1909. Her central target was the formula of "the right of nations to self-determination" which she said gave "no practical guidelines for the day to day politics of the proletariat, nor any practical solution of nationality problems".[12] Socialists should resist national oppression, as women's oppression, not because of any special 'rights' but simply because they were opposed to any form of social inequality. To speak of national 'rights' was akin to the liberal 'rights of man', and made as much sense as saying that workers had the 'right' to eat off gold plates. She urged a return to "the sober realism, alien to all sentimentalism" which Marx applied to the national question. Nations were not homogeneous, they were divided into antagonistic classes, so could have no unified interest. In fact, "Polish Social Democracy never had any pretensions to be speaking in the name of the 'nation' ".[13] This is radically different from Gramsci's strategy of building proletarian hegemony over the whole population. For Luxemburg, the nation-state was simply the historical form through which the bourgeoisie passed from the defensive to the offensive:

> without exception all of today's 'nation-states' fit this description, annexing neighbours or colonies, and completely oppressing the conquered nationalities.[14]

In these circumstances "the right of nations to self-determination" was either an empty non-committal phrase which meant nothing, or else, it was false if it implied the unconditional duty of socialists to support all national aspirations.

Undoubtedly her best known polemic on the national question was in the famous *Junius Pamphlet*, on the crisis of social democracy, published anonymously in 1916, which seemed to rectify her pre-war underestimation of the power of nationalism. She began to accept the policy of self-determination if not the actual phrase:

> International socialism recognises the right of free independent nations, with equal rights. But socialism alone can create such nations, can bring self-determination of their peoples.[15]

National self-determination was impossible under capitalism, and socialists could not adopt the point of view of the nation in fixing their policies. That was because "in the present imperialistic milieu there can be no wars of national self-defence".[16] National unity and the national state belonged to the era of rising capitalism. Their historic role as expression of a growing bourgeoisie was now over: "today the nation is but a cloak that covers imperialistic desires . . . ."[17] Even small nations such as Serbia which, on formal considerations, had the right of national defence on their side, were filled with expansionist desires. As to the dilemma between the national interests and the international solidarity of the proletariat, which supposedly haunted social democracy when the war broke out, this was a mere figment of the imagination:

> between the national interests and the class interests of the proletariat, in war and in peace, there is actually complete harmony. Both demand the most energetic prosecution of the class struggle . . . .[18]

This could be interpreted as a move towards Marx's conception of the 'national class' which expressed the development of society as a whole.

Lenin applied all his powers of polemic against the *Junius Pamphlet*. He did not consider it was a clear-cut denunciation of opportunism and Kautskyism, but he thought it wrong specifically on the national question. Against Luxemburg's argument that national wars under capitalism were no longer possible he wrote that "national wars waged by colonies and semicolonies in the imperialist era are not only probable but *inevitable*".[19] These national liberation movements were progressive and revolutionary. Even in Europe national wars could not be ruled out. The danger was that the arguments in the *Junius* could lead to a "downright reactionary attitude or indifference to national movements".[20] Lenin went on to say that "it would be unfair to accuse *Junius* of indifference to national movements", comparing it favourably with "the narrow-mindedness and caricature of Marxism now espoused by certain Dutch and Polish Social Democrats who deny the right of nations to self-determination under socialism".[21] Ironically, Lenin was comparing one Luxemburg (*Junius*) favourably with another (Polish social democrat). Lenin's critique of Luxemburg completed that previously begun by Kautsky in the article *Finis Poloniae?* which was directed at her early work.[22] He agreed that the restoration of Poland and the maintenance of Turkish unity was no longer a necessity for European democracy. Nor was national independence an aspiration of the working class to be unconditionally defended in all circumstances. Yet social democracy could not abstract from the national factor. The practical tasks of social democracy demanded a clear-sighted appraisal of the real influence of nationalism in the ranks of the working class. Nor could Luxemburg evade this duty by simply saying that the national question could not be resolved under capitalism.

Luxemburg welcomed the October revolution of 1917, but in *The Russian Revolution* of 1918 she once again took issue with the Bolshevik policy on self-determination. According to Luxemburg, this slogan was leading to the disintegration of Russia and creating many difficulties for the new Soviet state. Instead of opposing all forms of separatism and defending the integrity of the Russian Empire as an area of revolution, the Bolsheviks

> by their hollow nationalistic phraseology concerning the 'right of self-determination to the point of separation' have accomplished quite the contrary and supplied the bourgeoisie in all border areas with the finest, the most desirable pretext, the very banner of counterrevolutionary efforts.[23]

The Finnish bourgeoisie, like the Ukrainian one, would prefer the violent rule of Germany to national freedom, if that were associated with Bolshevik rule. As class antagonisms sharpened, the Bolsheviks were simply confusing the masses in the border countries and delivering them up to the demagogy of the bourgeoisie. She simply could not understand the "obstinacy and rigid consistency" with which Lenin and his comrades maintained the slogan of self-determination while their general organizational principles were rigidly centralist.

Certainly, in the early stages of the revolution, many of the border nations did separate from the central government and the Bolsheviks had some difficulty in winning them back (see Chapter 4). But there is no evidence that this was because of the policy of self-determination in itself, and generally this work of Luxemburg's suffers from a lack of concrete reference. It was the last shot in the running battle between Lenin and Luxemburg (who was murdered in 1919) on nationalism.

For Luxemburg, Ukrainian nationalism after the October revolution

> was a mere whim, a folly of a few dozen petty bourgeois intellectuals without the slightest roots in the economic, political or psychological relationships of the country; it was without any historical tradition, since the Ukraine never formed a nation or government, was without any national culture . . . .[24]

This hostile invective is reminiscent of Engels' diatribe against the South Slavs, and it is significant that Luxemburg never dissociated herself from the 1848 category of 'non-historic' nations. Trotsky in the chapter on 'The Problem of Nationalities' in his *History of the Russian Revolution* took Luxemburg to task on the Ukrainian issue.[25] It was, wrote Trotsky, a very serious historical error to think that the Bolshevik formula of self-determination had artificially created a 'national question' in the Ukraine. The February 1917 democratic revolution had effectively led to the political awakening of the peasantry. They "had not made national demands in the past for the reason that the Ukrainian peasantry had not in general risen to the height of political being".[26] The oppressed classes and nations of Russia could now speak out. In the circumstances

> this political awakening of the peasantry could not have taken place otherwise, however, than through their own native language — with all the consequences ensuing in regard to schools, courts, self-administration.[27]

This defensive nationalism could not be opposed by "a false banner of internationalism". Social contradictions sometimes took national disguises, but the conflict of nationalities was an essential element in destabilizing the February regime and making the October revolution possible. As Trotsky noted, "in these circumstances the national antagonisms whenever they coincided with class contradictions became especially hot".[28]

Having examined the complexity of Luxemburg's positions on the national question, can we simply say she was 'wrong', as the upholders of Leninist orthodoxy are tempted to do? If we begin with Luxemburg's method of analysis we can say that it suffered from a certain 'economism', as did virtually all the theoreticians of the Second International. This was apparent in her doctoral dissertation on Polish industrialization which determined "with the iron strength of historical necessity" the reactionary nature of Polish nationalism. In a subsequent article on social-patriotism in 1902, she argued that the economic tendency of Poland to unite with Russia would "therefore" lead to political unity.[29] In the one word "therefore", Luxemburg betrayed a heavily determinist economic analysis — there was an almost total lack of mediation between the economic 'base' and the political 'superstructure'. Luxemburg often spoke of "iron necessity" and the inevitability of natural laws. She was *not*, however, as inconsistent as her respective positions on Poland and Turkey might lead us to believe. She had broken with the earlier liberal attitude of socialists towards nationalism and posed a coherent alternative based on an analysis of the concrete situation and the interests of the class struggle. The practical interests of social democracy always took precedence over their natural inclination to support all those aspiring to freedom. In Turkey, these two criteria coincided and national liberation would lead to the development of the forces of production. In Poland, on the other hand, national independence had ceased to be a revolutionary demand, and it did not correspond with the necessity of social development.

It is common to read that Luxemburg 'underestimated' nationalism.[30] In a sense this is undeniable, in particular where her earlier writings are concerned. Yet in her post-1905 writings we do get an occasional glimpse of nationalism's real strength. In her foreword to the 1905 anthology she wrote:

> To the credit of mankind, history has universally established that even the most inhumane *material* oppression is not able to provoke such wrathful, fanatical rebellion and rage as the suppression of intellectual life in general, or as religious or national oppression.[31]

There was never any doubting of socialist condemnation of this "intolerably barbaric oppression". The point Luxemburg made was that only the working class was in the material social position which made possible an effective struggle against all forms of oppression. In this she was following Marx's footsteps. Even sympathetic writers, such as Löwy, have argued that

> Luxemburg saw only the anachronistic, petty-bourgeois and reactionary aspects of national liberation movements and did not grasp their revolutionary potential against Tsarism.[32]

In fact, Luxemburg did recognize, at least partially, what Löwy calls "the complex and contradictory dialectic of the *dual nature* of these nationalist movements".[33] In 1908 she had explicitly argued that "the working class is interested in the *cultural* and *democratic* content of nationalism . . . ."[34] Against a common view that she was personally hostile to Polish national ideals she had also written earlier that "today our national identity cannot be defended by national separatism; it can only be secured through the struggle to overthrow despotism . . . ."[35]

The major misinterpretation of Luxemburg's work on the national question has been perpetuated by her biographer J.P. Nettl for whom "Rosa Luxemburg elaborated the theoretical foundations of her anti-nationalist position, and extended it beyond the context of Poland".[36] Firstly, Luxemburg's position cannot be described as 'anti-nationalist'; but more generally we cannot accept the idea that she universalized from her Polish experience (Turkey being the one contrary example). Frölich is closer to the point when he notes that she "did not accept any dogma or universally applicable formula for the solution of national questions".[37] National movements could be progressive or reactionary according to the international context, and their social composition. There was no immutable socialist attitude towards nationalism. Nettl further states that for Luxemburg "national and Socialist aspirations were incompatible".[38] Posed in these terms Luxemburg's position does not make sense because it was not an attempt to reconcile the national factor in politics with the class struggle. In fact, Luxemburg only followed Marx to the letter in distinguishing between right and necessity, between principle and tactics. Nettl is wrong in this context to write that national self-determination was the first of Luxemburg's "indices of an opportunism which held Socialism to the chariot of the class enemy . . . ."[39] Luxemburg supported national freedom but she was opposed to elevating the slogan of self-determination to a principle as a 'right'. Class positions could be the only foundation of socialist politics: the attitude towards the national question would be determined by historical circumstances.[40]

The radical left

Apart from Rosa Luxemburg, it was Joseph Strasser and Anton Pannekoek who most consistently criticized socialist adaptation to nationalism, particularly, as they saw it, in the work of Otto Bauer. We consider both of these writers in turn, showing how they stressed the primacy of class over national divisions.

After the 1907 elections for the Austrian Reichsrat, the pan-national trade union movement, and later the social democratic party, began to break up under the onslaught of a nationalist revival. The Czech trade unions took the first step, demanding the independence of the Prague confederation from the Vienna centre which they accused of 'pan-Germanism'. It was in this context that the editor of *Vorwärts* in Bohemia, Joseph Strasser, published *The Worker and the Nation* in 1912.[41] His main target was Otto Bauer's strategy of national autonomy within the Austrian social democratic party as the best way to combat nationalism. To this, Strasser counterposed a frontal attack on nationalism as an ideology foreign to the working class.

Strasser argued that Czech and Slovak social democracy had 'fallen under the spell' of nationalist conceptions. Nationalist demagogy had drawn back the proletariat to its mythical 'national duty'. Strasser went through the nationalist arguments one by one to show how the proletariat had essentially different interests from those of the 'nation'. The working class had different cultural interests from those of the bourgeoisie; even the language question should not give rise to dissension if treated from a 'proletarian perspective'. Even if the national territory was attacked, worker and bourgeois would defend it for different reasons. National character was not an ahistorical homogeneous entity; it was capable of changing, and the division of the nation into classes made a "community of interests" (Bauer) a myth. Workers mocked nationalism and its mean reactionary politics — "for the worker, the world of nationalism is too narrow . . . he is a born internationalist . . . ."[42] Socialists could only recognize one source of sovereignty, the social whole, and they were opposed to any form of national autonomy. The separation of Czech workers from the central trade union body could only lead to a decline in their wages and a worsening of working conditions.

For Strasser, the relation of socialists to the nation was analogous to that *vis-à-vis* religion and the church. Against nationalism, it was no use counterposing the internationalism of the revisionists, this was merely "a morally purified nationalism, the supreme perfection and superlative of nationalism".[43] Nationalism should rather be treated as any other non-proletarian ideology and therefore socialists could only "counterpose to nationalist ideology the ideology of intransigent internationalism".[44] This would not be difficult, because the class conscious workers always judged things from a class perspective and not as Germans, Catholics or whatever. In fact, "if a person's national and economic interests enter into contradiction, economic interests prove to be stronger".[45] Sporadic exceptions to this rule may appear amongst isolated individuals who are detached from their class, but never amongst the mass of workers.

Otto Bauer was to write a spirited reply to Strasser's radical-left redefinition of the national question. He reiterated the importance of the nation and national struggles, which could not be assessed from a "shopkeeper's perspective". That was a reference to Strasser's economism and his point that the good German-Austrian patriot would shop in Czech stores if they were cheaper. Nor was proletarian internationalism indifferent to the destiny of the nation – on condition that the expansion of one nation was not at the expense of another. A vital point he made was that the liberation of the working class "is the liberation of the human species, and its particular interest is the true common interest of all individuals and of all peoples".[46] Though sympathic to Strasser's attack on German chauvinism, he argued that a lack of understanding of the national question on the part of socialists would only push workers into the hands of the bourgeois nationalism. Strasser appealed to Kautsky's orthodoxy in replying to Bauer's attack. He argued that the idealism implicit in nationalism always had material roots — "any cultural question is in the last instance an economic question".[47] Class interests and nationalism were basically incompatible. For Strasser, internationalism was incompatible with any form of nationalism; rather "*one* language, *one* nation, *one* humanity: that is the ideal of internationalism".[48] Social democracy, argued Strasser, did not represent 'nations' nor even the 'mass of the people', but only the proletariat. Though the *Communist Manifesto* could be quoted by Strasser in his support, Marx also wrote of the proletariat as the 'national class' which would lead the whole nation forward (see Chapter 1).

Anton Pannekoek was a Dutch astronomer, who, apart from his writings on the national question, wrote a remarkable critique of Lenin's philosophy and went on to become a leader of the council communism movement.[49] While Strasser's work on nationalism had been tied to a particular context, Pannekoek painted on a much broader theoretical canvas. Along with Rosa Luxemburg, he was one of the first to criticize the 'Marxist centre' led by Kautsky on a wide range of questions, including the national question. It was in this context that his *Class Struggle and the Nation* was published in 1912.

For the bourgeoisie, wrote Pannekoek, nations represented natural differences between people; for social democracy the nation was a human grouping produced simply by a common history, and, above all, by economic circumstances.[50] The modern nation-state was a product of capitalism: a combat organization of the rising bourgeoisie. The 'essence of the nation' lay in people's spiritual development, itself a product of material circumstances. For the bourgeoisie this entailed the need for a national base to engage in competition; but "the proletariat has nothing in common with this need for competition of the bourgeois classes, with their national aspiration".[51] The development of the class struggle leads inevitably to a disappearance of the "community of destiny" which had characterized the nation at its formation. The class struggle unites workers in their own "community of destiny" overcoming all national differences and rivalries. The future socialist society would extend this community throughout the world, with the organization of production on a global scale making the nation a relic of the past. For the working class, the national pertains to tradition and history; it has no material roots in the present.

Pannekoek then drew radically different conclusions from those of Bauer on the strategy of socialism *vis-à-vis* nationalism. He accused Bauer of 'national opportunism'. Pannekoek, for his part, argued that nationalism "as any bourgeois ideology, constitutes a brake on the class struggle, whose prejudicial effect must be eliminated as far as possible . . . ."[52] National aims and objectives detract from those of the working class and must be resolutely opposed. National struggles prevent the development of social questions and proletarian interests in the political domain. No ideology from the past would resist "the omnipotence of real class interests".[53] It would be wrong for socialists to attempt to use national grievances to win the proletariat for socialism. From this level, Pannekoek descended to socialist tactics where he essentially supported the social democratic programme of national autonomy as a practical solution to cut the ground from under the nationalists. In the long run, the detrimental power of nationalism could not be overcome by this programme but only "by the strengthening of class consciousness".[54]

Bauer's response to Pannekoek's study was to refuse to publish it in his review *Der Kampf*, arguing that its theoretical content did little to clarify the concrete tasks of social democracy in the national domain. He wrote to Pannekoek saying that

> what we need today is not a discussion on the essence of the nation or on the question of knowing whether in the future national differentiation will increase or not, but to discuss a quite different question, that of knowing how the Austrian proletariat should conduct itself with regard to the present national struggles within the bourgeoisie. It is that discussion which is the most urgent.[55]

This pragmatic response certainly reflected the order of priorities amongst the majority of social democrats. The theoretical weaknesses of Pannekoek's discourse seem evident, but they were not squarely confronted. This reflected, as Haupt points out, "a refusal and incapacity to reason theoretically, and the reticence to include the national question in their [social democracy's] theoretical field",[56] Pannekoek had in fact replaced the idealism of nationalism with another 'Marxist' idealism which saw the inexorable development of the forces of production entering into contradiction with the relations of production; and the emergence of a proletariat which would be the bearer of a new mode of production, quite uncontaminated by the impurities of the old. With the First World War this historical evolutionism seemed confirmed: the era of national movements was at a close; henceforth only the international struggle of the proletariat could overcome the problem of the oppressed nations. This evolutionist and, in some way optimistic perspective was to have an effect even in the Russian Bolshevik party, in spite of that party's official support for the policy of national self-determination.

In the Bolshevik party there was a group around Nikolai Bukharin and Grigori Piatakov which argued against the idea of self-determination during the First World War, on the basis that it was meaningless under capitalism and harmful under socialism. In their 1915 *Theses on the Right of Self-Determination*, they argued that

> Tne slogan of 'self-determination of nations' is first of all *utopian* (it cannot be realized *within the limits* of capitalism) and *harmful* as a slogan which *disseminates* illusions.[57]

For the proletariat to deflect its attention from the class struggle to the settling of 'national problems' was considered harmful. The task of social democracy was to put forward a "propaganda of indifference" with respect to the nation (be it great power or oppressed nations). Another set of *Theses* by Karl Radek, issued in 1916, was even more explicit:

> Tied hand and foot, corrupted politically by nationalism, the proletariat of the oppressed nation turns into a *defenceless object of exploitation* and at the same time a dangerous competitor (wage-cutters, strike breakers) to the workers of the oppressing nation.[58]

Here the 'Radical Left' was coming near to the open social imperialism of right-wing social democracy (see Chapter 2). It was no excuse to say that "in the *oppressed nations*, the slogan of the right to self-determination could serve as a bridge to social patriotism".[59] For this group of workers the right of self-determination can only arouse hopes that cannot be fulfilled under capitalism. Under socialism, national oppression will disappear "because it removes the class interests that furnish the driving forces of such oppression".[60]

At the Eighth Party Congress of the Bolsheviks in 1919, Bukharin returned to the argument that the interests of the world proletariat were paramount. Piatakov, for his part, now in charge of the Ukraine, condemned the slogan of national self-determination as essentially reactionary. Against the traditional slogan of national self-determination, Bukharin proposed "Self-determination of the toiling masses of each nationality", and the phrase 'self-determination' was actually removed from the Bolshevik programme. The idea of self-determination for the working class made little sense as a goal because it was included in the aims of socialism. What it meant in practice was demonstrated by Piatakov who argued that Soviet Russia must, in the interest of the world revolution, maintain the hold of its power in the Ukraine, even if this meant denying national autonomy to the Ukrainian proletariat.[61] Lenin, on the other hand, urged patience and tolerance for nationalist aspirations. Piatakov, who had even wanted a uniform education programme for the nationalities drew his bitter comment — "Such a Communist is a Great Russian chauvinist".[62] Was this the 'logical conclusion' of Luxemburg's point of view, as Davis argues?[63] There is no way to provide a definitive answer, but this episode, which led to Piatakov's removal in 1920, demonstrated the grave dangers of a 'super-internationalist' response to the national question. Again, despite all its inconsistencies (see Chapter 4), Lenin's adherence to the right of nations to self-determination did provide the rudiments of a principled yet flexible proletarian policy towards nationalism.

The young Trotsky also held what might be called a 'Luxemburgist' conception of the national question. Trotsky essentially considered the nation-state an historical anachronism destined to be swept aside by the rising tide of economic development. We have already seen (see Chapter 2) how in *The War and the International* (1914) he argued that

> The present war is at bottom a revolt of the forces of production against the political form of nation and state. It means the collapse of the national state as an independent economic unit.[64]

He later argued that the war, in "breaking up the nation-state, was also destroying the national basis for revolution".[65] In his major study of Trotsky, Knei-Paz writes with some exaggeration that, as regards the national question, "he wrote virtually nothing on this question either before or after 1917".[66] Even more sympathetic writers like Isaac Deutscher find Trotsky dismissive of the national dimension in favour of a somewhat abstract internationalism. In 1915 he did, however, write two articles on 'Nation and Economy' in *Nashe Slovo*.[67] Here he supported the right to national political independence, even accepting that "the nation is a powerful and extremely stable factor in human culture".[68] But he still argued that the "needs of economic development" would lead to the demise of the nation-state.[69] European nations would disappear into the 'United States of Europe', although nations would be granted rights to self-determination in the cultural sphere. By 1917, Trotsky had become a somewhat uncritical supporter of the Leninist position on the right of nations to self-determination. This marked a more extreme neglect and under-estimation of the national question than Luxemburg's.

Economism was a methodological 'deviation' shared by Strasser, Pannekoek, Bukharin, Piatakov, Radek and the young Trotsky. For them, nationalism had either economic or ill-defined cultural roots, but they neglected the political dimension. It was Lenin's unequalled political realism which was to allow him to develop a more fruitful analysis (see Chapter 4). Though these writers shared with Lenin an analysis of the new era of imperialism, they did not recognize that this would lead to an increase in national wars, not a cessation. Essentially, they tended to confuse national wars and imperialist wars. Likewise, they equated the urge to national self-determination with the growing phenomena of 'social patriotism' amongst the social democrats of the imperialist nations. They followed the evolutionist trend of Marxism, and accepted the category of 'non-historic' nations. Marx had also, of course, begun to distinguish between oppressed and oppressor nations when dealing with the Irish question. The full implications of this distinction were only really drawn out by Lenin. Finally the 'Radical Left' did not have a sufficiently subtle appreciation of the radical potential implicit in some nationalist movements: nationalism was reduced to pure and simple bourgeois ideology. In the imperialist era, more than ever before, there was to be a complex interaction between national and social claims, something Connolly had appreciated in practice in 1916.

Marxism against nationalism

Karl Radek, seen above in support of Rosa Luxemburg, was amongst those European socialists who viewed the Irish rising of 1916 as an adventurist *putsch*. Connolly had predicted that his fellow socialists in Europe would not understand why he had taken part of the labour movement into a nationalist uprising. With Connolly dead it was left to Lenin to assess the real revolutionary role of the Easter Rising.[70]

While Radek argued that the rising had "not much social backing", Lenin showed that the long-standing struggle for national independence in Ireland had

> expressed itself in street fighting conducted by a section of the urban petty bourgeoisie and a *section of the workers* after a long period of mass agitation, demonstrations, suppression of papers, etc.[71]

Only hardened reactionaries or doctrinaire socialists, who did not understand social revolution as a living phenomenon, would call such an uprising a *putsch*, the work of a circle of conspirators or stupid maniacs. In contrast, Lenin understood that a real revolution would not take a 'pure' form:

> To imagine that a social revolution is *conceivable* without revolts of small nations in the colonies and in Europe, without the revolutionary outbursts of a section of the petty bourgeoisie *with all its prejudices*, without the movement of non-class-conscious proletarian and semi-proletarian masses against the oppression of the landlords, the church, the monarchy, the foreign yoke, etc. — to imagine that is tantamount to *repudiating social revolution*. Only those who imagine that in one place an army will line up and say 'we are for socialism' and in another place, another army will say, 'we are for imperialism' and believe that this will be the social revolution, only those who hold such a ridiculously pedantic opinion could vilify the Irish rebellion by calling it a 'putsch'.[72]

The working class, especially in an oppressed nation, could hardly be expected to spring up fully clad in Marxist colours to lead a proletarian revolution. Even the prejudices of the nationalist petty bourgeoisie were nothing to be surprised about. The role of nationalism was crucial:

> The dialectics of history are such that small nations powerless as an *independent* factor in the struggle against imperialism, play a part as one of the ferments, one of the bacilli which facilitate the entry into the arena of *real* power against imperialism, namely, the socialist proletariat.[73]

Here nationalism is seen as a detonator for the 'real' revolutionary force — the working class. Lenin, furthermore, distinguished between national revolts in Europe and those in the colonies:

> The struggle of the oppressed nations *in Europe*, a struggle capable of going to the lengths of insurrection and street fighting, breach of military discipline in the army and martial law, 'sharpens the revolutionary crisis in Europe' infinitely more than a much more complete rebellion in a single colony.[74]

Here too Lenin had not gone as far as he would later on with the 'Eastern question' in supporting national movements. Yet the general impact of his analysis of 1916 is clear:

> The misfortune of the Irish is that they rose prematurely, when the European revolt of the proletariat had *not yet* matured . . . [But] only in revolutionary movements which are often premature, partial, sporadic, and, therefore, unsuccessful, will the masses gain experience, acquire knowledge, gather strength, get to know their real leaders, the socialist proletarians, and in that way prepare for the general onslaught, in the same way as separate strikes, demonstrations, local and national, mutinies in the army, outbreaks among the peasantry, etc., prepared the way for the general onslaught in 1905.[75]

In Ireland itself labour leaders were on the whole just as baffled by Connolly's role in the rising as were the European, and especially the British, socialists. One of Connolly's comrades in the Irish Citizen Army, the playwright Sean O'Casey, expressed a common feeling when he wrote that in the build-up to 1916

> Jim Connolly had stepped from the narrow byway of Irish Socialism on to the broad and crowded highway of Irish Nationalism . . . .The Labour movement seemed to be regarded by him as a decrescent force, while the essence of Nationalism began to assume the finest element of his nature.[76]

Did Connolly forsake internationalism for a narrow Catholic nationalism? None of his writings in the period leading up to 1916 indicate anything other than a 'Leninist' attitude towards the national question. As we showed in Chapter 2, Connolly saw the task of socialists during the First World War as one of turning an imperialist war into a civil war. That, in colonial Ireland, would inevitably take a national form, and Connolly was well aware that his erstwhile allies in the nationalist movement would turn on labour if they were victorious. The myth of Connolly as nationalist is a powerful one, propounded by bourgeois nationalists and 'pure' socialists alike. A recent restatement of this position by Austen Morgan argues that

> In trying to construct a Marxist explanation of nationalism's area of concern, Connolly tumbled headlong into green cotton wool, apparently remaining ignorant of his fall . . . Connolly lived as a socialist and died a nationalist.[77]

We now turn to recent controversies on the 'Connolly heritage' regarding nationalism and socialism.

A group of contemporary historians, Paul Bew, Peter Gibbon and Henry Patterson, have individually and collectively developed a 'revisionist' position on Irish nationalism. They argue that Marx and Lenin supported Irish nationalism only under very precise conditions — the first as an aid to the English revolution, and the second in so far as it threatened international imperialism.[78] The Marxist approach to nationalism is neither economic (Luxemburg) nor ideological (Bauer), but rather political. It was the international context which determined whether a national struggle was progressive (i.e. democratic) or not. In short, the national question is held to be a variant form of the question of democracy. They then argue that "Imperialism's real impact upon Irish society has not been a substantial one" and furthermore that "struggles over the status of the north are no more automatically anti-imperialist than crimes against property are automatically anti-capitalist".[79] The second statement is undoubtedly correct in a formal sense; but the first flies in the face of all evidence of economic domination of Ireland north and south by international capitalism, the division of the country by partitition in the 1920s and the continued military occupation of six counties in the north-east.

It is precisely the question of national partition which these authors refuse to see as a question of democracy. Instead, the demand for Irish unity is presented as one for 'territorial integrity' or "irredentism". They argue that "contrary to common assumption there is nothing inherently reactionary about a national frontier which puts Protestants in a numerical majority".[80] Perhaps not if it had been agreed to by the majority of the Irish people; but it was imposed by military force. They further argue that if Irish unity is *not* achieved there will be

> democracy for three million in the south, albeit infringed by the 'sense of national grievance', accompanied by restrictions on democracy for a million and a half, in the north, the result of the forcible inclusion of a Catholic minority within the state's borders.[81]

This, however, seems preferable to them rather than the alternative of "territorial completion" with "the probability of restrictions on democracy for *four and a half million* as a consequence of the forcible inclusion of a Protestant minority within a thirty-two county republic".[82] There is a distancing from the "sense of national grievance" as though it was not real; even Rosa Luxemburg was not quite so detached. There is a further strange assumption that a united Ireland would automatically result in further restrictions on democratic rights. In fact, the whole method of a numerical head count is 'un-Marxist' — the main question should be whether a nationalist war is hindering or promoting the prospects of socialism. Most independent observers seem to agree that the war is destabilizing the bourgeois political structure of north and south. Irish unity would be achieved in this process as part of a much wider social revolution which would overthrow the structures of dependent capitalism.

One of the key assumptions of Bew *et al*. is that "the democratic, that is to say the *national*, stage of the Irish revolution seems to have been as complete as it ever could be in 1921".[83] To argue that the war of independence (1919-21) left the Irish revolution 'incomplete' is for them a simple tautology. They argue elsewhere that recent "urbanization and industrialization have relegated the national question to the margin of Irish politics . . . ."[84] There is thus little material basis for a national struggle in Ireland, and the issue of reunification is of purely sentimental significance. Certainly to say the national revolution is 'incomplete' is but a rough analogy — it means that the civil war which followed the struggle against Britain did not pit the fundamental classes against each other but merely two fractions of the petty bourgeoisie. In that sense, the tasks of the radical republican movement are incomplete; completion not being a territorial issue but a political one. As to the 'mythical' nature of the national question today nothing could be further from the truth. Not only has a revolutionary nationalist movement been waging a war in a Western European country for 15 years, but every single aspect of economic, political and ideological life in all parts of Ireland is overlaid by the national question. This applies above all to the working class. Until the national question is settled there can be no 'pure' class politics in Ireland. For that reason alone, if no other, socialists have an interest in the outcome of the Irish nationalist struggle.

The 'revisionist' case against nationalism is also advanced by Austen Morgan who argues that the strategy of the Irish left has always oscillated between a *class* and a *nation* perspective; where they have attempted a synthesis, following Connolly, "they have become enchanted by nationalism's lyrical but simple, heroic but foolish, problematic of Brits Out/a United Ireland . . . ."[85] Instead, Morgan advocates that the left should reappropriate 'red socialism' and advance an international perspective. Is the nationalist 'green socialism' such a naive and foolish perspective in Ireland today? If we take international criteria into account, a successful national revolution in Ireland would seriously weaken NATO — it is not merely propaganda that leads perceptive British politicians to speak of the danger of an 'Irish Cuba'. If we take democracy as the criteria, partition did lead to "a carnival of reaction" north and south, as Connolly predicted, and neither state is a paragon of democratic virtue today. Republicanism has a secular democratic programme (not reducible to Brits Out) which 'red socialists' are not really in a good position to dispute after the somewhat less than full, democratic experience of 'actually existing socialism'. There are no nuances in the anti-nationalist polemic of Bew and Morgan. It is not, after all, an undifferentiated nationalist movement which is waging a war, but a specific revolutionary nationalist or republican movement committed to democratic socialism. A 'pure' red socialism which sees class antagonists lined up neatly for a 'clean' war is as unlikely today as it was in 1916 when Lenin condemned the 'purists' of his day.

This does not mean that we should blur the lines between Republicanism and socialism as Purdie argues in an important article.[86] He had earlier stated that "a fusion between revolutionary Marxism and Republicanism is the future for the Irish revolutionary movement".[87] He later carefully demystified the ideas implicit in this strategy and denied that the national and socialist struggles could be fused. The democratic radicalism of Irish Republicanism could not be equated with Marxism. The political ideas of Republicanism were, he argued, incompatible with an advocacy of the class struggle. This is all undoubtedly true in a formal abstract sense, but again as in 1916, real revolutions are not made by political programmes but non-class-conscious masses with all their prejudices as Lenin recognized. The nature of republicanism is largely dictated by the tasks it faces as a revolutionary movement. To ignore the national question in Ireland in practice condemns any socialist movement to the sidelines. A small political group in the south, 'Socialists against Nationalism', voices this position. Marxists should recognize that internationalism does not preclude supporting a nationalist movement, as Marx and Engels stressed in the case of Poland and Ireland. Rosa Luxemburg's writings might be taken as support for the argument that socialists should work to democratize the two partition states and not concern themselves with national reunification — but in her Poland the nationalist movement was really a marginal phenomenon whereas in Ireland it affects most of the population in one way or another. Marxism *against* nationalism is no answer to 'social patriotic' tendencies.

Notes

1. H.B. Davis (ed), *The National Question: Selected Writings by Rosa Luxemburg* (Monthly Review Press, New York, 1976) p.77.
2. Ibid., p.62.
3. C. Herod, *The Nation in the History of Marxian Thought* (Martinus Nijhoff, The Hague, 1976) p.86.
4. V.I. Lenin, *Collected Works*, Vol. 20 (Progress Publishers, Moscow, 1964) p.430.
5. H. Davis (ed.), *The National Question*, p.57.
6. Ibid., p.58.
7. Ibid., p.67.
8. Ibid., p.72.
9. Ibid., p.85.
10. Ibid., p.96.
11. Ibid., p.97.
12. Ibid., p.109.
13. Ibid., p.148.
14. Ibid., p.163.
15. M.A. Waters (ed.), *Rosa Luxemburg Speaks* (Pathfinder Press, New York, 1970) p.305.
16. Ibid., p.305.
17. Ibid., p.307.

18. Ibid., p.315.
19. V.I. Lenin, *Collected Works*, Vol. 22 (Progress Publishers, Moscow, 1964) p.310.
20. Ibid., p.312.
21. Ibid.
22. K. Kautsky, 'Finis Poloniae?', *Nieue Zeit*, XIV, No. II, 1895-6.
23. M.A. Waters (ed.), *Rosa Luxemburg Speaks*, p.382.
24. Ibid.
25. L. Trotsky, *History of the Russian Revolution*, Vol. 3, (Sphere Books, London, 1967).
26. Ibid., p.47.
27. Ibid.
28. Ibid., p.51.
29. Cited in M. Löwy, 'Marxists and the National Question', *New Left Review*, No. 96, 1976, p.88.
30. E.g. P. Frölich, *Rosa Luxemburg, Ideas in Action* (Pluto Press, London, 1972) p.30 (he adds that she also "failed to recognise the psychological aspect of this question").
31. H. Davis (ed.), *The National Question*, p.96.
32. M. Löwy, *Marxists and the National Question*, p.88.
33. Ibid.
34. H. Davis (ed.), *The National Question*, p.175.
35. Ibid., p.97.
36. J.P. Nettl, *Rosa Luxemburg* (Oxford University Press, 1969) p.503. For another 'universalist' interpretation see J. Petrus, 'The Theory and Practice of Internationalism: Rosa Luxemburg's Solution to the National Question', *East European Quarterly*, Vol. IV, No. 4, 1981.
37. P. Frölich, *Rosa Luxemburg*, p.29.
38. J.P. Nettl, *Rosa Luxemburg*, p.503.
39. Ibid.
40. For a development of this topic see G. Haupt, 'Dynamisme et conservatisme de l'ideologie: Rosa Luxemburg a l'orée de la recherche marxiste dans le domain national', *Pluriel*, No. 11, 1977.
41. In R. Calwer *et al.*, *La Segunda Internacional y el Problema Nacional y Colonial (segunda parte)* (Siglo XXI, Mexico, 1978).
42. Ibid., p.221.
43. Ibid., p.231.
44. Ibid., p.237.
45. Ibid., p.230.
46. Ibid., p.253.
47. Ibid., p.239.
48. Ibid., p.241.
49. For an introduction to Pannekoek and Herman Görter (who also wrote on the national question) see D. Smart (ed.), *Pannekoek and Görter's Marxism* (Pluto Press, London, 1978).
50. In 'Lucha de clases y nación' in R. Calwer *et al.*, *La Segunda Internacional y el Problema Nacional y Colonial*.
51. Ibid., p.275.
52. Ibid., p.290.
53. Ibid., p.293.

54. Ibid., p.303.

55. Cited in G. Haupt, 'Les Marxistes face à la question nationale: l'histoire du problème', in G. Haupt, M. Löwy and C. Weill (eds.), *Les Marxistes et la Question Nationale 1848-1914* (Maspero, Paris, 1974) p.51.

56. Ibid.

57. O. Gankin and H. Fisher, *The Bolsheviks and the World War: The Origin of the Third International* (Stanford University Press, 1960) p.219.

58. 'Theses of the Editors of Gazeta Robotnicza', Appendix to H. Davis (ed.), *The National Question*, p.304.

59. Ibid., p.311.

60. Ibid., p.310.

61. R. Daniels, *The Conscience of the Revolution* (Simon and Schuster, New York, 1969) p.97.

62. Ibid.

63. H. Davis (ed.), *The National Question*, p.28.

64. L. Trotsky, *The War and the International* (Wesley Publications, Wellawate, 1971) p.VII.

65. Cited in I. Deutscher, *The Prophet Armed, Trotsky: 1879-1921* (Oxford University Press, 1970) p.237.

66. B. Knei-Paz, *The Social and Political Thought of Leon Trotsky* (Clarendon Press, Oxford, 1979) p.547.

67. In *International*, Vol. 3, No. 4, 1977.

68. Ibid., p.56.

69. Ibid.

70. In 'The Discussion of Self-Determination Summed Up' *Collected Works*, Vol. 22 (Progress Publishers, Moscow, 1964).

71. Ibid., p.355.

72. Ibid., pp.355-6.

73. Ibid., p.357.

74. Ibid., pp.356-7.

75. Ibid., p.358.

76. S. O'Casey, *The Story of the Irish Citizen Army* (Oriole Editions, New York, 1919) p.52.

77. A. Morgan, 'Socialism in Ireland — Red, Green and Orange', in A. Morgan and B. Purdie (eds.) *Ireland: Divided Nation, Divided Class* (Ink Links, London, 1980) p.179 and p.178.

78. 'Marxism and Ireland', in P. Bew, P. Gibbon and H. Patterson, *The State in Northern Ireland 1921-72* (Manchester University Press, 1979).

79. Ibid., p.25 and p.24.

80. Ibid., p.221.

81. Ibid., p.19.

82. Ibid.

83. Ibid.

84. P. Bew, P. Gibbon and H. Patterson, 'Some Aspects of Nationalism and Socialism in Ireland: 1968-1978', in A. Morgan and B. Purdie (eds.), *Ireland: Divided Nation, Divided Class*, p.160.

85. A. Morgan, *Socialism in Ireland*, p.181.

86. B. Purdie, 'Reconsiderations on Republicanism and Socialism', in A. Morgan and B. Purdie (eds.), *Ireland: Divided Nation, Divided Class*.

87. B. Purdie *Ireland Unfree* (IMG Publications, London, 1972) p.37.

4. Leninism

Of all the debates within Marxism on nationalism, Lenin's concept of the right of nations to self-determination is the most famous and the one which has had most practical effect. In this chapter we trace Lenin's development of the principle of national self-determination against the 'leftist' views of Rosa Luxemburg and the 'rightist' line of Bauer and Renner. What did this right of nations to separation amount to if Lenin did not actually expect them to secede? Lenin's sometimes contradictory and pragmatic writings on nationalism have been elevated to a pinnacle of polished proletarian policy. It was Stalin, however, who elaborated the orthodoxy of 'Leninism', in particular through his unduly influential pamphlet *Marxism and the National Question* which we shall consider next. Finally, we turn to developments in the Russian Empire after the revolutions of 1917, and Lenin's last confrontation with Stalin before his death in 1924.

The national minorities had played a major role in breaking up the old empire between the February and October revolutions of 1917. Now, as the right to self-determination was put to the test, the Bolsheviks turned to a more centralist policy, and redefined self-determination to apply only to the workers of the oppressed nationalities. Stalin, as People's Commissar for Affairs of Nationalities, played a major role in suppressing the national revolts; though Lenin at first backed this policy, he began to develop grave objections. In confronting Stalin, Lenin sowed many doubts as to whether 'Leninism' had in fact resolved the relations between socialism and nationalism.

The right to self-determination

The first congress of the Russian Social Democratic and Labour Party (RSDLP) in 1898 made no reference to the national question; but its second congress in 1903 drew up a programme which included the famous Article 9 which demanded "The right of all nations in the state to self-determination". This new-found interest in the national question was largely the result of the demand made in 1901 by the Jewish workers' organization, the Bund, to be recognized as the sole representative of Jewish workers within the party.[1] The Bund supported the minority position taken by the South Slavs at the 1898

Brünn Congress, namely for extraterritorial or 'personal' national autonomy. The demand for national cultural autonomy proposed by the Bund was shortly to be taken up by the Byelorussian socialists, the Georgian socialist federalist party and the Dashnaktsutiun movement in Armenia. The response of the Socialist Revolutionaries (SR) at their first congress in 1905 was to support a federalist solution and to recognize the principle of national cultural autonomy. The RSDLP, for its part, strenuously opposed any concessions to federalism within and outside the party. It did, however, establish the general principle of the right of nations to self-determination, which it took from the 1896 platform of the Second International adopted in London (see Chapter 2). As yet, 'national self-determination' was more a declaration of principles, rather than a fully worked out programme.

The 1905 revolution was to bring the national question more fully into the centre of social democratic politics. The 'Leninist' theory of self-determination was not fully elaborated until Lenin moved to Polish Cracow in 1912 and began a thorough investigation of the national question. Before that Lenin had not been fully aware of the socialist literature on the national question, and had simply advocated a pragmatic alliance between the working class and the minority nationalities. He argued in 1903 that

> Class antagonism has now undoubtedly relegated national questions far into the background, but, without the risk of lapsing into doctrinairism, it cannot be categorically asserted that some particular national question cannot appear temporarily in the foreground of the political drama.[2]

A conditional and temporary alliance between the social democrats and the nationalist movements was possible in these circumstances. As yet, this position fell squarely within the framework of the Second International's approach to the national question. From 1912 onwards, under the impact of events in the Balkans and rising international tensions, Lenin was to elaborate a considerably more complex national programme. Referring to the 1896 recognition of national self-determination by the Second International, Lenin stressed "the particularly urgency of this demand under imperialism", the distinction between oppressor and oppressed nations, and "the inconsistent, purely verbal recognition of self-determination by the opportunists and the Kautskyites".[3] Lenin arrived at his position by way of a polemic against the Austro-Marxist and the 'Luxemburgist' position on the national question.

Lenin's attack on the Austro-Marxist positions was in fact motivated by internal party disputes, particularly with the Bundists. Against the demand for Jewish national cultural autonomy, Lenin argued that whoever, directly or indirectly, put forward the slogan of Jewish national culture "[was] (whatever his good intentions may be) an enemy of the proletariat, a supporter of all that is *outmoded* and connected with *caste* among the Jewish people . . . ."[4] In promoting the national cultural slogan of "the rabbis and the bourgeoisie", the Bundists were effectively acting as "instruments of bourgeois nationalism among the workers".[5] Likewise, if Ukrainian socialists counterposed Ukrainian culture to Greater Russian culture as a whole. They would be betraying the interests of the proletariat. Against Otto Bauer's ideas (see Chapter 2) Lenin counterposed the argument that "There are two national cultures in every national culture",[6] that of the bourgeoisie and that of the proletariat. Lenin's hostility to the demands of cultural autonomy for the minority nationalities extended to their schools, against which Lenin directed what seems a disproportionate amount of energy. He wrote in 1913 against the plan for national schools proposed by the Bund and several minority nationalities, "We must most emphatically oppose segregating the schools according to nationality, no matter what form it may take".[7] He abusively compared the Bund's proposal for Jewish schools with the segregation of black and white children in the former slave states of the USA.[8] This opposition had its roots in the Bund's position within the RSDLP. The Bund had left the party in 1903 but, as Lenin writes,

> when the Bund in 1906 again returned to the Party, the Party stipulated the condition that separatism would cease, ie that there should be local unity of all the Marxist workers of *whatever* nationality.[9]

He compared the separatist tendencies of the Bund with those of the Czech workers (see Chapter 2) which, Lenin argued, "destroyed the unity that had previously existed between the Czech and the German workers".[10] At this stage Lenin would not recognize that Czech separatism might be a product of German chauvinism. His main concern was with the unity of Russian social democracy, the rigid centralism which would make the Bolsheviks such a powerful revolutionary instrument after they split with the Mensheviks in 1912. While he attacked the Austro-Marxists for promoting separatism he also argued, somewhat paradoxically, that their proposals for national cultural autonomy were inadequate to deal with the national problem in the Russian Empire, where only self-determination (in practice the right to separation) would suffice.

While Lenin faced up to the Austro-Marxists on his 'right' flank, the supporters of Rosa Luxemburg within the ranks of Russian social democracy attacked him from the 'left'. It is as well to recall here that Lenin's position on nationalism was not widely accepted within the party. We have already noted in Chapter 3 the basis of Lenin's argument with Rosa Luxemburg on the national question. While recognizing the correctness of Luxemburg's struggle against Polish 'social nationalists', Lenin wrote that

> Carried away by the struggle against nationalism in Poland, Rosa Luxemburg has forgotten the nationalism of the Great Russians, although it is *this* nationalism that is the most formidable at the present time.[11]

While in his argument with the Bund he stressed their 'nationalist' deviations, now Lenin was concerned with an abstract leftist denial of national oppression. Luxemburg's position, if applied to Russia, was "*in fact* assisting the Great-Russian Black Hundreds. She is in fact assisting opportunist tolerance of the privileges (and worse than privileges) of the Great Russians".[12] Having despatched the 'opportunists' of the right who promoted bourgeois nationalism within the working class (the Bund) and those of the left who tolerated the excesses of the Black Hundreds, what alternative did Lenin advance? In the pages which follow we will try to systematically unravel Lenin's conception of national self-determination, which E.H. Carr has bemusedly referred to as "somewhat nebulous".[13] Trotsky on the other hand wrote that

> whatever may be the further destiny of the Soviet Union — and it is still far from a quiet haven — the national policy of Lenin will find its place among the eternal treasures of mankind.[14]

Lenin, like other Marxists before him, closely related the nation to the rise of capitalism. The rising bourgeoisie had to capture the home market and establish a politically united territory. For Lenin

> the tendency of every national movement is towards the formation of *national states*, under which these requirements of modern capitalism are best satisfied.[15]

The nation-state is seen as the normal and typical political form of bourgeois rule as it emerges from feudalism. Against abstract or 'legal' definitions of the nation Lenin counterposed this concrete analysis of the historical economic conditions under which national movements emerge. Capitalism was seen to promote centralization in the political domain as much as in the economic aspects analysed by Marx in *Capital*. For Lenin,

> The great centralised state is a tremendous historical step forward from medieval disunity to the future socialist unity of the whole world, and only *via* such a state (*inseparably* connected with capitalism), can there be any road to socialism.[16]

That is why Lenin, following Marx and Engels, argued in 1913 that "*Other conditions being equal*, the class conscious proletariat will always stand for the larger state".[17] Though Lenin qualified this by saying that it was 'democratic centralism' that he was advocating on the national question, the same reservations must be applied to him as to Marx; namely that he held a somewhat evolutionist view of capitalism, and granted dubious universal validity to centralization and the larger state.

Lenin summed up the argument when he said

> From the standpoint of national relations, the best conditions for the development of capitalism are undoubtedly provided by the national state.[18]

This recalls the statement that democracy is "the best possible shell" for capitalism. Lenin did not, however, stop there, and went on to apply this basic Marxist dictum to the new era of imperialism. He argued that

> Developing capitalism knows two historical tendencies in the national question. The first is the awakening of national life and national movements, the struggle against national oppression and the creation of national states. The second is the development and growing frequency of international intercourse in every form,

the break-down of international barriers, the creation of the international unity of capital, of economic life in general, of politics, science, etc.[19]

According to Lenin, Marxism must take *both* tendencies into account, advocating the equality of nations on the one hand, and the struggle against bourgeois nationalism on the other. The first tendency, which predominates with the early development of capitalism, leads to the basic democratic principle of national self-determination. The second, with the internationalization of capital which Marx foresaw, and Lenin followed closely, breaks down national barriers and makes anything but the most resolute internationalism a regressive policy.

It therefore follows that national independence was for Lenin a basic democratic demand, but no longer a task which pertained to the proletariat as such. The national question was, in short, an element which was 'external' to the struggle of the working class. It was in this context that Lenin developed his basic pragmatic attitude towards nationalism:

> Increased national oppression under imperialism does not mean that Social Democracy should reject what the bourgeoisie call the 'utopian' struggle for the freedom of nations to secede but, on the contrary, it should make greater use of the conflicts that arise in this sphere, *too*, as ground for mass action and for revolutionary attacks on the bourgeoisie.[20]

As Lenin constantly stressed, in a Russia which was "a prison of peoples", national antagonisms had a vast potential to increase pressure against the Tsarist regime. It was the national and agrarian questions, as much if not more than the socialism of the workers, which led to the democratic revolution of February 1917. Conservative writers have argued that Lenin was basically an opportunist about nationalism. Smal-Stocki wrote that self-determination was "a tactical propaganda trick to deceive [the non-Russians] and to bring about the 'speedy extinction of their national feelings' ".[21] Self-determination *was* a tactical weapon, it was an 'exception' to a general support for centralization, and it was subordinate to the interests of the working class, as expressed through the social democratic movement.

But Lenin was more than a simple pragmatist, as we can see in his attitude to Marx and Engels' writings on Ireland (see Chapter 1). Lenin wrote that

> The policy of Marx and Engels on the Irish question serves as a splendid example of the attitude the proletariat of the oppressor nation should adopt towards national movements, an example which has lost none of its *practical* importance.[22]

Though Marx did not make a fetish of the national question, nor raise national independence to an absolute right, he recognized that it was a basic democratic task of the proletariat. The conclusion Lenin drew was that

> *Insofar as* the bourgeoisie of the oppressed nation fights the oppressor, we are always, in every case, and more strongly than anyone else, *in favour*, for we are the staunchest and the most consistent enemies of oppression.[23]

This is an unequivocal statement in support of national rebellion. It is not diminished at all when Lenin goes on to point out that "insofar as the bourgeoisie of the oppressed nation stands for *its own* bourgeois nationalism, we stand against".[24] What we see emerging from this discussion on Ireland, which Lenin takes up after Marx and Engels, is a clear-cut distinction between oppressed and oppressor nations, which completely replaced the earlier Marxist categories of historic and non-historic nations.

For Lenin,

> the focal point in the Social-Democratic [national] programme must be that division of nations into oppressor and oppressed which forms the *essence of* imperialism . . . .[25]

It is from this division that Lenin's definition of the 'right of nations to self-determination' in the age of imperialism flows. It was a division which was ignored by the 'social chauvinists' who spoke of the same right to self-determination but only to "justify and defend the oppression of the majority of the world's nations by the Great Powers".[26] Socialism for Lenin "will remain a hollow phrase if it is not linked up with a revolutionary approach to all questions of democracy, including the national question".[27] It was in this context that Lenin developed a three-fold categorization of countries, where self-determination took on a different meaning:

1) the advanced capitalist countries of Western Europe and the United States, where progressive national movements had already run their course;
2) the multi-national states of Austria, the Balkans and Russia, where the class struggle was combined with the democratic tasks of national self-determination;
3) the colonial and semi-colonial countries, where the democratic movement has barely begun, and where socialists should support the movement for national liberation.[28]

It was on the basis of this three-fold distinction that Lenin began to forge a concrete national programme for the workers' movement, and brought to the fore the relation between the colonial question and the national question, which would henceforth be inseparable.

For some, this apparently 'pro-nationalist' side of Lenin's thought contradicts his forthright condemnation of nationalism on other occasions. Lenin rejected this accusation and argued for a 'dialectical' policy: workers in the oppressor nations should fight for the independence of the oppressed nations, whereas

> the Social-Democrat of the oppressed nations must attach prime significance to the unity and the merging of the workers of the oppressed nations with those of the oppressor nations . . . .[29]

In this context he supported Marx's position on Ireland which was to demand the right of separation for Ireland, but also to argue for a subsequent "free union" with Britain. It is possible to see how, in a modern context, the apparent contradictions would be resolved: in the case of the Falklands/Malvinas war of 1981 it was quite correct for British socialists to argue the case of the oppressed nation, while socialists in Argentina could equally strenuously oppose a war waged by their bourgeoisie.

A further contradiction arises, however, when we consider that Lenin supported the 'right' to separation without actually advocating separation. He argued that it was like a divorce law, which allowed for separation but did not promote it.[30] In a telling phrase, Lenin wrote that

> the proletariat confines itself, so to speak, to the negative demand for recognition of the *right* to self-determination, without giving guarantees to any nation . . . .[31]

Though it might not be practical, it was for Lenin the only democratic solution to the national question. Lenin's position is clear:

> Socialist parties which did not show by all their activity, both now, during the revolution, and after its victory, that they would liberate the enslaved nations and build up relations with them on the basis of a free union — and free union is a false phrase without the right to secede — these parties would be betraying socialism.[32]

The right of the oppressed nations to self-determination means categorically the right to free political separation. But, and here is the catch, socialists in the *oppressed* nations might play into the hands of bourgeois nationalism if they adopted this slogan. Whereas workers in the imperialist countries had the duty to strive against colonial annexations, the social democrat of the small nation

> must fight *against* small-nation narrow-mindedness, seclusion and isolation, consider the whole and in general, subordinate the particular to the general interest.[33]

What this means in practice is that the socialist movements of the big nations fight for the right of nations to self-determination, whereas the socialists in the small nations must emphasize voluntary integration of nations. For Lenin there is no contradiction between the "freedom to secede" and the "freedom to integrate". This position could only make sense in the Russian context, which shaped Lenin's ideas as much as Poland did for Rosa Luxemburg. He was trying to establish a viable democratic policy for the national question, which would not conflict with the need for a centralized proletarian party. Too often Lenin's 'right to self-determination' has been taken as an abstract timeless formula, divorced from the particular historical context in which it was developed.

It is necessary to bear in mind this context when assessing the general value of Lenin's contribution to a Marxist theory of nationalism. Lenin added nothing new, following Kautsky in his historical analysis and emphasizing, like him, the importance of language. Nationalism was not viewed as an independent and self-sufficient issue, but seen as subordinate to class politics. But Lenin contributed a concrete policy in relation to nationalism and socialism — the right of nations to self-determination. This was opportunist and contradictory for its detractors, realistic and dialectical for its supporters. Alfred Low is one of those who simply cannot understand Lenin's approach:

> An all-pervading dichotomy characterizes Lenin's thought on nationality. On the one hand, there is his pure negativism in regard to nationality and the national state . . . . On the other hand, there is his insistence, in spite of all qualifications, on national self-determination.[34]

In a sense, Lenin was using the national question to supersede nationalism, or, to put it another way, in fighting for national independence, socialists were not fighting *for* nationalism. The Institute for Marxism-Leninism admits quite bluntly that Lenin's interest was chiefly in using national movements for the purpose of promoting socialism.[35] From this perspective it is perfectly coherent to advance different tasks for the workers of oppressed and oppressor nations. It is also possible to replace the accusation of opportunism with the virtue of political realism.

What can be said without fear of contradiction is that Lenin's work on the national question "placed politics in command", as Löwy notes.[36] Self-determination could not be reduced to cultural autonomy, but belonged to the realm of political democracy. Though there are traces of economism in his theory of nationalism, Lenin does recognize for the first time in Marxist discourse the "relative autonomy" of the national question. Lenin was not overly concerned to define the category of nation or nationalism, precisely because it was not a theoretical problem but one of political practice. But this failure was partly the effect of Lenin's firm conviction that the nation was a transient phenomenon, which was bound to disappear under socialism. In his desire to counter any subjectivism Lenin defined the nation solely in economic and political terms and ignored the cultural dimension. He believed that economic factors would prevent multi-national states like that of Russia from breaking up. The whole conception of a 'national culture' was repugnant to his internationalist outlook. His belief that once capitalism was overthrown, the international culture of the proletariat would come to the fore and replace any separatist tendencies inherent in 'national culture' was to prove wrong after 1917. But before we can turn to the post-revolutionary period, we must consider Stalin's contribution towards the construction of an orthodox 'Leninist' position in the national question.

Stalin's orthodoxy

Stalin was a prolific writer on nationalism — only 2-3% of the writings of Marx and Engels deal with this topic, as opposed to 25% of Lenin's output, and Stalin's 50%. In one of his early works, *How Does Social Democracy Understand the National Question* (1904), he made the interesting point that in different epochs the national question serves distinct interests and adopts different nuances according to the class that poses it and the moment at which it is posed.[37]

On the strength of this work and because he was a Georgian, Lenin asked Stalin to produce a pamphlet on the national question in 1912. This work, *Marxism and the National Question* (1913), came eventually to be considered the definitive Marxist treatise on the question, cited as authoritative by even the most ardent opponents of everything else Stalin stood for.

Stalin's essay deals in the main with the Austro-Marxist approach to the national question, which was then having considerable influence on the Bund and several minority groups in Russia. Nationalism is identified closely with the bourgeoisie: "The fate of the national movement, which is essentially a bourgeois movement, is naturally connected with the fate of the bourgeoisie".[38] Though national oppression can only be overcome by socialism, democratization under capitalism can reduce the national struggle to a minimum: "This is borne out by the examples of Switzerland and America".[39] One of Stalin's major concerns was to define the nation; it was "a historically evolved, stable community of language, territory, economic life, and psychological make-up manifested in a community of culture".[40] This definition was based almost completely on previous characterizations by Kautsky, Bauer and the Bund theorist V. Medem. Stalin's main interest, however, was not in a theoretical debate but in making political criticisms of Bauer and Renner. To that purpose he used Strasser's 'leftist' critique of Bauer (see Chapter 3) to undermine Bauer's 'evolutionary national' policy. His argument is based on the incorrect premise that the 1899 Brünn programme had granted personal non-territorial autonomy to the nationalities in the Austrian Empire. These ideas as taken up by the Bund would similarly disrupt class unity, and would spread to other groups "unable to withstand the nationalist 'epidemic' ".[41] To this 'liquidationist' perspective Stalin counterposed the right of nations to self-determination. When the Caucasian Social Democrats argued that national cultural autonomy was not incompatible with this principle, Stalin replied through an analogy with the Marxist attitude towards religion: freedom to practise it but opposition to it as an ideology. So, while

nations have the right to arrange their affairs as they please ... that does not mean that Social-Democrats will not combat and agitate against the pernicious institutions of nations and against the inexpedient demands of nations.[42]

This meant that the party would fight against national cultural autonomy for the Caucasian nations because it was contrary to the interests of the Caucasian proletariat.

We must assess Stalin's essay at two levels: its substantive content and its status within Marxism. On the first count the main problem is Stalin's famous definition of the nation. This has quite correctly been attacked for its formalism and reductionism, its undialectical and scholastic approach.[43] Löwy notes that "Stalin gave his theory a dogmatic, restrictive and rigid character which one never finds in Lenin".[44] The historian Pierre Vilar, however, rejects this line of attack, praises his "acute intelligence" and argues that we should not "allow ourselves to be mystified by a sanctimonious revisionism".[45] Stalin's definition is indeed more than just an inventory of empirical categories and his work does have a considerable coherence. Carrère d'Encausse has further argued that "Stalin's approach to the nation was much more positive than Lenin's. Stalin believed in the permanence of the nation."[46] The implication is that Stalin was more of a 'nationalist' whereas Lenin always adopted a pragmatic attitude towards nationalism. This interpretation *can* be derived from Stalin's definition of the nation; but it is undermined by his continuous attacks on nationalism and his statement that "a nation is not merely a historical category but a historical category belonging to a definite epoch, the epoch of rising capitalism".[47]

One of the most serious criticisms of Stalin's essay is that it fails to distinguish between the nationalism of the oppressed and that of the oppressor. The actual phrase 'oppressed nation' occurs; but as so often in Stalin's work, the stated position is contradicted in practice. So, in the text of the essay he refers to "the rising tide of militant nationalism above . . . [which] evoked an answering tide of nationalism below, which at times took the form of crude chauvinism".[48] Thus the Tsarist pogroms are seen as equivalent to the nationalism of Jewish workers. Stalin's main task was "to resist nationalism" and he saw little difference between nationalism from above and that from below. His attitude becomes clearer when juxtaposed with that of David Ananoun, an Armenian Marxist who advanced an Austro-Marxist line. Ananoun took up several points in Stalin's 1904 essay, where he had stated that "the national problem in the Caucasus can be solved *only by drawing the backward nations and peoples into the common stream of higher culture*".[49] Ananoun criticized Stalin for his imperious disdain for 'national peculiarities' and argued that his denial of Jewish nationalism in particular was "in effect to desire or cooperate in their burial as a nation".[50] Ananoun wanted to see a cultural revolution in the Russian Empire and insisted that "Democracy leaves the solution of the fate of nationalities to the future. It does not coerce or destroy anything which does not hinder its own movement".[51] Stalin, on the other hand, wrote,

> Just think: to 'preserve' such 'national peculiarities' of the Transcaucasian Tatars as self-flagellation at the festival of Shakhsei-Vakhsei; or to 'develop' such 'national peculiarities' of the Georgians as the vendetta![52]

Stalin would not accept that customs might bind a community together and be a means of resistance to oppression; he only wished to drag them into 'civilization'.

The debate on the standing of Stalin's essay within Marxism revolves around the extent of Lenin's responsibility for and agreement with it. The negative case is put by Pipes for whom the essay

> though undoubtedly written under Lenin's instructions and very likely with some of his assistance, did not, on the whole, represent Lenin's opinions.[53]

Pipes views the essay as an unoriginal polemic, "a not so intelligent restatement of old arguments, replete with errors in fact and in reasoning".[54] Certainly, though Lenin praised the work by "the wonderful Georgian", he carried on working on the national question himself and corrected several errors such as Stalin's interpretation of the Brünn programme. Yet it was Lenin who elevated Stalin to a position as head of the Peoples Commissariat for Affairs of Nationalities in 1917. It would thus be wrong to minimize the link between Stalin's and Lenin's positions on the national question. It is part of the myth of 'Leninism' that Lenin could not possibly have approved of such a defective work; yet he explicitly wrote that Stalin's article "stands out in first place" in theoretical Marxist literature on nationalism.[55] Indeed, Lenin's responsibility for the Stalin essay could be greater if we accept Deutscher's findings that not only had Lenin "probably suggested to him the synopsis of the essay, its main arguments and conclusions" but he had also "almost certainly pruned the essay of the stylistic and logical incongruities with which the original must have bristled".[56]

Does this mean that Lenin was effectively the co-author of Stalin's essay and that we are really dealing with the 'Lenin-Stalin theory of nationalism', as Stalin was keen to claim in later years? In the following section we will see how Lenin disagreed with Stalin in practice over the national question after 1917. Yet, even before this, though there were no explicit theoretical or political disagreements between Lenin and Stalin on the national question their work is by no means similar. The theme of democracy runs clearly through Lenin's articles; with Stalin a purely pragmatic attitude comes to the fore. In Lenin's work there are many contradictions, and the principle of national self-determination is by no means a fully satisfactory one. With Stalin, contradictions disappear (though logical inconsistencies abound) and his approach to questions of national oppression is far from sensitive. Stalin produced a dogmatic definition of the nation which was later used as a checklist to assess whether a people met the criteria to become a nation. It never occurred to Stalin that a community might decide for itself to be a nation. As the classical writer Ernest Renan stressed, a nation was 'a daily plebiscite' in which people consented and clearly expressed the desire to continue a common life.[57] Or, as Trotsky wrote in one of his rare insights into the national question: for Blacks in the United States, "an abstract criterion is not decisive in this case: much more decisive are historical consciousness, feelings and emotions".[58]

Lenin confronts Stalin

Lenin was realistic enough to recognize in 1916 that

> By transforming capitalism into socialism the proletariat created the *possibility* of abolishing national oppression; the possibility becomes *reality* 'only' — 'only'! — with the establishment of full democracy in all spheres . . . .[59]

For a series of historical reasons — such as the bloody imperialist intervention

— as well as Stalin's role as head of the Nationalities Commissariat, the national question was not really 'solved' by the October Revolution. Instead, it led to a considerable change in the very principles underlying the slogan of self-determination.

The 'national question' centred around the subject peoples in the border regions of the empire who constituted over half the total population. The democratic revolution of February 1917 had led to the disintegration of the empire and a burgeoning of national movements in many of these border areas. While the Provisional Government acted to preserve a degree of state unity, the Bolsheviks encouraged separatist movements as a means of undermining the new regime. The national and agrarian questions combined in the border areas where resentment was focused on the Russian colonists. The native populations of the Ural region, the Northern Caucasus and the Steppe districts of Central Asia had, as Pipes explains, "expected that the new democracy would at once remedy the injustices of the past by returning to them the properties of which they had been deprived".[60] The Bolsheviks also encouraged the development of national units in the army. Gradually organs of self-rule were developed by the national minorities, and when the Bolsheviks seized power in October 1917 they were faced with the practical consequences of having encouraged the right of national self-determination.

The Bolsheviks in power were faced with the independence of Finland, Lithuania, Latvia and Estonia, and vast areas such as the Siberian Republic and the Northern Caucasus where autonomy was proclaimed. Economics was one of the main problems. Trotsky had taunted the Provisional Government, saying that it "could not possibly agree to the 'autonomy' of Ukrainian grain and the ores of Krivorog",[61] but the Bolsheviks, too, had to contend with the economic inter-dependence of the Russian nationalities. At the political level, the very basis of 'self-determination' was being drawn into question, because Lenin always assumed that without coercion free union would result. Using local Bolsheviks and Russian troops the new regime vowed to stifle the centrifugal tendencies. A hostile observer such as Pipes can note quite correctly that

> the dissolution of the Belorussian Rada; the attempted coup in Transcaucasia; the invasion of the Ukraine; as well as the suppression of the Moslem governments of Kukand, Crimea the Alash Orda, and the Bashkir republic . . . were all a complete violation of the principle of national self-determination.[62]

By 1920, the failure of the world revolution to materialize was evident. The failure of the Polish proletariat to rise when the Red Army reached the gates of Warsaw was a bitter blow. Now the main task for the new Soviet government was to build a coherent and stable territorial unit and consolidate the reversal of the previous tendency towards national dispersal.

The traumatic experience of 1917-20 was bound to lead to a revision of Bolshevik doctrine on nationalism. Lenin had argued in 1913 that "Marxists will never, under any circumstances, advocate either the federal principle or decentralisation".[63] Now, in 1918, Lenin prepared a resolution for the Third

Congress of Soviets which read: "The Soviet Russian Republic is established on the basis of a free union of free nations as a federation of Soviet national republics". Stalin's report on the national question to this same congress launched a more far-reaching revision of the principle of self-determination, arguing for "the necessity of interpreting the principle of self-determination as a right not of the bourgeoisie, but of the working masses of the given nation".[64] The implications were clear: self-determination would be completely subordinated to the interests of the working class. Self-determination for the working class was a formulation which Bukharin had raised in 1915 and which Lenin then criticized severely (see Chapter 3). When the Bolsheviks held their Eighth Party Congress in 1919, Lenin won a battle to return to the old party principles. Part of his resolution dictated that

> On the question who is to express the nation's will to secede, the Russian Communist Party adopts the class-historical viewpoint, taking into consideration the stage of historical development of the given nation . . . .[65]

The implications were clear: when fighting against feudalism the national bourgeoisie was progressive, but under the struggle for socialism that mantle passed to the working class. In this period the 'right to unite' was beginning to take precedence over the 'right to secede'.

In the successive struggles in the Ukraine after 1917 we can see how these doctrinal issues were derived from a very complex situation.[66] With the collapse of the old regime, the Ukrainian Central Rada (Soviet) shared power with the Bolshevik-dominated city Soviets. The Ukrainian nationalists wanted to preserve national culture, folklore and language. At first the Bolsheviks accepted self-determination for the Ukraine willingly; but later the Rada began to co-operate with the counter-revolutionary activities of the Don Cossacks. Nor could the Bolsheviks accept Ukrainian units in the Red Army fighting a fierce war against imperialist intervention. When the Kiev Soviet was repressed by the Rada in 1918, the Bolsheviks decided to move. German occupation of the Ukraine postponed the final confrontation between nationalists and communists till 1919. The invasion of the Ukraine was undertaken without Lenin's approval and he launched a serious attack on 'Great Russian chauvinism' at the Eighth Party Congress. While Lenin was being criticized for his undue concessions to minority nationalists he was seriously troubled by the handling of the Ukrainian question. The nationalists there expressed genuine popular interests, in spite of their serious political weaknesses. The communists had failed to significantly extend their influence beyond the cities and their ultimate reliance on military power was a sign of weakness. With the establishment of a "dictatorship of the toiling and exploited masses of the proletariat and the poor peasants" the Ukraine was settled; but national grievances were now transferred to the interior of the Bolshevik movement.

One of the main exponents of 'national-communism' was Sultan Galiev of the Tatar Communist Party who was taken on to Stalin's Commissariat of Nationalities in 1918. Sultan Galiev had become the most influential Muslim in Soviet political life by 1920, and was in a key position to reconcile socialism with the Muslim religion and tradition of the Eastern borderlands. He began to doubt, however, whether the world-wide socialist revolution would indeed lead to the liberation of the colonial peoples. In an early version of the 'Third Worldist' position he wrote that

> the formula which offers the replacement of the world-wide dictatorship of one class of European society (the bourgeoisie) by its antipode (the proletariat) . . . will not bring about a major change in the social life of the oppressed segment of humanity . . . .In contradiction to this we advance another thesis: the idea that the material premises for a social transformation of humanity can be created only through the establishment of the dictatorship of the colonies and semi-colonies over the metropolises.[67]

Eventually Sultan Galiev was arrested in 1923, and though he recanted his heresy, he became one of the early victims of the Stalinist purge. The handling of this affair, over and above Sultan Galiev's particular ideas, demonstrated the failure of the Bolsheviks' national programme. One of the delegates to the conference where Sultan Galiev was 'tried' by Stalin, argued that to prevent nationalist deviations, it was necessary to destroy the national inequalities and injustices present in the Soviet system.

The final and explosive confrontation between Lenin and Stalin over the national question was about Georgia, which, like the Ukraine, passed through a period of independence, German (then British) occupation and then Soviet conquest. Lenin, and the local Bolsheviks, were extremely reluctant to move against the Georgian Menshevik regime which had been established in 1920, but in 1921 the Soviet divisions moved in. Lenin was particularly concerned in case Ordzhonikidze, who was placed in charge of Georgia, used the same methods he had employed in Armenia and alienated the local population. He therefore cabled Ordzhonikidze, urging

> not the application of the Russian pattern, but a skilful and flexible elaboration of a special original tactic, based on large-scale concessions to all kinds of petty-bourgeois elements.[68]

He argued in particular for concessions towards the Georgian intellectuals, petty traders and the Georgian Mensheviks. Ordzhonikidze also met opposition from the Georgian Bolsheviks who were concerned to maintain an element of national independence. As Lenin notes, they

> were anxious to gain popular support in a Caucasus in which national and nationalistic feelings were particularly deep-rooted and had recently been reawakened by the experience of independence under a Menshevik government that had been crushed by force.[69]

More than any other group in the party, the Georgian Bolsheviks were determined to make a reality of national self-determination within the Soviet system. Ordzhonikidze, for his part, was acting like a Roman pro-consul subjugating his new domain.

In 1922 the 'Georgian affair' reached a peak when Ordzhonikidze moved to set up a Transcaucasian Federation embracing Georgia, Armenia and Azerbaijan. The Georgian Congress of Soviets responded with a declaration of the inviolability of their national independence. Now a full scale debate erupted over the future of the whole national policy of the new Soviet regime. The entire central committee of the Georgian Communist Party resigned, and Lenin was forced into an investigation of Stalin's handling of the Georgian question. Lenin was not at first over-concerned with the methods being used to force Georgia into economic union with its neighbours, nor with the conduct of Ordzhonikidze. However, when Stalin was charged with preparing a constitution for the new Union of Soviet Socialist Republics in 1922, Lenin proposed a less centralist scheme. At this stage Lenin thought merely that Stalin was being too "impatient" in centralizing the new state; but Stalin responded by accusing Lenin of "national liberalism".[70] Eventually, the ailing Lenin was forced to draw the relevant conclusions on Stalin's conduct during the 'Georgian affair'. He realized that the national question was simply being suppressed rather than resolved and proceeded to lay out an alternative with far-reaching implications.

In Lenin's *Testament* (or *Letter to the Congress*) written in December 1922, he was to give considerable attention to the national question.[71] He began with a sustained attack on 'the Great Russian chauvinist' and the need to protect the minorities from them. He reiterated that the nationalism of the oppressed nation (Georgia) and that of the oppressor must always be distinguished: "In respect of the second kind of nationalism we, the nationals of a big nation, have nearly always been guilty . . . of an infinite number of cases of violence . . . ."[72] He castigated that Georgian (Stalin) who accused others of "social chauvinism" while being himself a crude imperialistic Derzhimorda (a symbol of brutal police mentality and methods). Lenin then advanced what amounts to a policy of 'reverse discrimination' for the oppressed nations:

> In one way or another, by one's attitude or by concessions, it is necessary to compensate the non-Russians for the lack of trust, for the suspicion and the insults to which the government of the 'dominant' nation subjected them in the past.[73]

Internationalism for Lenin now meant more than observing the 'formal equality' of nations, as he became aware of the deeply entrenched feelings of 'national injustice'. It was better by far to give too much rather than too little to the national minorities. A formal treatment of the national question could never remove the barrier to international proletarian solidarity caused by 'offended nationals'. In practical terms, Lenin made several immediate suggestions:

1) Stalin had to assume "political responsibility for this truly Great-Russian nationalist campaign" and Ordzhonikidze was to be subject to "exemplary punishment";

2) The Union of Soviet Socialist Republics was to be preserved but at the next Congress of Soviets it might be retained "only for military and diplomatic affairs and in all other respects restore full independence to the individual Peoples Commissariats";

3) To not "ourselves lapse ... into imperialist attitudes towards oppressed nationalities" exceptional resourcefulness and sincerity would be required and, for example, "the strictest rules must be introduced on the use of the national language in the non-Russian republics.".[74]

Early in 1923, when it became clear that his health would not allow him to attend the Twelfth Party Congress, Lenin requested Trotsky to take charge of the 'Georgian affair'. Trotsky agreed, but then proceeded to arrange the 'rotten compromise' with Stalin that Lenin had explicitly warned him against. Having sought an alliance with Lenin to fight against the bureaucracy which was beginning to tighten its grip on the Bolshevik party, Trotsky threw away the chance to confront Stalin. As Deutscher writes, "All he asked of Stalin was that he should mend his ways: let him behave loyally towards his colleagues ... and let him stop bullying the Georgians".[75] Stalin agreed to tone down the criticisms of "local nationalism" (i.e. Georgian) in his report to the forthcoming congress, and inserted a ritual condemnation of 'Great Russian chauvinism'. The Georgians and Ukrainians would be given bland assurances that henceforth their national rights would be respected. Lenin fell victim to another stroke and died ten months later. At the Twelfth Party Congress Trotsky

> gave not a nod of encouragement to the disheartened Georgians; and when the debates over nationalities opened he left the assembly, excusing himself on the ground that he was busy preparing his own report to the congress.[76]

Lenin had left the confrontation with Stalin till too late, but he handed Trotsky all the ammunition necessary to expose Stalin's undemocratic practices. Trotsky failed to do so for a number of reasons; one of these was his undoubted lack of sensitivity to nationalism. During the wars of intervention Trotsky had written that the Bolsheviks supported the principle of self-determination when directed against feudal or imperialist states, but

> wherever the fiction of self-determination, in the hands of the bourgeoisie, becomes a weapon directed against the proletarian revolution, we have no occasion to treat that fiction differently from the other 'principles' of democracy invented by capitalism.[77]

Here, self-determination is reduced to a 'bourgeois fiction' to be swept aside when it conflicted with the "unifying tendencies of socialist economic construction".

Early in 1921 Trotsky had protested against the conquest of Georgia engineered by Stalin but, in Deutscher's words, "then Trotsky reconciled himself to the accomplished fact and even defended the conquest in a special pamphlet".[78] At the Eleventh Party Congress in 1922 he did not intervene in the debate when dissident Bolsheviks accused the government of forsaking the principle of self-determination. He later developed doubts about the pace of centralization imposed by Stalin and his open abuse of power; yet when his chance came to confront Stalin, with Lenin's full support, in 1923, he failed to do so. Lenin's notes on the Georgian question were suppressed, and the possibility of an alternative democratic course on the national question was lost.

A forgotten aspect of the whole Georgian question was the role of the local Bolsheviks, whose leader Filipp Makharadze had ironically maintained 'Luxemburgist' positions prior to 1921. Such was the mishandling of the national question in Georgia that he, and the other leading Bolsheviks, developed a 'national-communist' line. Makharadze wrote a letter to the Russian Communist Party late in 1921 showing how Ordzhonikidze had disregarded Lenin's recommendations to tread softly, had failed to win the sympathies of the Georgian population to the Soviet cause, and by not involving local Bolsheviks had made the move against the Menshevik government appear as a foreign invasion.[79] Had this letter been heeded the Soviet Union might have followed more democratic policies towards its rebellious nationalities. The problems it mentions make it hard to accept the verdict of the 1938, Stalin-inspired, *History of the Communist Party of the Soviet Union* that, at the Twelfth Party Congress,

> Comrade Stalin stressed the international significance of our policy on the national question. To the oppressed peoples of the East and West, the Soviet Union was a model of the solution of the national question and the abolition of national oppression.[80]

Notes

1. For a history of the Bund see H. Tobias, *The Jewish Bund in Russia: From its Origins to 1905* (Stanford University Press, California, 1972).
2. V.I. Lenin, *Collected Works*, Vol. 6 (Progress Publishers, Moscow, 1964) p.61, pp.59-60.
3. V.I. Lenin, *Collected Works*, Vol. 22 (Progress Publishers, Moscow, 1964) p.155.
4. V.I. Lenin, *Collected Works*, Vol. 20 (Progress Publishers, Moscow, 1964) p.26.
5. Ibid.
6. Ibid., p.32.
7. V.I. Lenin, *Collected Works*, Vol. 19 (Progress Publishers, Moscow, 1964) p.532.
8. Ibid., p.504.
9. Ibid., p.87.
10. Ibid., p.88.
11. V.I. Lenin, *Collected Works*, Vol. 20, p.412.
12. Ibid.
13. E.H. Carr, *The Bolshevik Revolution 1917-1923*, Vol. 1 (Penguin, Harmondsworth, 1971) p.435.
14. L. Trotsky, *History of the Russian Revolution*, Vol. 3 (Sphere Books, London, 1967) p.62.
15. V.I. Lenin, *Collected Works*, Vol. 20, p.396.

16. Ibid., p.46.
17. Ibid., p.45.
18. Ibid., p.400.
19. Ibid., p.27.
20. V.I. Lenin, *Collected Works*, Vol. 22, p.146.
21. R. Smal-Stocki, *The Captive Nations: Nationalism of the Non-Russian Nations in the Soviet Union* (Bookman Associates, New York, 1960) p.43.
22. V.I. Lenin, *Collected Works*, Vol. 20, p.442.
23. Ibid., pp.411-12.
24. Ibid., p.412.
25. V.I. Lenin, *Collected Works*, Vol. 21 (Progress Publishers, Moscow, 1964) p.409.
26. Ibid.
27. Ibid., p.413.
28. Ibid., p.151.
29. Ibid., p.409.
30. V.I. Lenin, *Collected Works*, Vol. 20, p.422.
31. Ibid., p.410.
32. V.I. Lenin, *Collected Works*, Vol. 22, p.143.
33. Ibid., p.347.
34. A. Low, *Lenin on the Question of Nationality* (Bookman Associates, New York, 1958) p.126.
35. Institute of Marxism-Leninism (Central Committee CPSU), *Leninism and the National Question* (Progress Publishers, Moscow, 1977) p.93.
36. M. Löwy, 'Marxists and the National Question', *New Left Review*, No. 96, 1976, p.97.
37. Cited in P. Vilar, 'Nationalism', *Marxist Perspectives*, No. 5, 1979, p.25.
38. J. Stalin, *Marxism and National Question* (Foreign Language Publishing House, Moscow, 1945) p.24.
39. Ibid., p.24.
40. Ibid., p.11.
41. Ibid., p.57.
42. Ibid., p.66.
43. E.g. H.B. Davis, *Toward a Marxist Theory of Nationalism* (Monthly Review Press, New York, 1978) pp.70-5.
44. M. Löwy, 'Marxists and the National Question', p.95.
45. P. Vilar, 'Nationalism', p.27.
46. H. Carrère d'Encausse, 'The Bolsheviks and the National Question (1903-1929)', in E. Cahm and V.C. Fisera (eds.), *Socialism and Nationalism*, Vol. 3 (Spokesman, Nottingham, 1979) p.117.
47. J. Stalin, *Marxism and the National Question*, p.17.
48. Ibid., p.6.
49. Cited in M. Matossian, 'Two Marxist Approaches to Nationalism', *The American Slavic and East European Review*, No. 4, 1957, p.492.
50. Ibid., p.492.
51. Ibid., p.495.
52. Ibid., p.492.
53. R. Pipes, *The Formation of the Soviet Union: Communism and Nationalism 1917-1923* (Harvard University Press, Cambridge, Mass., 1954) pp.40-1.

54. Ibid., p.41.

55. V.I. Lenin, *Collected Works*, Vol. 24 (Progress Publishers, Moscow, 1964) p.223.

56. I. Deutscher, *Stalin — A Political Biography* (Penguin, Harmondsworth, 1972) p.126, p.131.

57. E. Renan, 'Qu'est-ce qu'une nation', *Oeuvres Complètes*, Vol. 1 (Calmann-Levy, Paris, 1947).

58. L. Trotsky, *Trotsky on Black Nationalism and Self-Determination* (Pathfinder, New York, 1967) p.16.

59. V.I. Lenin, *Collected Works*, Vol. 22, p.325.

60. R. Pipes, *The Formation of the Soviet Union*, p.51.

61. L. Trotsky, *History of the Russian Revolution*, Vol. 3, p.45.

62. R. Pipes, *The Formation of the Soviet Union*, p.108.

63. V.I. Lenin, *Collected Works*, Vol. 20, p.46.

64. Cited in E.H. Carr, *The Bolshevik Revolution*, p.272.

65. Ibid., p.274.

66. See J. Borys, *The Sovietization of Ukraine 1917-23* (Toronto University Press, 1983).

67. Cited in R. Pipes, *The Formation of the Soviet Union*, p.261.

68. Ibid., pp.239-40.

69. M. Lewin, *Lenin's Last Struggle* (Pluto Press, London, 1975) p.45.

70. Ibid., p.52.

71. 'The question of Nationalities or "Automisation" ' in V.I. Lenin, *Collected Works*, Vol. 36 (Progress Publishers, Moscow, 1966) pp.605-11.

72. Ibid., p.607.

73. Ibid., p.608.

74. Ibid., p.611 and p.610.

75. I. Deutscher, *The Prophet Armed; Trotsky: 1921-1929* (Oxford University Press, 1970) p.91.

76. Ibid., p.98.

77. L. Trotsky, *Social Democracy and the Wars of Intervention: Russia 1918-1921* (New Park Publications, London, 1975) p.94.

78. I. Deutscher, *The Prophet Armed*, p.49.

79. Cited in R. Pipes, *The Formation of the Soviet Union*, p.264.

80. C.C. of the CPSU (B), *History of the Communist Party of the Soviet Union* (Foreign Language Publishing House, Moscow, 1939) p.263.

5. The Third International

It was the Third, or Communist, International which brought the 'national question' into the forefront of Marxist politics. In this chapter we trace the theoretical positions of the International, and some of their practical consequences, from its founding congress in 1919 to its dissolution in 1943. The basic issues are the role of what is now known as the Third World in the international socialist revolution, and the revolutionary potential, or otherwise, of the indigenous or national bourgeoisie in those countries. To focus the debate, a second section examines some salient aspects of the communist movement in Latin America. Its early pioneers, such as the Peruvian José Carlos Mariátegui, tackled their national reality with a great insight. Later, the 'Stalinization' of the International imposed its heavy-handed schemas on its Latin American sections, and we see a general failure to adopt a consistent revolutionary attitude towards nationalism. Finally, we turn to the Chinese revolutions: that of 1927 where Stalin's line of alliance with the Kuomintang led to disaster, and that of 1949 which was victorious under an independent national communist leadership. The critical tone of this chapter should not prevent us from recognizing that the theory and practice of the Third International contains some of the most fruitful contacts between Marxism and nationalism. Even in its failures and hesitations, the experience of the International and its national sections merits renewed attention today.

The 'national question'

Whereas for Marx and the Second International nationalism and colonialism were two distinct phenomena, for Lenin there was no fundamental distinction between nationalism in Europe and the colonies. The Third International viewed the national and colonial questions as essentially one, recognizing no essential difference between revolution in Ireland and in Asia. Since its emergence in 1919, the new Communist International placed a major emphasis on the 'East', which covered not only Asia, but Africa and Latin America as well. Lenin himself had recognized the new trends in the world revolution in 1913:

Throughout Asia a mighty democratic movement is growing, spreading and gaining in strength . . . . *Hundreds* of millions of people are awakening into life, light and freedom.[1]

The First Congress of the Third International (or Comintern) in 1919 was essentially a European affair, as the Bolsheviks garnered support for their struggling revolution. All eyes focused on the labour movement in advanced Germany, to the neglect of the colonies. In its manifesto, drafted by Trotsky, the Comintern recognized that the colonial question was a pressing one but argued that:

The emancipation of the colonies is conceivable only in conjunction with the emancipation of the working class in the metropolises. The workers and peasants not only of Annam, Algiers and Bengal, but also of Persia and Armenia, will gain the opportunity of independent existence only in the hour when the workers of England and France, having overthrown Lloyd George and Clemenceau, will have taken state power into their own hands.[2]

While capitalist Europe had dragged the colonies into the capitalist mode of production, a socialist Europe would facilitate the transition to a socialist economy in those countries. Clearly, national liberation was seen as a subordinate task for the world revolutionary movement.

The Second Congress of the Comintern in 1920 saw the first sustained theoretical debate on the national and colonial questions. The two main figures in this debate were Lenin himself and the young Indian Marxist, M.N. Roy. The central element in Lenin's presentation was that

We, as Communists, should support the bourgeois movements for liberation in the colonies only in the cases when these movements are really revolutionary, when they are not opposed to our enlightening and organising the peasantry and the great masses of the exploited for revolutionary purposes.[3]

Lenin wished to deal not with 'bourgeois democratic' movements, but only with 'revolutionary nationalist' movements. Thus began the long career of the 'national bourgeoisie', that "white blackbird", as Claudin calls it,[4] which was at once capitalist and revolutionary. For the workers' movement in the colonies the problem was how to unite *with* this class in pursuit of national liberation while also fighting *against* it for social liberation. In his *Supplementary Theses on the National and Colonial Questions*, which Lenin also accepted, Roy developed a somewhat different perspective. He argued that

There are to be found in the dependent countries two distinct movements, which every day grow further apart from each other. One is the bourgeois democratic national movement . . . and the other is the mass action of the ignorant and poor peasants and workers for their liberation from all sorts of exploitation.[5]

The first inevitably tries to control the latter, and while communists may agree to collaborate with the bourgeois nationalists for the overthrow of foreign capitalism, "the foremost and necessary task is the formation of Communist

Parties which will organise the peasants and workers".[6] Whereas Lenin stressed that the weak communist parties were bound to support the nationalist movement, Roy stressed that

> if from the outset the leadership is in the hands of a Communist vanguard, the revolutionary masses will not be led astray, but go ahead through the successive periods of development of revolutionary experience.[7]

During the Second Congress debate on the national question several different positions were put forward. The Persian delegate Sultan Zade argued that "in view of the weakness of the bourgeoisie [in the colonies] the next national upheaval may easily turn into a social revolution".[8] While recognizing this potential, he thought that this did

> not justify the conclusion that the triumph of Communism in the rest of the world depends upon the success of the Social Revolution in the Orient, as Comrade Roy asserts . . . .[9]

Sophisticated discussions on Ireland, the Dutch East Indies and other situations were marred by the Italian delegate Serrati who took an extreme 'Europeanist' attitude and did not hide his lack of interest in the national/colonial question. With an argument reminiscent of the Second International, Serrati stated that

> on the whole, the entire struggle for national liberation carried on by the democratic bourgeoisies, even when insurrectionary methods are employed, is not a revolutionary movement. It usually serves the interest of national imperialism striving to rise to the surface.[10]

This position was, however, now in retreat, as the Bolshevik revolution turned more to the East with each setback for the European revolution.

One of the major practical confrontations over the national question came at the First Congress of the Peoples of the East at Baku in 1920 attended largely by Muslims from Central Asia. The leaders of the Comintern wooed the revolutionary nationalists assiduously: "Brothers, we summon you to a holy war primarily against British imperialism!" proclaimed Zinoviev, while the delegates brandished their sabres and revolvers to the cries of "Jihad" and "Long live the renaissance of the East."[11] In more sober vein, Zinoviev called on the movement of the oppressed nationalities "to rid itself of its nationalist prejudices" and merge into the current of world revolution. The Eastern delegates were by no means uncritical of the Comintern, with Narbutabekov complaining that

> We Turkestanis state that we have never before seen either Comrade Zinoviev or Comrade Radek or the other leaders of the revolution. They should come and see for themselves what is happening in our country, what exactly the local authorities, whose policies drive the working masses away from the Soviet power, are up to.[12]

The Eastern delegates furthermore stressed the *national* nature of their revolution which could only occur "in accordance with its religious, human, social and economic circumstances", according to Narbutebekov.[13] Comintern leaders such as Karl Radek showed little understanding of these national peculiarities and basically saw the national revolutions as a secondary complement to the proletarian revolution in the West. As E.H. Carr notes, even in 1922 the "Comintern was still interested in the national question primarily as it affected Europe . . . ."[14]

The Third Congress of the Comintern in 1921 was decidedly more 'European' than the previous one and treated the national and colonial questions so cursorily that Roy was forced to make an energetic complaint on this account. The anti-imperialist struggle had been proceeding rapidly in the intervening years and on the surface this neglect was inexplicable. Essentially the new Soviet *state* had begun to develop alliances which conflicted with the interests of the world revolution. In 1920 the nationalist government in Turkey led by Mustafa Kemal had appealed for Soviet military and financial aid which resulted in a treaty of friendship in 1921. Before the treaty was signed, Kemal had arrested the Communist leadership in Turkey, executing 15 of them, and launched a fierce repression against the peasant movement for agrarian reform. In 1922 Radek could still say to the Comintern that

> We do not regret for a moment that we said to the Turkish communists: your first duty, once you have organised yourselves in an independent party, will be to support the national liberation movement.[15]

Radek had clearly come a long way from his earlier 'Luxemburgist' positions on the national question (see Chapter 3). A more direct reason for the silence at the Third Congress was the trade agreement signed with Britain in 1921, which included a clause which pledged the Soviets to abstain from any propaganda which might incite the peoples of Asia to act contrary to British interests.[16] The point here is not whether compromises of this nature were necessary, but that the national interests of the Soviet state were taking precedence over the world revolution, even before the death of Lenin.

The Fourth Congress of 1922 was charged with adapting the resolutions of the Second Congress and setting them in a more practical context. As the proletarian united front was adopted in the West so the 'anti-imperialist united front' became the watchword for the East. One of the *Theses on the Eastern Question* declared that

> Taking full cognizance of the fact that those who represent the national will to State independence may, because of a variety of historical circumstances, be themselves of the most varied kind, the Communist International supports every national revolutionary movement against imperialism.[17]

Yet, in apparent contradiction, it elsewhere stated that "the ruling class among the colonial and semi-colonial peoples are unable and unwilling to lead the struggle against imperialism".[18] The fact is that the final resolution was a compromise one because radically opposed positions had been put forward during the debate. Tan Malaka, from Java, criticized the Comintern's earlier hostility towards Pan-Islamism arguing that

> It corresponds to the national liberation struggle, for Islam is everything to the Muslim . . . . Just as we wish to support national wars, we also wish to support the war of liberation of the 250 millions of extremely active and extremely combative Muslims against the imperialist powers.[19]

Previous co-operation between communists and Muslims had been damaged by the Comintern's hostility, argued Malaka. M.N. Roy, however, took a diametrically opposed view of the national movement, pointing out that it was too late for the bourgeoisie to play a revolutionary role:

> The nationalist revolutionary movement, in these countries where millions and millions of human beings aspire to national liberation, and want to free themselves economically and politically from imperialism . . . cannot achieve victory under the leadership of the bourgeoisie.[20]

Roy argued that the leadership of the national revolution had to be assumed by the proletariat. In the end both Malaka and Roy were accommodated in the Comintern resolutions.

There was a consistent analysis of the role of the working class *vis-à-vis* nationalist movements from the Second to the Fourth Congresses. At the Second Congress Lenin had argued for closer collaboration with the nationalist movement that Roy wanted only because the workers' parties were as yet weak. The final resolution was, however, quite clear that

> The Communist International should collaborate provisionally with the revolutionary [nationalist] movement of the colonies and backward countries, and even form alliances with it, but it must not amalgamate with it; it must unconditionally maintain the independence of the proletarian movement, even if it is only at an embryonic stage.[21]

In short, the Comintern support for nationalism was explicitly limited to the rallying of the constituent elements of the future proletarian parties. At the Fourth Congress this position was made more explicit:

> The workers' movement in the colonial and semi-colonial countries must first of all win for itself the position of an independent revolutionary factor in the anti-imperialist front as a whole. Only when its importance as an independent factor is recognised and its political independence secured, are temporary arrangements with bourgeois democracy permissible and necessary.[22]

The Fourth Congress was the last one attended by Lenin, and henceforward there was to be a growing accommodation with the national bourgeoisie, and less emphasis on the independent organization of the working class in the colonial countries. From 1924 onwards, Stalin's conception of 'socialism in one country' would dictate much of Soviet foreign policy.

At the Fifth Congress of 1924, Manuilsky argued that whereas earlier congresses had only put forward general principles, it was now possible to "base oneself on the rich experience of the Russian Leninist-Stalinist school regarding the treatment of the national question".[23] Stalin now stressed the need for an alliance with the 'national bourgeoisie', with few of the caveats which had been added by earlier congresses. Roy argued vigorously that the colonial world was not an undifferentiated category, and that with the capitalist penetration the indigenous bourgeoisie would lose its nationalist inclinations:

> Surely, then, we cannot continue to insist on a formula which holds that the colonial bourgeoisie is an objectively revolutionary force which we should support and with which we should establish relations.[24]

Nationalist movements could not be supported regardless of which class led them. Manuilsky accused Roy of holding a "nihilistic theory on the national question" and supporting the discredited notion advanced in 1919 by Bukharin that self-determination should apply to workers and not nations (see Chapter 3). The diversity of Marxist positions on the national question reflected in the Comintern can be seen from two debates which arose at the Fifth Congress. Nguyen Ai Quoc, later to become known as Ho Chi Minh, berated the metropolitan communist parties for neglecting the colonies:

> Comrades have not thoroughly grasped the idea that the destiny of the world proletariat, and especially that of the colonizing countries, is closely bound up with the destiny of the oppressed classes in the colonies.[25]

On the other hand, the French CP section from Sidi-bel-Abbès in Algeria reflected the persistent hold of ideas from the Second International: given "that the Arab bourgeoisie profess[ed] nationalist and feudal principles", rather than supporting national independence for Algeria, they argued that "the liberation of the native proletariat of North Africa [would] be the fruit only of the revolution in the mother country . . . ."[26]

Between the Fifth and Sixth Congresses of the Comintern, the Chinese revolution had suffered the major setback of 1927 (see below). In Europe, the workers' movement had also suffered major defeats. Consequently, the 1928 Congress decided on an ultra-left turn — "class against class" — which saw social democracy as the main enemy in the metropolitan countries and 'national reformism' in the colonies. The main resolution on the national and colonial question began by distinguishing between a section of the national bourgeoisie which directly served the interests of imperialism (the comprador bourgeoisie) and that vacillating national reformist sector which supported the national movement. Though of "little significance in themselves", open conflicts between the national reformist bourgeoisie and imperialism could provide openings for the proletariat. So, while

> the formation of any kind of bloc between the communist party and the national-reformist opposition must be rejected; this does not preclude temporary agreements and the co-ordination of activities in particular anti-imperialist actions . . . .[27]

As to the 'national revolutionary' movement of the petty bourgeoisie, temporary alliances were permissible, "provided that the latter is a genuine revolutionary movement".[28] This congress also made the general theoretical point that

> The bourgeois-democratic revolution in the colonies is distinguished from the bourgeois-democratic revolution in an independent country chiefly in that it is organically linked with the national liberation struggle against imperialist domination.[29]

The national factor was seen as exerting a major influence on the revolutionary process in the colonial world. Finally, this Congress consecrated the formula which declared the colonies 'a powerful auxiliary force' in the socialist world revolution behind the Soviet Union and the labour movement in the capitalist countries.

One of the most interesting debates which arose at the Sixth Congress centred around Roy's thesis of 'decolonization'. The discussion focused on whether imperialism was promoting or retarding industrialization in India. Roy's argument, which he had developed at several successive congresses, was that the basic trend was one of increased capitalist penetration and therefore of decolonization. Most of the British delegates agreed that Britain was industrializing India to take advantage of the cheap labour there. Otto Kuusinen, official Comintern spokesperson on the national question, argued against this position:

> Real industrialization of the colonial country ... which would promote the independent development of its productive forces, is not encouraged but, on the contrary, is hindered by the metropolis.[30]

Behind this debate lay two different conceptions of the 'national bourgeoisie', interpreted in a thoroughly economistic manner as the political reflection of its economic role. If the decolonization thesis was accepted, then the national bourgeoisie was to be seen as a thoroughly counter-revolutionary force not in the least contradictory with imperialism. Kuusinen drew no such conclusion; he argued that there *was* a fundamental difference of interests between the indigenous bourgeoisie and the imperialists. Effectively, all participants in this debate denied the relative autonomy, in both economic and political senses, of the Indian bourgeoisie. As Banaji comments,

> as long as the national capitalists retained and even expanded their autonomous base within the economy ... *there could be no question of the bourgeoisie finally* compromising with imperialism, betraying the national movement, giving up the goal of independence.[31]

How far the Comintern went in ignoring this is testified by its 1930 labelling of Gandhi as "a prime agent of British imperialism".

The ultra-left course set by the Comintern in 1928 was eventually reversed at the Seventh Congress in 1935, which proclaimed the line of the 'Popular Front'. The main resolution declared resolutely that "It is the duty of the communists actively to support the national liberation struggle of the oppressed peoples of the colonial and semi-colonial countries . . . ."[32] In the case of China specifically, the national liberation front should be extended "to draw in all the national forces that are ready to repulse the robber campaign of the Japanese and other imperialists".[33] The struggle against fascism entailed not only a downgrading of the anti-imperialist struggle so as not to break the front of 'democratic nations', but also a careful avoidance of divisive class issues within the national liberation fronts. In India this meant that Gandhi ceased to be "an agent of British imperialism", and a "progressive role" was attributed to him. When the Second World War broke out in 1939, the Indian CP inevitably supported the British war effort, at a time when the Indian nationalists were languishing in British jails. Not surprisingly, there was a sharp divorce between the nationalist and communist movements, as the latter began unconditionally to follow the dictates of Soviet foreign policy. Indian communists collaborated with British imperialism, Latin American communists allied with US imperialism and in China a revolution succeeded only because Stalin's dictates were disregarded (see below). The ease with which Stalin dissolved the Comintern in 1943 only confirmed that by then it had become a branch of the Soviet state's foreign policy.

The attitude of the Seventh Congress towards national liberation struggles in the colonies was exemplified by the practice of the French CP *vis-à-vis* Algeria. Party leader Thorez spoke in 1937 of how "the decisive question of the moment is the victorious struggle against fascism, the interest of the colonial peoples lies *in their union* with the French people . . . ."[34] Recalling a formula of Lenin's (see Chapter 4), Thorez proclaimed that the right of the colonial peoples to national independence, like the right to divorce, need not be exercised. In 1939 Thorez referred to "the Algerian nation which is taking form historically and whose evolution can be facilitated, aided by the efforts of the French Republic".[35] This position was no different from the benign paternalism that Kautsky had suggested the successful British revolution would display towards India and which Engels had castigated so forthrightly (see Chapter 1). The French CP effectively supported the infamous Blum-Violette plan aimed at reforming the colonial state in Algeria, and its chosen allies in Africa were the bourgeois nationalist partisans of assimilation or integration centred around Ferhat Abbas. The "defence of the Algerian people" proclaimed by Thorez entailed their subordination to the interests of the metropolitan communist party. This type of episode, and many others described above, makes it hardly surprising that "the Comintern was to end its life without having succeeded in establishing solid and influential bases in the great majority of the countries under imperialist domination", as Claudin writes.[36] A major element in this was the failure to adopt a principled yet flexible policy towards nationalist movements.

Latin American communists

By examining selected aspects of communism in Latin America we can better understand how Comintern policy affected its national sections. José Carlos

Mariátegui from Peru was a pre-eminent figure amongst the early Communist leaders. His *Seven Interpretative Essays on the Peruvian Reality* (1927) matches the work of Antonio Gramsci in its originality and sensitivity. In 1929, a year before his death, he submitted an essay on *The Anti-Imperialist Perspective* to the First Congress of Latin American Communist parties. He squarely confronted the dominant Comintern tendency of seeking allies among the national bourgeoisie. Mariátegui argued that

> The Latin American bourgeoisie . . . [was] totally unwilling to consider the idea that a second struggle for independence [was] necessary . . . the ruling class [had] no yearning for a greater degree of national autonomy.[37]

In his outline programme for the Peruvian Socialist Party, Mariátegui made clear the political consequences which followed from this analysis:

> Only proletarian action can stimulate first and later realize the tasks of the bourgeois-democratic revolution, which the bourgeois regime is incapable of developing and accomplishing.[38]

In short, the national tasks of the revolution in dependent countries could only be accomplished by the working class, as the bourgeoisie was now thoroughly integrated with imperialism. Against a vague nationalist anti-imperialism, Mariátegui declared,

> We are anti-imperialists because we are Marxists, because we are revolutionaries, because we oppose socialism to capitalism, believing them to be antagonistic systems and that socialism must follow upon capitalism.[39]

The other major independent communist was Julio Antonio Mella who also died in 1929. The Comintern leaders were seeking Latin American equivalents of the Chinese Kuomintang, with whom local communists could ally. A prime candidate was the bourgeois nationalist APRA movement in Peru led by Haya de la Torre. In a short polemical pamphlet *What is the APRA* (1928), Mella put forward a strikingly radical reading of Lenin's thesis on the national question at the Second Congress of the Comintern. He argued that "absolute national liberation will only be obtained by the proletariat, and it will be by means of the workers' revolution".[40] While the Comintern was seeking the "progressive national bourgeoisie" Mella analysed the position of this class with great clarity:

> In their struggle against imperialism — the foreign thief — the bourgeoisies — the national thieves — unite with the proletariat, good cannon fodder. But they end up understanding that it is better to make an alliance with imperialism, which, when all is said and done, pursues a similar interest. From progressives they become reactionaries.[41]

While Lenin, in his debate with Roy, had maintained a flexible attitude towards the national bourgeoisie, the Comintern had, after 1924, stressed the 'progressive' aspect which Mella pours scorn on. After the ultra-left 'class against class' period of 1929-34, which resulted in a premature rising in El

Salvador in 1932, the Comintern in Latin America settled down to the task of wooing the 'progressive' national bourgeoisie.

At the Seventh Comintern Congress in 1935 the example of the National Liberation Alliance established in Brazil was held up as an example for other Third World countries. By underestimating the importance of the national question, communists in Latin America had effectively isolated themselves from the mass struggle. Now, however, it was not merely a united front which was sought with bourgeois nationalism, in so far as the Popular Front entailed holding back the mass movement within the limits set by its bourgeois components. The Brazilian CP called for 'national unity against fascism' and in the trade unions its anti-strike policy left the labour movement powerless in the face of an offensive by the state. In 1945 party leader Luis Carlos Prestes declared:

> The only way out of the economic and social crisis that we are going through is without doubt the *peaceful* and progressive implementation, in a framework of *law and order*, of a programme of national unity . . . . All together, *workers and progressive employers, peasants and landowners*, democrats, intellectuals and military men.[42]

During the 1950s the Brazilian CP moved even closer to bourgeois nationalism, stating in 1958 that "in the present conditions of our country, *capitalist development* corresponds to the interests of the proletariat".[43] As elsewhere in Latin America, the Brazilian communists defined the revolution as anti-imperialist and anti-feudal, with the main priority being the formation of a broad nationalist front. In accordance with the conception of a 'revolution by stages' socialism was postponed to an undefined future.

The communist movement's analysis of Latin America from the 1920s onwards was of a 'dual society', where feudalism was being gradually driven back by a progressive national bourgeoisie. But a whole series of concrete studies have shown that there is no material basis in Latin America for this democratic/anti-imperialist revolution based on alliance with a progressive wing of the indigenous bourgeoisie. Nor can it be conceived as a distinct and clearly delimited 'stage'. The material interests of the 'national bourgeoisie' have led it into competition with international capital but not into an irreconcilable conflict. Likewise, the 'feudal' agricultural sector has in fact always been highly integrated with the urban/industrial economy, and is again not a source of deep contradictions. The 'national bourgeoisie' has simply sought to defend its interests in the best way possible, sometimes confronting imperialism with the aid of the working class, at other times simply accepting the role of dependent partner. The Bolivian trade union federation adopted a Trotskyist-inspired programme in 1952 which pointed out that

> any attempt at collaboration with the exploiters, any concession to the enemy amounts to a betrayal of the workers. Class collaboration implies the renunciation of our objectives.[44]

The *Thesis of Pulacayo* argued that the so-called national bourgeoisie could at best pursue the revolution halfway, and that once its immediate objectives were achieved it would turn on its erstwhile allies. Latin American Trotskyists were, however, just as divided on what attitude to maintain towards the nationalist movement: some proposed a tactical alliance while others maintained an uncompromising opposition.

After Stalin dissolved the Comintern in 1943 as a gesture of goodwill to the West, he proceeded to negotiate respective 'zones of influence' with the imperialist powers. When accused of Soviet expansionism in Eastern Europe his lieutenant Molotov replied:

> It is known that the United States of America is also pursuing a policy to strengthen its relations with neighbouring countries — for instance Canada, Mexico, and also other countries of America — which is fully understandable.[45]

With Latin America ceded passively to the US sphere of influence, the communist parties of the area were forced to tone down their support for nationalism. The shadowy Cominform, which replaced the Comintern in 1947 as the highest organ of international communism, declared that the Latin American CPs "must use every means in the struggle to ensure stable and prolonged peace; they must subordinate all their activities to this paramount task of the day".[46] As mass nationalist movements were arising in many Latin American countries, the CPs busied themselves collecting signatures for the Stockholm 'peace appeal' and strenuously opposed any discussion of national independence within the peace movement. The highpoint of this strategy was the phenomenon known as 'Browderism' — after the leader of the United States CP, Earl Browder, who advanced the view that imperialism no longer existed and that communist parties were therefore redundant — which had a considerable influence in Latin America.

The Comintern had often taken a sectarian attitude towards nationalist movements in Latin America. In 1929 the concept of 'national fascism' was applied to the nationalist government of Lázaro Cardenas in Mexico. In the 1930s Leon Trotsky, by then in exile in that country, advanced a more subtle interpretation:

> In the industrially backward countries foreign capital plays a decisive role. Hence the relative weakness of the *national* bourgeoisie in relation to the *national* proletariat.[47]

This gave rise to a Bonapartist type of state such as the Cardenas government, which carried out an important series of nationalization measures. Trotsky did not believe that a negative stance towards this nationalist regime was justified. Turning slightly later to India he made this position clear:

> The main task in India is the overthrow of British domination. This task imposes upon the proletariat the support of every oppositional and revolutionary action directed against imperialism. This support must be inspired by a firm distrust of the national bourgeoisie.[48]

As Lenin in 1920, Trotsky in 1938-9 was calling for the seemingly contradictory policy of uniting with the national bourgeoisie against imperialism, while continuing the struggle against them. For the post-Lenin Comintern such subtlety was impossible. During the depression of the 1930s, when broad sections of the petty bourgeoisie were being radicalized, the Latin American CPs refused any form of class alliances. Thus during the US occupation of Nicaragua (1926-34), when Augusto César Sandino had mobilized a powerful revolutionary nationalist guerrilla force, the Comintern concluded, with no justification, that "the struggle ended by the capitulation of Sandino and his passage over to the side of the counter-revolutionary government of Sacasa".[49]

A later example of a sectarian attitude towards a nationalist movement occurred in Argentina when Juan Perón came to power in 1946 at the head of a labour-nationalist coalition. The entry of the Soviet Union into the Second World War in 1941 — after the disastrous Nazi-Soviet pact — led the Comintern in general to adopt an 'anti-fascist' line. This orientation was to be faithfully applied in Latin America, regardless of the fact that imperialism, and not fascism, was the main enemy there. The CP in Argentina applied the 'fascism versus democracy' scheme mechanically in Argentina, concluding that Perón was a fascist because he did not support the Allied war effort. The CP formed an alliance with the most pro-imperialist sections of the ruling classes, thus isolating itself from the labour movement for many years to come. The CP even distinguished between 'democratic' firms such as the railways and meat-packing plants (in British and US hands) where strikes were strenuously discouraged, and 'fascist' firms such as Bayer and Siemens owned by German capital. The official party history could only say lamely in explaining Perón's immense appeal amongst the working class that "he was able to cleverly exploit the anti-imperialist sentiments of our people".[50] But the anti-imperialist stance of nationalist regimes was not negated by the war. Effectively, in this as in other episodes, the Latin American communists isolated themselves from the forces of nationalism and their socialist potential. As Debray notes,

> Whatever the reasons for this split between nationalism and socialism . . . its effects distorted both. On the one hand it kept socialism apart from the mass of the people, and on the other it gave a certain fascist tinge to all the nationalist and anti-imperialist movements; in fact the two effects are inseparable.[51]

Debray, in common with many left-wing nationalists, goes on to blame this on the 'foreign' nature of the communist parties rather than on mistaken political conceptions.

The Comintern had come quite late to an interest in Latin America — a Latin American Secretariat was not set up until 1924. Its somewhat undifferentiated view of the 'East' led it to place Latin American in the semi-colonial category. The unique combination of class struggle and national struggle in Latin America was not clearly grasped by the early Comintern. According to Kermit McKenzie, it was not until 1928 that the Comintern revived Lenin's term "dependent country" (used by Lenin in *Imperialism: The Highest Stage of Capitalism* to characterize Argentina) on the prompting of Ricardo Paredes to cover those areas which had been penetrated economically by imperialism but which still retained a higher degree of political independence than the colonies and semi-colonies.[52]

The analysis of the Latin American social formation was often quite crude and lacking in concrete knowledge. An impoverished 'Marxism-Leninism' transposed a schema based on the European experience — revolutionary role of the bourgeoisie, struggle against feudalism, formation of the nation-state — and applied it mechanically to the recalcitrant reality of Latin America. On top of that, the policy of each national communist party in Latin America unswervingly followed the Comintern policy of the time, whether it corresponded with local conditions or not. The nationalist or revolutionary nationalist movements of Peronism in Argentina, Lázaro Cardenas in Mexico and Sandino in Nicaragua were all condemned by the Comintern at a time when communists could have made a decisive intervention. At other times communists entered into subordinate alliances with nationalist forces. Thus during the Chilean Popular Front period (1938-48), the Chilean communists strove to restrain strikes in order to protect 'national industry'. In Brazil, during a succession of nationalist governments from 1955 to 1964, the CP became one of the most active propagandists of nationalism, a nationalism which remained an empty slogan, devoid of revolutionary social content. With the working class beginning to forge a place for itself in the political arena, the Brazilian CP was objectively shackling the unions and the working class to the bourgeois nationalist political apparatus. Since the defeat in Chile in 1973, the communist parties of the area have been recalling the decisions of the Seventh Congress of Comintern to launch a broad 'anti-fascist' alliance, in yet another mechanical transposition from another time and another place.

The Chinese revolution

Commenting on the dissolution of the Comintern in 1943, Mao Tse-tung stated that,

> Since the Seventh World Congress of the Communist International in 1935, the Communist International has not intervened in the internal affairs of the Chinese Communist Party. And yet, the Chinese Communist Party has done its work very well, throughout the whole Anti-Japanese War of National Liberation.[53]

With this understatement Mao was pointing to a long history of Soviet intervention before 1935 and the growing independence of Chinese communism after that date. It is that history which we will now briefly survey as a 'case-study' of Comintern attitudes towards the national/colonial question.

From 1922 onwards a succession of Soviet advisers in China forged an alliance with the bourgeois nationalist Kuomintang (KMT) movement. The fledgling Chinese Communist Party (CCP) was quite reluctant to enter an alliance with the Kuomintang but it eventually did so in 1924, under Comintern orders. In Gruber's judgement, Stalin's policy on China "left the CCP no role save that of hand-maiden of the nationalist cause".[54] E.H. Carr, for his part, argues that the alliance was essentially between the Chinese national revolution and the Soviet state "with the CCP as an often reluctant partner — and instrument — of the alliance".[55] The Second Congress of the CCP in 1922 had indeed decided to seek a united front with the Kuomintang, but the Comintern argued that they should join it as individuals as the KMT was not a bourgeois party but rather a coalition of the bourgeoisie, petty bourgeoisie, peasantry and proletariat. Thus the Comintern forced a reluctant Chinese Communist Party to accept the theory of the KMT as a "bloc of four classes". A Comintern Executive Committee resolution of January 1923 still insisted that the CCP "must retain its independent organization . . . while avoiding any conflict with the national-revolutionary movement".[56] The CCP meanwhile, having rid itself of the opponents to entry into the KMT, held its Third Congress in June 1923 and stated that "the KMT should be the central force of the national revolution and should assume its leadership".[57] This was the perspective which predominated in practice, as the Soviet Union threw its weight behind Sun Yat-Sen and his successor Chiang Kai-Shek.

The Soviet-KMT alliance explicitly stated that the Soviet Union would not sponsor communism in China and, though Sun Yat-Sen's principles were rewritten to make them more acceptable to the Chinese communists, this agreement was essentially kept to. The Soviet leadership supported the nationalist offensive of the KMT with finance and military aid for its own 'reasons of state'. This may well have been the correct policy, but it could not justify accepting the KMT into Comintern membership in 1926 and making Chiang Kai-Shek an honorary member of its ruling Praesidium. From 1925 onwards the Chinese communists had grown increasingly uneasy with their subordinate role in the nationalist movement. But Stalin insisted in 1926 that in countries like China, communists

> must pass from a united national front policy to the policy of a revolutionary bloc of the workers and the petty bourgeoisie. This bloc . . . can take the form of a single party, a workers' and peasants' party of the Kuomintang type . . . .[58]

Subsequent events led to the deletion of the words 'of the Kuomintang type' from future reprintings of this article.

From 1924 onwards the class struggle in China greatly accelerated with a series of strikes, peasant mobilizations and nationalist risings. The KMT began to question the alliance with the communists as armed militias were formed by the unions and workers took over the management of some foreign firms. The inevitable confrontation came in 1927 when a workers' insurrection took over the city of Shanghai. As the Nationalist Army of Chiang Kai-Shek moved into Shanghai a situation of dual power developed, with the CCP attempting to maintain a precarious balance. The communists continued to treat Chiang Kai-Shek as a great revolutionary leader and strove to keep the mobilization of the workers within tolerable limits. Stalin and the Comintern were well aware that the alliance between the CCP and the KMT was an unstable one, but were determined to maintain it as long as Chiang Kai-Shek remained favourably disposed towards the Soviet Union. Chiang Kai-Shek, for his part, acted to defend the position of the 'national bourgeoisie' and in a bloody coup on April 12, took over the city of Shanghai. When cries of 'betrayal' were raised by the Comintern, Trotsky quite rightly noted that Chiang Kai-Shek had not betrayed his class but rather the illusions of the Comintern. A wave of anti-communism swept through China, as Chesnaux describes:

> The unions were dissolved, strikes were banned, the peasant unions were liquidated, the Communists were hunted down, and military workers were fired. A few weak attempts at retaliation were immediately crushed. A new chapter had begun.[59]

The divorce between the bourgeois nationalists and the communists seemed complete.

The reaction of the Comintern to the 1927 debacle was to blame the Chinese CP for a faulty implementation of their correct directives. Bukharin, leader of the Comintern, but by now completely subordinated to Stalin, wrote how

> it was possible for a time to march together with the national bourgeoisie but at a certain stage of development *it was necessary to foresee imminent changes* . . . .[60]

The "opportunist blunders" Bukharin referred to, such as the CCP becoming a simple accessory to the KMT and its role as a brake on the mass movement, were, however, dictated by Comintern policy-makers. A Comintern declaration in July 1927 stated ingeniously that "the present leadership of the Chinese Communist Party has recently made a number of profound political mistakes", listed these, and then went on to say that the Comintern had warned them about these mistakes all along.[61] That Comintern policy had not really changed is demonstrated in that same declaration which said that the CCP "should not leave the Kuomintang. They must remain in it . . . ."[62] At the Sixth Congress of Comintern in 1928, China received comparatively little attention in the debate. One delegate did urge the Indian CP to learn the lesson of China: "The national bourgeoisie will betray you even at the beginning of the revolutionary movement".[63] But in presenting the main resolution, Kuusinen defended Comintern policy towards the KMT; it had merely been wrongly executed by the Chinese communists. As to the future, participation of the national bourgeoisie in the revolutionary movement was unlikely, but not impossible.

Leon Trotsky, for his part, developed some severe criticisms of Comintern orthodoxy on the basis of the 1927 events. As E.H. Carr notes there is some dispute as to when this criticism began: "Exactly when Trotsky began to think of the entry of the CCP into Kuomintang as a grave political error remains uncertain".[64] Certainly, by mid-1926 he was arguing that national oppression was insufficient justification in itself for a communist party to ally itself with a national revolutionary party. Trotsky made the obvious point that a "national revolution in the sense of a struggle against national dependency is achieved through the mechanics of classes".[65] When the CCP was a small propaganda society, it was "perfectly correct" to enter the KMT and take part in the ongoing national liberation struggle. When the rise of the mass movement began, however, it was indispensable to maintain an independent working-class organization. Trotsky admitted in a letter to Radek that his knowledge of China was insufficient to state with precision whether that withdrawal should have occurred in 1923, 1924 or 1925.[66] Whatever his inconsistencies, Trotsky did however, in a sustained argument with Stalin on the lessons of the Chinese revolution, raise the important general question of whether

> the bourgeoisie of a colonial or semi-colonial country in an epoch of struggle for national liberation must be more progressive and more revolutionary than the bourgeoisie of a non-colonial country in the epoch of the democratic revolution.[67]

Lenin had raised the national liberation movement to the level of the bourgeois democratic revolution, argued Trotsky: but it was sheer Menshevism to argue that the fact of colonial oppression made the national bourgeoisie more progressive. This general debate is still relevant today.

After the 1927 coup, the Comintern line on China changed dramatically, as the 'class against class' policy of the Comintern was faithfully put into practice. A new leadership in the CCP first launched the Nanchung insurrection in a major provincial capital, then the Autumn Harvest Uprising among the peasants of Hunan. Both were routed by the nationalist troops. Towards the end of 1927, the CCP prepared for yet another insurrection, this time in the city of Canton where they still had a strong influence within the working class. Stalin and the Comintern delegates in China were impatient for a victory, partly at least to quell Trotsky's insistent criticisms. The Soviet government of Canton was, however, shortlived, and in the repression which followed the Chinese working class was basically knocked out of the revolutionary process. A concerted rising in 1930 failed just as severely. This whole adventurist strategy (in the context of the 1927 defeat) was not applied consistently because the Chinese communists remained part of the KMT government in Wuhan. While Stalin recognized the desertion of the national bourgeoisie after Chiang's coup he discerned a revolutionary wing in Wuhan. Agrarian revolution and arming of the masses would be subordinated to this new Kuomintang left. Helmut Gruber shows how the "leaders of the KMT left were one of the many myths with which Stalin decked out his self-serving approach to the Chinese revolution".[68] Nor did Wuhan represent the petty bourgeoisie: in fact, the Comintern never carried out a rigorous analysis of the class forces involved in the Chinese national revolution. Not surprisingly the alliance with the KMT 'left' did not last more than a few months.

By 1935 the Chinese communists, and in particular Mao Tse-tung, had developed an alternative strategy to overcome the errors of 1927 and the adventurist attempts which had followed. Already in 1927 in his *Report on the Peasant Movement in Hunan*, Mao had pointed to the inevitably important role which the peasantry would play in any Chinese revolutions. He further recognized that the struggle would be a long one and that it would be centred on the 'red bases' of the countryside. When the Second World War broke out, the Soviet government signed a military aid pact with the Kuomintang government and called on Mao to end the undeclared civil war. The communists were in the forefront of the anti-Japanese resistance but refused to follow Stalin's directives unconditionally — they would probably have led to a new debacle on the lines of 1927. The Maoist leadership did not believe that the united front against Japan precluded an ongoing struggle for predominance over its temporary nationalist allies. After the collapse of Japan, the civil war resumed at full intensity, even though Stalin continually pressurized for a compromise settlement, in accord with the post-war agreement with the imperialist powers. The Chinese communists pressed on until ultimate victory in 1949. As Claudin writes,

> the ultimate goal of Mao's strategy was not the limited one of national liberation; it included social revolution. It is well known that the close connection between these two aspects was the secret of the Communist victory in China.[69]

Mao's line on the national bourgeoisie was quite different from Stalin's, even when he was adopting the accepted formulations of the Comintern. In 1938 he wrote of how "Chinese Communists must . . . combine patriotism with internationalism" and how the united front meant there was "relative independence" in "the relationship between the class struggle and the national struggle".[70] The following year he argued that the proletariat should form a united front with the national bourgeoisie and maintain it "as far as possible".[71] Foreign oppression made this possible but "in other historical circumstances, the Chinese national bourgeoisie will vacillate and defect because of its economic and political flabbiness".[72] In other words, the national bourgeoisie was a weak and vacillating force and in any alliance with it the proletarian party should retain full independence of action. The national bourgeoisie had for Mao a dual character determined by its position between the proletariat and imperialism, an analysis strikingly similar to that Trotsky carried out in Mexico. What this meant in terms of the political line of the Communist Party "was the policy both of unity with the bourgeoisie and of struggle against it".[73] This was essentially Lenin's strategy outlined at the Second Congress of Comintern, a pragmatic alliance with nationalism while retaining full consciousness that the ultimate aims of bourgeois nationalism and socialism were quite distinct. After 1949, Mao argued that there was only a "non-antagonistic contradiction" between the national bourgeoisie and the proletariat; but that is something we must examine in the next chapter.

Even before the victory of the Chinese revolutions, attempts were being made to raise 'Maoism' to the level of a new Marxist orthodoxy. In 1945 Liu Shao-ch'i reported to the Seventh Congress of the CCP that

> the *Thought of Mao Tse-tung* is a further development of Marxism in the national-democratic revolution in the colonial, semi-colonial and semi-feudal countries of the present epoch. It is an admirable model of the nationalization of Marxism . . . .[74]

It is as well to recall the overwhelming importance of the national factor in the Chinese revolution: its success was due in no small part to the Kuomintang's failure to achieve national independence and an integrated modern nation. Its success, furthermore, was due to the 'nationalism' of the Chinese communists which led them to break with the Comintern and develop their own independent strategy. But was 'Maoism' truly going to lead to "the emancipation of the peoples of all countries" as Liu Shao-ch'i claimed? Just as the 'lessons of October' had been universalized to an undue extent by the Comintern, so now the undoubted success of the Chinese revolution was leading to a similar exercise. This was to lead to the 'Third Worldism' we analyse in the next chapter. Mao had forged a powerful synthesis between Marxism and China's national peculiarities; he had established a pragmatic yet consistent alliance with national capitalists; but his advance on Comintern orthodoxy was an empirical one never fully theorized. The continued veneration of Stalin in China, and the silence over many of the episodes from 1924 onwards, testify to an incomplete break.

Notes

1. 'Backward Europe and Advanced Asia', cited in H. Carrère d'Encausse and S. Schram (eds.), *Marxism and Asia* (Allen Lane The Penguin Press, London, 1969) p.139.

2. L. Trotsky, *The First Five Years of the Communist International*, Vol. 1 (New Park Publications, London, 1973) p.49.

3. *The Second Congress of the Communist International* (Publishing Office of the Communist International, America, 1921) p.117.

4. F. Claudin, *The Communist Movement: From Comintern to Cominform* (Penguin, Harmondsworth, 1975) p.265.

5. *The Second Congress of the Communist International*, p.120.

6. Ibid., p.120.

7. Ibid., p.121.

8. Ibid., p.135.

9. Ibid.

10. Ibid., p.160

11. H. Carrère d'Encausse and S. Schram (eds.), *Marxism and Asia*, p.173.

12. Ibid., p.160.

13. Ibid., p.174.

14. E.H. Carr, *Socialism in One Country 1924-1926*, Vol. 3 (Penguin, Harmondsworth, 1972) p.634.

15. H. Carrère d'Encausse and S. Schram (eds.), *Marxism and Asia*, p.193.

16. F. Claudin, *The Communist Movement*, p.252.

17. J. Degras (ed.), *The Communist International 1919-1943 — Documents*, Vol. 1, 1919-1922 (Frank Cass, London, 1971) p.385.

18. Ibid., p.385.

19. H. Carrère d'Encausse and S. Schram (eds.), *Marxism and Asia*, p.190.

20. Ibid., p.192.

21. J. Degras (ed.), *The Communist International*, p.144.

22. Ibid., p.390.

23. Cited in D. Boersner, *The Bolsheviks and the National and Colonial Question (1917-1928)* (Hyperion Press, Westport, Conn., 1981), (originally published 1957) p.154.

24. H. Carrère d'Encausse and S. Schram (eds.), *Marxism and Asia*, p.203.

25. Ibid., p.199.

26. Ibid., p.197.

27. J. Degras (ed.), *The Communist International 1919-1943 — Documents*, Vol. 2 1923-1928 (Frank Cass, London, 1971) p.541.

28. Ibid., p.542.

29. Ibid., p.537.

30. Ibid., p.534.

31. J. Banaji, 'The Comintern and Indian Nationalism', *International*, Vol. 3, No. 4, 1977, p.34.

32. J. Degras (ed.), *The Communist International 1919-1943 — Documents*, Vol. 3 1929-1943 (Frank Cass, London, 1971) p.377.

33. Ibid., p.377.

34. H. Carrère d'Encausse and S. Schram (eds.), *Marxism and Asia*, p.249.

35. Ibid., p.250.

36. F. Claudin, *The Communist Movement*, p.294.

37. J.C. Mariátegui, 'The Anti-Imperialist Perspective', *New Left Review*, No. 70, 1977, p.67.

38. J.C. Mariátegui, *Ideologia y Politica* (Biblioteca Amauta, Lima, 1969), p.160.

39. J.C. Mariátegui, 'The Anti-Imperialist Perspective', p.72.

40. J.A. Mella, *Que es el APRA* (Editora Educacion, Lima, 1975) p.24.

41. Ibid., p.24.

42. Cited in C. Rossi, *La Revolution Permanente en Amérique Latine* (Cahiers Rouge, Paris, 1972) p.162.

43. Ibid., p.163.

44. Cited in G. Lora, *A History of the Bolivian Labour Movement 1848-1971* (Cambridge University Press, 1977) p.247.

45. Cited in F. Claudin, *The Communist Movement*, p.472.

46. Ibid., p.580.

47. L. Trotsky, *Writings, 1938-39* (Pathfinder Press, New York, 1974) p.326.

48. L. Trotsky, *Writings, 1939-40* (Pathfinder Press, New York, 1973), p.109.

49. Cited in L. Aguilar (ed.), *Marxism in Latin America* (Alfred Knopf, New York, 1968) p.119.

50. *Esbozo de Historia del Partido Communista de la Argentina* (Ediciones Anteo, Buenos Aires, 1947) p.125.

51. R. Debray, *A Critique of Arms: Vol. 2, The Revolution on Trial* (Penguin, Harmondsworth, 1978) p.225.

52. K. McKenzie, *Comintern and World Revolution, 1928-1943* (Columbia University Press, New York, 1974), p.81.

53. S. Schram, *The Political Thought of Mao Tse-tung* (Penguin, Harmondsworth, 1969) p.423.

54. H. Gruber (ed.), *Soviet Russia Masters the Comintern* (Anchor Books, New York, 1974) p.404.

55. E.H. Carr, *Foundations of a Planned Economy 1926-1929*, Vol. 3 - III (Macmillan, London, 1978) p.701.

56. J. Degras (ed.), *The Communist International 1919-1943: Documents*. Vol. 2 1923-1928, p.6.

57. Ibid., p.25.

58. H. Carrère d'Encausse and S. Schram (eds.), *Marxism and Asia*, p.226.

59. J. Chesnaux, F. Le Barbier and M.C. Bergere, *China: From the 1911 Revolution to Liberation* (Harvester, Brighton, 1977) pp.174-5.

60. Cited in F. Claudin, *The Communist Movement*, p.275.

61. J. Degras (ed.), *The Communist International 1919-1943 — Documents*, Vol. 3 1929-1943, p.395.

62. Ibid., p.395.

63. Ibid., p.529.

64. E.H. Carr, *Foundations of a Planned Economy*, p.754.

65. L. Trotsky, *Leon Trotsky on China* (Pathfinder Press, New York, 1976) p.145.

66. Ibid., p.122.

67. Ibid., p.294.

68. H. Gruber (ed.), *Soviet Russia Masters the Comintern*, pp.450-1.

69. F. Claudin, *The Communist Movement*, p.554.

70. Mao Tse-tung, *Selected Readings from the Works of Mao Tse-tung* (Foreign Languages Press, Peking, 1967) pp.113, 117.

71. Ibid., p.137.

72. Ibid.

73. Ibid., p.138.

74. H. Carrère d'Encausse and S. Schram (eds.), *Marxism and Asia*, p.260.

6. The Third World

After the Second World War and the collapse of the Third International, the epicentre of the world revolution seemed to shift to those countries in the so-called Third World fighting against colonialism and neo-colonialism. In Africa, Amílcar Cabral was to become the most articulate spokesman for the need to adapt Marxism to the reality of nationalist aspirations. The first section of this chapter explores his main ideas on the relationship between nationalism and socialism and some of the key practical tests of it in practice. In Latin America, the Cuban revolution provided an impetus to both nationalism and socialism, articulated most clearly by the almost mythical figure of Che Guevara. Behind the myths and the arguments with the orthodox communist parties we find the still unresolved classical dilemmas. Finally, we turn again to the Chinese revolution taking up the post-revolutionary development of Maoism and the ideology which became known as 'Third Worldism'. With this, the original Marxist tendency to distinguish between 'historic' and 'non-historic' nations was turned on its head, with the 'revolutionary' nations of Africa, Asia and Latin America being seen as the new bearers of the socialist cause. This chapter will examine the positive and negative contributions made by Third World theorists to our understanding of nationalism, previously viewed through a somewhat Eurocentric optic.

Cabral and the African revolution

A recent biographer writes that Amílcar Cabral "was first and foremost a nationalist. Nationalism, not communism, was his cause".[1] Yet the leader of the anti-imperialist movement in Guinea-Bissau worked within an explicitly Marxist discourse. This meeting between Marxist theory and nationalist practice produced one of the most fruitful and open-ended analyses of the African type of revolution. It was in a speech to the First Solidarity Conference of the Peoples of Africa, Asia and Latin America held in Havana in 1966 that Cabral set out his ideas on national liberation most clearly.

The 1966 speech, known as *The Weapon of Theory*, begins by reinserting the Third World into the process of world history, against the still lingering ideology of the 'non-historic' nations. To assert that the history of humankind is the history of class struggle, means according to Cabral,

> that various human groups in Africa, Asia and Latin America were living without history or outside history at the moment they were subjected to the yoke of imperialism.[2]

It is as well to recall this point when Eurocentric history still teaches that Columbus 'discovered' America, ignoring the peoples who lived there before. Cabral then goes on to question the then orthodox Marxist position on imperialism, arguing that it has accelerated the accumulation of capital in the periphery, "thus contributing, by a process which some would call dialectical, to sharpening the contradictions within the societies in question".[3] Having said that, he did not believe that the Third World bourgeoisie could become a genuine national bourgeoisie and freely guide the development of the productive forces.

The struggle against imperialist domination by the national liberation movement was for Cabral a clearly defined phenomenon. National liberation was, in short, a process

> in which a socio-economic whole rejects the denial of its historical process . . . the regaining of the historical personality of that people, it is their return to history through the destruction of the imperialist domination to which they were subjected.[4]

The theme is similar to Otto Bauer's description of how a people regains its historical role (see Chapter 2). Cabral is dismissive of the subjective formulations of international law which refer to national liberation as "the right of all peoples to decide their destiny freely".[5] In this he follows Rosa Luxemburg's rejection of the phrase regarding the 'right' of nations to self-determination (see Chapter 3). Cabral reasserts the 'orthodox' Marxism of the 1859 Preface when he argues that the only objective definition of national liberation is that "the national productive forces have been completely freed from any kind of foreign domination".[6] Because it demands a development of the forces of production, the phenomenon of national liberation "necessarily corresponds to a revolution".[7] But does a revolution not imply a shift in the *relations* of production and an overthrow of the relations of domination and exploitation? We can approach this question by turning to Cabral's analysis of the social forces involved in the national liberation movement.

Cabral wrote often of the 'nation-class', that broad alliance of nationalist forces which would lead the anti-colonial struggle. The leading role in this class bloc would, according to Cabral, inevitably be the petty bourgeoisie, given the underdevelopment of the working class. It is here that Cabral advances his well-known, and controversial, thesis that

> In order to play completely the part that falls to it in the national liberation struggle, the revolutionary petty bourgeoisie must be capable of committing *suicide* as a class, to be restored to life in the condition of a revolutionary worker completely identified with the deepest aspirations of the people to which he belongs.[8]

The dilemma of the petty bourgeoisie in the national liberation struggle was whether to betray the revolution or commit suicide as a class. We might well ask if this was ever a realistic prospect. On the one hand, Cabral's emphasis on the development of the forces of production led to a type of 'stages theory' in which, quite simply, "the nation gains its independence and theoretically adopts the economic structure it finds most attractive".[9] Only under neo-colonialism is the socialist solution appropriate. Yet the agent for this struggle remains the petty bourgeoisie, through a development of its revolutionary consciousness, as happened in Cuba, according to Cabral. We have here a certain technological determinism which focuses on the material aspect of production, and on the other hand, a certain subjectivism which relies unduly on the 'moral' commitment of the middle class.

In 1970 Cabral presented a lecture on *National Liberation and Culture* which pointed to the crucial relation between the two phenomena. He made the point that

> Whatever the conditions of subjection of a people to foreign domination and the influence of economic, political and social factors in the exercise of this domination, it is generally within the cultural factor that we find the germ of challenge which leads to the structuring and development of the liberation movement.[10]

Cabral was one of those Marxists who placed a great stress on national culture and the development of hegemony in the course of the struggle. Indeed, for Cabral "the armed liberation struggle is not only a product of culture but also a *factor of culture*".[11] Or, as he puts it at another point, "The armed liberation struggle implies a veritable forced march along the road to cultural progress".[12] Less well defined in this essay is how the 'cultural reconversion' or 're-Africanization' of the petty bourgeoisie will take place. There is also the question of how far the necessary forging of national cultural resistance across classes — "the harmonizing and development of these [different] values within a national framework"[13] — is compatible with the struggle for socialism. Jock McCulloch has indeed argued that,

> The major difference between the arguments presented in *The Weapon of Theory* (1966) and *National Liberation and Culture* (1970) is Cabral's changed attitude to the role of the class struggle. In the later essay he has abandoned completely the role of class struggle as the motive force of history, as he calls dialectical materialism.[14]

The discourse of nationalism seemed to impose its logic, but as Cabral died in 1973 we cannot be sure of how he would have seen the post-colonial phase.

We must now turn to another African revolutionary writer who made an important contribution to our understanding of nationalism — Frantz Fanon. Better known for his exaltation of revolutionary violence and praise of the lumpen proletariat, Fanon also produced a realistic appreciation of nationalism. The experience of post-revolutionary Algeria taught him that

National consciousness instead of being the all-embracing crystallization of the innermost hopes of the whole people . . . will be only an empty shell, a crude and fragile travesty of what it might have been.[15]

The cruel reality of neo-colonialism would reimpose its grip after the victory of the national liberation movement. Fanon stated the obvious: "The objective of nationalist parties . . . is strictly national. They mobilize the people with slogans of independence, and for the rest leave it to future events".[16] The socio-economic system to be adopted is left vague and undefined. The national petty bourgeoisie, which Cabral thought might commit suicide as a class, is not credited with such altruism by Fanon. This 'underdeveloped' social class takes over power at the end of the colonial regime, but it lacks the attributes Fanon considers necessary for it "to fulfill its historic role of bourgeoisie".[17] In short,

Its mission has nothing to do with transforming the nation; it consists, prosaically, of being the transmission line between the nation and a capitalism, rampant though camouflaged, which today puts on the mask of neo-colonialism.[18]

We may question the implied idealizing of the rising European bourgeoisie contrasted with the "meanness of outlook" and "cheap-jack's function" of its African counterpart; but Fanon does paint a picture which corresponds well with the reality of post-colonial Africa.

Fanon, like any African revolutionary, could not have a one-sided view of nationalism. On the one hand it did act as a factor promoting social unity, overcoming ethnic divisions, and as a detonator of the anti-colonial struggles. It is well to recall with Fanon that "in the first phase of the national struggle colonialism tries to disarm national demands by putting forward economic doctrines".[19] Economic concessions are used to delay the emergence of national consciousness; class demands are more easily defused than national ones. Fanon even argues that it "can be dangerous when they [the people] reach the stage of social consciousness before the stage of nationalism".[20] Yet after the victory of the national liberation movement other dangers present themselves. Fanon writes that in some cases , "From nationalism we have passed to ultra-nationalism, to chauvinism, and finally to racism".[21] This type of admission is rare indeed from a revolutionary nationalist. Most far-reaching of all is Fanon's conclusion that

If nationalism is not made explicit, if it is not enriched and deepened by a very rapid transformation into a consciousness of social and political needs . . . it leads up a blind alley.[22]

If national consciousness does not develop and acquire a social dimension it is reduced to a "sterile formalism", to use Fanon's phrase. The collective building of a people's destiny is reduced to the sordid history of repression, poverty and the resurgence of tribalism which has characterized most of post-colonial Africa.

It is precisely that historical experience which must ultimately be the judge of Cabral's and Fanon's political theses. For Tanzanian Marxist Issa Shivji, nationalism was essentially a sham:

> The slogans of nationalism and freedom, equality, etc. that the petty bourgeoisie shouted on the eve of independence were merely echoes of the ideology of the metropolitan bourgeoisie without their social or economic content.[23]

This takes us back to Fanon's view that nationalism is, as it were, an empty shell into which different social classes put their hopes and aspirations. Nationalism, which has a positive role to play during the anti-imperialist struggle, later prevents, or denies, the emergence of class conflicts. African socialism for long argued that the continent was classless, and indeed many liberation movements profess to believe this even in the contemporary period. Yet nationalism retains within it a contradiction. A recent study of Algeria points out how in that country, "nationalism, instrument of social consensus, has also created a dynamic of demands directed towards the state: work, education, social needs".[24] The myth of nation was a vital element in forging a post-colonial Algeria. Nationalist ideology has been internalized to such an extent that its democratic components cannot be easily denied. Social cohesion and the political legitimacy of the state depend crucially on nationalism, yet that nationalism is now irredeemably fissured with emerging class contradictions.

National and class contradictions have always been intertwined: it is the task of social analysis to separate them. Clegg writes, in relation to Algeria again, how in the course of the liberation struggle there was an

> attempted elision of a national and a class struggle through the identification of the European settlers as the oppressors and the indigenous population as the oppressed.[25]

Of course this reductionism had its appeal because it corresponded to the needs of the struggle. It should not lead us to confuse a national liberation war with a class war. Later, in the 1970s, the Algerian political leadership stressed the need for national solidarity against imperialism — the external enemy. Against the traditional concept of non-alignment in international affairs, President Boumedienne advanced the theory that the world was divided into rich and poor, with "proletarian nations" such as Algeria confronting the rich bourgeois nations of the West. Internal contradictions were denied and the whole 'Algerian nation' was portrayed as a victim of imperialism.

What we are saying, of course, is that socialism and nationalism cannot be fused; they are distinct social and political phenomena. The myth of 'African socialism' was rapidly punctured by the first post-colonial regimes. Hopes were more persistent where a long armed struggle and more explicit Marxist language was used, such as in the Portuguese colonies of Angola, Mozambique and Guinea-Bissau. Cabral argues that these movements "were thus the first African nationalist parties in a position to replace, rather than simply inherit, the colonial state".[26] The new states had, therefore, a greater potential role as an instrument for revolution. Two questions arise: to what extent was any liberation war a class struggle, and who managed the state after independence and for whose benefit? To the first question Anthony Smith provides a forthright, if possibly overstated, answer. Referring to the 1980 coup in Guinea-Bissau he writes that

> Ethnicity has, in this instance, proved stronger than marxism, revealing the essentially nationalist foundations of the liberation struggle, in the hearts and minds of the masses who followed the PAIGC [Partido Africano da Independencia da Guiné e Cabo].[27]

There is little from the experience of Angola (witness the ethnic base of Savimbi's opposition movement) or Mozambique which would fundamentally alter that picture. As to the state, we must first note the obvious: that socialism cannot be built from above, by the state or a benevolent revolutionary leader. Nor have we seen the petty bourgeoisie, who seized the state apparatus, "committing suicide", as Cabral had hoped. To the contrary, as Gabriel points out, we have witnessed a renaissance of their real values: authoritarianism, paternalism, and bureaucratism.[28] The state in Guinea-Bissau, as in the other 'popular states', is indeed a breeding ground for the formation of bureaucratic petty bourgeois cliques and the consolidation of a genuine bourgeois state. The harsh verdict must be that neo-colonialism has reimposed its grip on most of the post-colonial countries.

Even so, does nationalism not lay the basis for socialism? Arrighi and Saul argue persuasively that

> Nationalism, so potentially mystifying an element on the African scene, can in certain contexts be revitalized, used (and controlled) as a progressive instrument providing the rationale for struggle and/or the framework within which social reconstruction proceeds.[29]

The second part of this statement is undoubtedly true: nationalism is a potent mobilizing agent and the necessary framework for the transition to socialism in societies dominated by imperialism. The problem is that nationalism has more often used or controlled socialism than vice versa. Marxism-Leninism is a useful ideology of modernization in many so-called socialist countries: this does not mean that the dictatorship of the proletariat prevails. By claiming the mantle of revolutionary nationalism many of these movements simply evade the issue of class. As Trotsky noted in the case of China (see Chapter 5), the bourgeois democratic nationalist movements in the Third World are neither more nor less 'progressive' than their metropolitan counterparts. The great appeal of the 'liberation movement' was that it promised a short cut for socialists. We may conclude with a quote from Cabral in a more sceptical mood than usual: "to hope that the petty bourgeoisie will just carry out a revolution when it comes to power in an underdeveloped country is to hope for a miracle".[30]

Guevara and the Latin American revolution

Ernesto 'Che' Guevara was the internationalist *par excellence*; yet his memory in Latin America is inextricably bound up with the history of nationalism.

Guevara called for the creation of "Two, three, many Vietnams" in Latin America in a bold internationalist venture. Yet most of those who followed in his footsteps after his death in 1967 built 'National Liberation Armies' which had *Patria o Muerte* (Fatherland or Death) as their main slogan.

Guevara's attitude towards nationalism and socialism was shaped by the Cuban revolution. Much has been said about the social composition of this revolution and we may now accept a much greater role for the working class and the urban population generally.[31] We may also accept that the revolution had a socialist dynamic from the start. However, in its origins, personnel and programme, the Cuban revolution was an essentially nationalist phenomenon, uniting broad social sectors against a common foreign enemy (US imperialism) and its local representative (the dictator Batista). That is why Guevara could write,

> We do not believe one can consider exceptional the fact that the bourgeoisie, or at least a good part of the bourgeoisie, favoured the revolutionary war against the tyranny . . . .[32]

Likewise, for him,

> It [was] understandable that the national bourgeoisie, oppressed by imperialism and by a tyranny whose troops pillaged their holdings, should look with sympathy when the young rebels of the mountains punished the armed servants of imperialism who composed the mercenary army.[33]

Such tolerance towards "the young rebels" was only possible because these had not declared themselves socialists and took their stand instead on the democratic principles of the French Revolution and nationalism.

In the 1960s, Guevara was to inspire a much more radical stance towards the vexed issue of the 'national bourgeoisie'. As we saw in Chapter 5 this class was, for the orthodox communist parties, a progressive element. In his 1967 *Message to the Tricontinental*, Guevara argued that

> The autochthonous bourgeoisie have lost all their capacity to oppose imperialism — if they ever had it — and they have become the last card in the pack. There are no alternatives: either a socialist revolution or caricature of revolution.[34]

That same year the Latin American Solidarity Organisation (OLAS) launched a declaration that broke decisively with traditional communist conceptions of the national bourgeoisie. It was analysed as weak and indecisive, indissolubly linked with the traditional landowning oligarchy. So,

> It would be absurd to suppose that, under such conditions, the so-called Latin American bourgeoisie could develop political action independent of the oligarchies and imperialism in defence of the interests and aspirations of the nations.[35]

It was now being argued that genuine national liberation could only be brought about through socialist revolution. The hope that the national bourgeoisie would first build a stable democratic national capitalism was shattered. Yet the

'Guevarist' organizations clung to a nationalist discourse which even sometimes obscured their socialist message.

The Tupamaros in Uruguay and the People's Revolutionary Army (ERP) in Argentina took their stand on grounds of patriotism. Indeed, they saw their task as that of accomplishing the Second Independence, the first being achieved in the early 19th Century against colonial Spain. The Revolutionary Coordinating Committee, which grouped together the Tupamaros, the ERP, the Chilean MIR and the Bolivian ELN, declared at its founding congress in 1974 that

> The cowardly creole bourgeoisie and their armies did not know how to honour the revolutionary liberationist legacy of the glorious anti-colonial struggle of our people which, led by heroes like Bolivar, San Martin, Artigas, and many others, won independence, equality and liberty.[36]

Of course the 'equality and liberty' they won were for the aspiring local merchants, not the impoverished masses. More importantly, we note that the 'Guevarist' organizations placed themselves in a line of continuity with the pantheon of nationalist heroes, not those of socialism. In practice these organizations were based on quite restricted radicalized sectors of the population; yet their discourse was predominantly nationalist. Nationalism was in many ways seen as the 'lowest common denominator', so that the ERP was the nationalist anti-imperialist 'army' of the more openly socialist Revolutionary Workers' Party (PRT). The question still remains as to why these organizations constantly strove to build National Liberation Fronts and the like, in conditions where they were not really appropriate.

The answer must be sought in the deep mystifications surrounding the term 'anti-imperialism', which as Bill Warren has acidly commented, can be a cover for the worst type of capitalism.[37] The Revolutionary Coordinating Committee, referred to above, had developed in many respects an acute understanding of nationalism:

> Bourgeois nationalism is a current approved by imperialism which supports it as a demagogic variant to distract and divert the struggle of the peoples when counter-revolutionary violence loses its effectiveness.[38]

The verbal anti-imperialism of many Latin American regimes is indeed a foil for their continued accommodation — both economic and political — with imperialism. To continue appealing to nationalism meant redefining a 'genuine' or 'revolutionary' variant. If 'bourgeois nationalism' was defined quite clearly as an enemy of the people, it was hard to conjure up a positive variant using the same symbols and language. In fact, nationalism had fundamentally taken over and dominated the discourse of the Guevarist organizations, with the partial exception of the Chilean MIR.[39]

We have already noted in the quotes above a certain voluntarism. Imperialism deliberately 'chooses' bourgeois nationalism as a strategy to mislead the masses. Did the local capitalist classes not have their own objective economic interests in pursuing nationalist policies? Even more significantly, the language of voluntarism tended to downplay the significance of class. Reformism was reduced to cowardice, rather than a coherent and, within limits, quite viable political strategy. Appeals to mobilize were not couched in class terms generally but in the vague mythological terms of nationalism. This adaptation towards nationalism obviously had serious practical effects. In Peru, most of the left supported the 'nationalist' policies of the military dictatorship which came to power in 1968. In Uruguay, the Tupamaros sought allies amongst the 'nationalist' sectors of the army even while they were being crushed in 1972. In Argentina, nearly all the left supported the 1982 takeover of the Malvinas islands by a military dictatorship which had butchered tens of thousands. Abroad, political exiles who had been tortured in Argentina laid wreaths on the tomb of national hero San Martín alongside the diplomatic representatives of the dictatorship. The list is a long one, and it is not meant as facile criticism. The point is, that the Guevarist organizations were small radical movements committed to armed struggle, and they were completely overwhelmed by nationalism. It was hard to stop and ask if Argentina really was a semi-colonial country where a 'National Liberation Front' could commence a guerrilla war in the hills in a bid to replicate Vietnam. Nor were the huge complex societies of Mexico, Brazil or Colombia comparable to Cuba in 1959. The anti-imperialist perspective tended to flatten national peculiarities and it reduced class contradictions to moral ones.

This critique should not prevent us from recognizing that Guevara developed an essentially correct analysis of the 'national bourgeoisie' at various times. He recognized firstly that

> There are objective contradictions between the national bourgeoisies struggling to develop and the imperialism which inundates the markets with its products in order to destroy in unequal competition the national industrialists . . . . [40]

This is undoubtedly true and something which the OLAS declaration tended to neglect. There was indeed a tendency in Guevarist circles to deny that the national bourgeoisie even existed. That it was not nationalist in the sense desired by the communists did not make this class any less real. Guevara goes on to say that "In spite of these conflicts the national bourgeoisie are not capable, in general, of sustaining a consequential struggle against imperialism".[41] That is because they fear the revolution more than imperialism. Certainly, the indigenous capitalist class has more to fear from an insurgent working class and peasantry than from the "despotic domination of imperialism, which destroys nationality, affronts patriotic sentiments, and colonizes the economy".[42] The first two do not concern a capitalist, and the third is faced every day of the week in the 'national' marketplace. Contradictions between international and national capital are 'secondary', to use the Maoist terminology.

Twenty years after the success of the Cuban revolution in 1959, the Sandinista revolution achieved victory in Nicaragua. What was the relationship between nationalism and socialism in this case and what were its implications for the rest of the continent?

The Sandinistas began, like other Guevarist organizations, by organizing isolated rural *focos* which were virtually doomed to fail.[43] After defeats in 1963 and 1967 they began a gradual reorientation of the movement. This included the appropriation of the 1930s war led by General Augusto Sandino against the invasion by US Marines. From then on the Sandinistas stressed their national roots and developed a strong base amongst the people. By 1978 they had forged a broad anti-dictatorial alliance with many democratic sectors of the bourgeoisie. The Broad Opposition Front (FAO) brought bourgeois sectors into the struggle against the dictator Somoza, for their own reasons. The bourgeoisie complained about Somoza's near monopoly of economic and political power and his fraudulent business practices. Their aim was a peaceful changeover of regimes and the re-establishment of normal conditions for capital accumulation. In 1979 the FAO was replaced by the National Patriotic Front (FPN), and the insurrectional phase of the revolution was launched. Though the main impetus of the rising was democratic and anti-imperialist, the insurrection had a profound effect on the political consciousness of the broad masses. The transition to socialism was a real prospect in the free Nicaragua.

The concentration of state power, political regime, and armed forces under Somoza meant that his collapse had far-reaching effects. The predominantly nationalist character of the struggle, however, set obvious limits on the Sandinistas' ability to lead an immediate transition to socialism. The alliance with the democratic and nationalist sectors of the bourgeoisie continued, and so did the mixed economy. For some commentators, this broad nationalist alliance "opened up a whole new chapter in the art of making revolution in Latin America".[44] Had Guevara's strictures on the 'national bourgeoisie' been superseded by events? In fact, Nicaragua, like Cuba before, was in a number of ways unique. Both victories took place in conditions where in Blackburn's words the "enemy was a starkly corrupt and asocial machine. Its character determined the conditions of its overthrow".[45] It does not follow from the Nicaraguan experience that socialist parties in the rest of Latin America should assiduously court bourgeois forces on the basis of a national democratic platform. Nor does the post-revolutionary situation in Nicaragua justify some of the excessive claims by Sandinista supporters that some new kind of alliance with private capital is possible in the transition to socialism.

Cuba had a relatively weak and unsophisticated national bourgeoisie, and a large and politically advanced proletariat. In Nicaragua there was a unique combination of local and international factors (e.g. the support of social democrats), which made a radical nationalist insurrection viable. This scenario would not, however, apply in Argentina and Mexico where the political sophistication of the bourgeoisie is legendary, civil society is of a great 'density', and the working class is organized in powerful reformist trade unions. Where nationalism becomes institutionalized, practically sanctified, as in both these countries, it is hardly a mobilizing revolutionary force. Nationalism may indeed remain a necessary factor in any struggle for socialism in Latin America; but it is not sufficient in itself.

Perhaps one of the clearest experiences that illustrates this was that of the Montoneros in Argentina during the mid-1970s.[46] Drawing on the revolutionary nationalist legacy of Peronism, this movement became one of the strongest on the continent (in many ways equivalent to the Palestine Liberation Organization). Yet it failed under democratic and dictatorial governments alike to gain a mass base and forge a permanent position for itself in the class struggle. This was essentially because its nationalist outlook tended to focus on events in a subjective and moralistic manner. The other side of this was an opportunism which led them to volunteer from prison to fight alongside the dictatorship's troops in the Malvinas. When the struggle against imperialism can lead to such a gross violation of basic political principles, we tend to end up agreeing with Bill Warren about the damage done by nationalism to socialism in the Third World.

Perhaps at this stage we can return to the difference between 'bourgeois nationalism' and 'revolutionary nationalism'. One way of resolving the general confusion is by looking at two variants of nationalism: one reformist, where its aims and objectives are not pursued to their final resolution and another, revolutionary, where they are. In other words, reformist and revolutionary refer to the methods employed and the degree to which nationalist objectives are fulfilled. Yet this tells us nothing about which class interests are being satisfied. Bourgeois nationalism in this sense is quite straightforward, or at least should be, in that it represents the national interests of the capitalist class. Revolutionary nationalism must then be understood as a struggle against all forms of exploitation suffered by a people within a national boundary. Argentinian 'national socialist' Ricardo Carpani writes that "the authentically national cannot be conceived independently of the satisfaction or frustration of the needs of all the individuals who make up a nation".[47] From this perspective the nation is understood as the product of the creative activity of the masses, to be recovered in struggle against foreign oppression and its internal counterparts. Bourgeois nationalism instead presents the nation as something abstract and symbolic, separating it from the concrete labour of those who have built it. The particular interests of the bourgeoisie cannot be equated with those of the nation, which is mainly composed of workers, peasants and artisans.

Maoism and Third Worldism

In the previous chapter we discussed how Mao had developed a sceptical interpretation of the 'national bourgeoisie' even while he was forging the broad nationalist alliance which led to victory in 1949. In the post-revolutionary period a new orthodoxy was to develop about the role of the national bourgeoisie.

In 1949, as the communists seized power, Mao Tse-tung elaborated the theory of the 'people's democratic dictatorship'. In what was later to become the famous 'bloc of four classes', the people were defined as the working class, the peasantry, the petty bourgeoisie and the national bourgeoisie. As to this last group,

> The national bourgeoisie at the present stage is of great importance . . . . To counter imperialist oppression and to raise her backward economy to a higher level, China must utilize all the factors of urban and rural capitalism that are

beneficial and not harmful to the national economy and the people's livelihood; and we must unite with the national bourgeoisie in common struggle.[48]

Here is posed with admirable clarity the problem of national economic development under socialism. It is a view not dissimilar to that adopted by the Sandinistas thirty years later when they seized power in another dependent nation. The first sentence is incontestable: the national bourgeoisie is of great importance. More questionable is the assumption that it is actually possible to distinguish the beneficial from the harmful effects of capitalism. Nor does it follow that workers and national capitalists must unite "in common struggle". As the recent experience of Nicaragua shows, no capitalist class wishes to retain a moderate economic role 'in the national interest' without the corresponding state power. The final point is the nationalist framework in which economic development is posed — "China must" ... — and the practically Manichean role attributed to imperialist oppression.

In 1957 Mao Tse-tung wrote *On the Correct Handling of Contradictions Among the People*, in which he claimed that, "In our country, the contradiction between the working class and the national bourgeoisie belongs to the category of contradictions among the people".[49] It was not explained how two social classes, proponents of two different modes of production which were mutually exclusive, could achieve such peaceful coexistence. Mao did argue that its dual character during the revolutionary phase — at once nationalist and conciliationist — could now be extended to the post-revolutionary era when it would seek profit and exploit the working class on the one hand, while being marked by "willingness to accept socialist transformation on the other".[50] The first contradiction was of course antagonistic — that between wage-labour and capital — but

> in the concrete conditions of China, this antagonistic class contradiction can, if properly handled, be transformed into a non-antagonistic one and be resolved by peaceful methods.[51]

These included "suitable educational methods" through which "we shall carry the work of educating [the national bourgeoisie] and remoulding them".[52] To those who claimed that the bourgeoisie now had only one side — i.e. progressive — Mao replied that they still had two sides to their character, but education would take care of their 'bad' side.

The general accommodation with nationalism on the internal front was bound to have repercussions in foreign affairs. In 1952 a short book was published in China on *The New Aspect of the War of National Liberation in the East*.[53] This strongly emphasized the role of China in the Third World and the universal validity of the Chinese experience. The 'people's democratic revolution' in China was going to influence the world as a whole and was a model for all subsequent national liberation struggles to follow. An Indian delegate at a trade union conference in China was quoted as saying that study of the thought of Mao Tse-tung was sufficient to equip him to gain victory in his own country. National independence and the 'new democracy' were to be the watchwords of a new revolutionary wave guided by China (the Soviet Union was already being relegated to a secondary position). In 1957, Chou En-lai made a report after a tour of Asia in which he hardly mentioned socialism. He spoke of how

> Our nations are humiliated and our people reduced to slavery. The independent development of our political life, of our economy, and our culture was arrested and trampled on . . . . We must struggle unremittingly to defend the sovereignty and independence of our countries . . . . We are all resolved to develop our native lands and reach the level of modern states . . . .[54]

From now on national interest and the pursuit of national grandeur would dictate China's foreign policy. Criticisms of Soviet 'revisionism' could not hide the basic fact, even though Maoist groups for long denied it, until their general demoralization in the 1970s.

China's foreign policy has been a subject of abuse from socialists for such a long time that we do not need to enter into detail here.[55] After the Sino-Soviet split in the 1960s, Chinese foreign policy was largely dictated by the belief that the Soviet Union was the Number One enemy of socialism. By the 1970s China saw world politics exclusively as a battle between the two superpowers, with the United States being considered the lesser evil compared with the 'social imperialists' of the Soviet Union. China supported Pakistan's military dictatorship against leftist rebels, and did likewise in Ceylon. President Nixon was fêted in Peking barely months after the mining of Haiphong by the US armed forces. In Angola, China supported the FNLA alongside the CIA and assorted Western mercenaries. In Chile they rapidly recognized the military dictatorship which overthrew the Allende regime, because the Soviet-line communist party was part of the government. In Western Europe, uncritical support was given to the EEC because it stood in the way of Soviet 'expansionism'. The world was divided into three areas: the first world was composed of the two superpowers, the second world was an 'intermediate zone' (the middle class) composed of the other advanced industrialized countries, and the third world was composed of the underdeveloped or 'proletarian' nations. This somewhat shaky distinction, based on nation-states rather than social classes, was to frame China's foreign policy.

It is one particular strand of China's foreign policy which interests us here, namely that which led to the development of 'Third Worldism'. This was articulated by Lin Piao in 1965 in an article entitled *Long Live the Victory of People's War*.[56] He began by recalling the major role of the peasants in China's national democratic revolution and how the imperialists were driven out of the countryside to the cities. Revolutionary bases were established in the country areas which then encircled the cities. This perspective was then globalized:

> Taking the entire globe, if North America and Western Europe can be called 'the cities of the world', then Asia, Africa and Latin America constitute 'the rural areas of the world' . . . . In a sense, the contemporary world revolution also presents a picture of the encirclement of the cities by the rural areas. In the final analysis, the whole cause of world revolution hinges on the revolutionary

struggles of the Asian, African and Latin American peoples who make up the overwhelming majority of the world's population.[57]

This articulates with admirable clarity the ideology of 'Third Worldism' which develops the pioneering analysis of Sultan Galiev (see Chapter 4) and, more importantly, expresses the growing self-confidence of revolutionary nationalist movements throughout the world. The pre-eminent role accorded to the Third World — on the dubious criteria of population — and the substitution of a nationalist for a class vocabulary were its main elements. We shall now examine its revolutionary and reformist variants and its effect in the metropolitan countries.

The Third Worldist euphoria probably began with the Algerian war of independence and its radical impact on Europe. It continued with the Cuban revolution, which shook the hegemony of US imperialism and it was epitomized by the long resistance of the Vietnamese people and their ultimate victory. Fanon wrote of "the colonial countries where a real struggle for freedom has taken place, where the blood of the people has flowed . . . ."[58] He went on to say that "it is a question of the Third World starting a new history of Man . . . ."[59] There was an almost mystical belief in the regenerating value of Third World struggles. There was an absolute confidence in ultimate victory — imperialism was 'a paper tiger'. There was far less consideration of the concrete basis of the 'Third World revolution'. The grinding poverty of the masses was not in itself sufficient to produce a revolutionary situation — these in the Leninist sense were few and far between. As Chaliand writes there was also

little analysis probing beneath the rhetoric of the leaders, getting at the actual matters at stake in a given conflict or the actual nature of the independence gained or lost.[60]

This criticism is a valid one. But this variant of Third Worldism was still revolutionary. The victory of the Vietnamese people, in their long struggle against the most powerful nation on the planet, attained mythical status but was based on hard facts. Revolutionary Third Worldism eventually faded but its reformist variant proved a sturdier breed.

By reformist Third Worldism we are referring to a diffuse movement launched by a series of statements and events which followed on the formation of the Movement of Non-Aligned countries at the Bandung Conference of 1955.[61] With the formation of the oil producers' cartel OPEC in 1964 this movement reached its peak. Concrete action in 1973 — the raising of oil prices by OPEC — stimulated a campaign to bring the natural resources of the Third World under national control. One slogan put forward was to call for "Two, three, many OPECs" in a pale economistic reflection of Guevara's clarion call. Later the campaign for a 'new international economic order' set as its aim a thorough re-articulation of 'North-South' relations through a policy of 'collective self-reliance' in the Third World. We may criticize the radical pseudo-democratic rhetoric of this enterprise, but not its rationality. The larger dependent capitalist states had much to gain from a level of economic and political co-operation against the former colonial powers. The ideology of Third Worldism helped express the grievances of the subordinated capitalist units and gave them a certain legitimacy in the international forums of debate. Of course this could not hide the fact that the 'Third World' was not an undifferentiated mass, nor that the beneficiaries of this movement would be each country's elite rather than the mass of the people. This reformist transformation of a radical ideology, should be a lesson to all socialists who try to 'use' nationalism.

Third Worldism had its greatest media impact in the 'cities' of the advanced industrialized countries it was threatening to engulf. Young people in Paris, Bonn and London demonstrated on behalf of the Vietnamese people, and stuck Che Guevara posters on their bedroom walls. Jean-Paul Sartre wrote a preface for Fanon's *The Wretched of the Earth* where he abased himself, praised the cleansing value of violence, agreed that Europeans were "estranged from themselves" and that "Europe is at death's door".[62] What lay behind all this was a profound pessimism amongst European socialists about the working class in their own countries. Workers were soft, bought-off and objectively part of imperialism: they were a 'labour aristocracy' helping to plunder the virtuous Third World. Anyway, more exciting things than trade union meetings and strikes were happening abroad: the armed struggle was going on (proof in itself of revolutionary virtues) and the 'world revolution' loomed on the horizon. This is by no means meant to mock the role played by the anti-Vietnam War movement in the USA and other countries. This one true act of internationalism was matched by many more pious illusions, evasions of responsibility, and a remarkable displacing on to others of genuine hopes and ambitions. In the cold economic climate of the 1980s, metropolitan Third Worldism is less in evidence, although some marginal political groups still persist in the illusions of an earlier era.

Why did Third Worldism emerge in the first place? Chaliand argues that it

> was a phenomenon born of the crisis of Stalinism and fed by the policy of peaceful coexistence. It prospered in the 1960s because of the new hopes in the spread of socialist revolution in the Third World. But it has turned out to be a myth.[63]

Orthodox communism seemed to be going nowhere following the dissolution of the Third International after the war; it was the colonial world that was making the running. The Soviet Union was playing a cautious diplomatic game, and China on the other hand appeared more adventurous. A tremendous international wave of enthusiasm focused on the national liberation movement, and Lin Piao's famous metaphor captured the mood of the period. Of course, nations do not rise up, but rather social classes; nations are not oppressed, social classes are. A cold analysis would show a great deal of difference between those who complained (justifiably) about "the pillage of the Third World", and those fighting for social and economic justice in those very same countries. The major characteristic of all the variants of Third Worldism was their subjectivism or sheer voluntarism. The will to accomplish completely overrode the objective situation. Marx spoke of the 1871 Paris Communards "storming the heavens";

but this kind of action cannot maintain a prolonged class war. For this, Marxist analysis and not revolutionary nationalist rhetoric is called for.

Today it is the metaphor of North and South which has replaced the 1960s version of Third Worldism. It slides over the heterogeneous economic and political objectives of the various social classes in the nations of the South. It never asks what type of social system will emerge from the new 'auto-dynamic' model of development, nor what type of government can or will promote it. By the 1979 Havana World Conference of the Non-Aligned Movement the serious rifts between the different nation-states of the South were evident. The material economic base of non-alignment was disappearing as the NICs (Newly Industrializing Countries) showed the benefits of dependency. The strategy of independent economic development with a self-sufficient internal market and effective protective measures to build up an industrial base was waning in popularity. As the model of dependent capitalist development spreads, so the very notion of a Third World will lose any value it may have. As Parboni writes,

> It is the end of an era: the development exigencies of world capital are destroying the dream of neutrality, peace and independent development in the Third World. War is becoming a permanent feature of capitalism.[64]

It seems that the reformist variant of Third Worldism will now fade as did its revolutionary counterpart earlier. China meanwhile slips into a more aggressive nationalist stance and assiduously practises the 'peaceful coexistence' for which it once criticized the Soviet Union.

Notes

1. P. Chabal, *Amilcar Cabral: Revolutionary Leadership and People's War* (Cambridge University Press, 1983) p.168.

2. A. Cabral, *Unity and Struggle* (Heinemann, London, 1980) p.124.

3. Ibid., p.128.

4. Ibid., p.130.

5. Ibid.

6. Ibid.

7. Ibid.

8. Ibid., p.136.

9. Ibid., p.133.

10. Ibid., p.143.

11. Ibid., p.153.

12. Ibid., p.152.

13. Ibid., p.147.

14. J. McCulloch, *In the Twilight of Revolution: The Political Theory of Amilcar Cabral* (Routledge and Kegan Paul, London, 1983) p.105.

15. F. Fanon, *The Wretched of the Earth* (Penguin, Hardmondsworth, 1969) p.119.

16. Ibid., p.121.

17. Ibid., p.122.

18. Ibid.

19. Ibid., p.167.

20. Ibid., p.164.

21. Ibid., p.125.

22. Ibid., p.165.

23. I. Shivji, *Class Struggles in Tanzania* (Heinemann, London, 1978) p.20.

24. Dersa, *L'Algérie en débat* (Maspero, Paris, 1981) p.198.

25. I. Clegg, *Workers' Self-Management in Algeria* (Monthly Review Press, London, 1971) p.178.

26. P. Chabal, *Amilcar Cabral*, p.218.

27. A. Smith, *State and Nation in the Third World* (Wheatsheaf Books, Brighton, 1983) p.121.

28. C. Gabriel, *Angola: le tournant africain?* (Editions La Brèche, Paris, 1978) p.50.

29. G. Arrighi and J. Saul, *Essays on the Political Economy of Africa* (Monthly Review Press, New York, 1973) p.91.

30. A. Cabral, *Revolution in Guinea* (Stage One, London, 1969) p.58.

31. Cf. J. Petras, 'Socialist Revolutions and their Class Components', *New Left Review*, No. 111, 1978.

32. J. Gerassi (ed.), *Venceremos! The Speeches and Writings of Che Guevara* (Panther Books, London, 1964) p.199.

33. Ibid.

34. Ibid., p.574.

35. OLAS General Declaration, *International Socialist Review*, Vol. 28, No. 6, 1967, p.52.

36. 'The Founding of the Revolutionary Coordinating Committee, 1974' in W. Ratcliff, *Castroism and Communism in Latin America, 1959-1976* (AEI-Hoover Policy Studies, Washington, 1976) p.210.

37. B. Warren, *Imperialism: Pioneer of Capitalism* (New Left Books, London, 1980).

38. 'The Founding of the Revolutionary Coordinating Committee, 1974', p.212.

39. For a broader discussion of 'Guevarism' see R. Munck, *Revolutionary Trends in Latin America*, Centre for Developing-Area Studies, McGill University, Montreal, Occasional Monograph Series No. 17, 1984.

40. J. Gerassi (ed.), *Venceremos!*, p.205.

41. Ibid.

42. Ibid.

43. For further detail see G. Black, *Triumph of the People: The Sandinista Revolution in Nicaragua* (Zed Books, London, 1981).

44. N. Chinchilla, 'Class Struggle in Central America', *Latin American Perspectives*, Vol. 7, No. 2/3, 1980, p.21.

45. Blackburn, 'Prologue to the Cuban Revolution', *New Left Review*, No. 21, 1963, p.21.

46. For a full history of this movement see R. Gillespie, *Soldiers of Perón: Argentina's Montoneros* (Oxford University Press, 1982).

47. R. Carpani, *Nacionalismo, Revolucionario y Nacionalismo Burgues*

(Zero, Madrid, 1976) p.52.

48. Mao Tse-tung, *Selected Readings From the Works of Mao Tse-tung* (Foreign Languages Press, Peking, 1967) p.312.

49. Ibid., p.352.

50. Ibid.

51. Ibid.

52. Ibid., p.310.

53. Extracted from H. Carrère d'Encausse and S. Schram (eds.), *Marxism and Asia* (Allen Lane The Penguin Press, London, 1969) pp.274-81.

54. Ibid., p.297.

55. Cf. N. Harris, *The Mandate of Heaven: Marx and Mao in Modern China* (Quartet Books, London, 1978) Part V: Proletarian Internationalism.

56. Reprinted in W. Chai (ed.), *Essential Works of Chinese Communism* (Bantam Books, New York, 1972).

57. Ibid., p.400.

58. F. Fanon, *The Wretched of the Earth*, p.36.

59. Ibid., p.254.

60. G. Chaliand, *Revolution in the Third World: Myths and Prospects* (The Harvester Press, Hassocks, 1977) p.xv.

61. For a history see P. Willetts, *The Non-Aligned Movement: The Origin of a Third World Alliance* (Frances Pinter, London, 1978).

62. F. Fanon, *The Wretched of the Earth*, p.12.

63. G. Chaliand, *Revolution in the Third World*, p.184.

64. R. Parboni, *The Dollar and its Rivals* (New Left Books, London, 1980) p.195.

7. Socialist States

It was once an article of faith amongst socialists that there could be no wars between socialist nations. After the bloody fratricidal wars in Indo-China since 1979 such complacency is no longer possible. So this chapter needs to come to grips with the persistence of the 'national question' under socialism. We begin with the Union of Soviet Socialist Republics, taking up our previous discussion of nationalism after the October Revolution (see Chapter 4). We examine the economic, political and cultural aspects of the 'national problem', as some Marxists persist in calling it. We look at the resolution of these issues in Yugoslavia, a truly multi-national state, where the socialist revolution was inextricably bound up with national unification. Yugoslavia gives us one of the first examples of a major confrontation between socialist states, as Stalin strove to isolate the non-conformist Tito. In Yugoslavia, as in the USSR, there was also an important advance in understanding national peculiarities (uneven development) and their handling under the transition to socialism. With this background we turn finally to the 'fraternal wars' in Indo-China following the heroic victory of the Vietnamese people over US imperialism. Can these tragic events be reduced to 'historic rivalries' between peoples, or is 'US manipulation' to blame? If Marxism has had difficulty in coming to grips with the phenomenon of nationalism, this is nowhere more true than its treatment of the issue in socialist states where it is decreed superseded by the dictatorship of the proletariat.

The USSR: the 'nationality problem'

According to Carrère d'Encausse, successive Soviet leaders have found that the "link between objective conditions in which society develops and social consciousness apparently does not exist so far as nationalism is concerned".[1] The paradox she sees is that the Soviet Union confronts nationalism from a Marxist perspective, while nationalism operates outside the historical dynamic which frames historical materialism. Certainly, Soviet national policy has often been contradictory: a combination of hope that development would destroy nationalism and concessions to it, for example in the cultural domain. Only a crude economic determinism would expect to find an immediate and direct relation between national conditions and ideology; but we cannot say that this link "does not exist". It is precisely that relationship which will frame our analysis of how the Soviet Union has dealt with the 'national problem'.

Lenin, as we have shown in Chapter 4, had an optimistic view of how nationalism would decline under socialism. After 1917 he gradually came to recognize that nationalism was not an easy tiger to ride. Its role in breaking up the old Russian Empire was beneficial; but afterwards the revolution required a certain degree of centralization for economic, political and military reasons. Stalin imposed this and then Lenin recoiled at the consequences for democracy; in his last political battle he confronted Stalin over the national question. In his last months of life he developed a democratic socialist policy towards nationalism, only improperly described by the term 'national liberalism'.

Under Stalin there was an unashamed promotion of Great Russian patriotism. A leading theoretician of the 1950s declared that

> Soviet patriotism constitutes the fusion of the progressive national traditions of the peoples with the common vital interests of all the toilers of the USSR . . . . The Party of Lenin and Stalin is the inspirer and teacher of Soviet patriotism . . . .[2]

Ivan the Terrible was rehabilitated, as were the expansionist tendencies of the old Russian Empire. For the minority nationalities this meant repression. During Stalin's great purge of 1937-8, the governments of thirty Soviet republics were liquidated totally or in part. Their sin was 'nationalist deviation'. During the Second World War whole peoples — the Crimean Tatars, the Volga Germans, the Kalmyks, the Chechens and several other Caucasian peoples — were exiled *en masse* by Stalin, again because he feared their disloyalty to the Russian centre. Certainly the war (the Great Patriotic War) united the Soviet people in a heroic drive against fascism; but we cannot forget the cost of this. Kruschev writes unashamedly of Russia's seizure of the Baltic states:

> We were all very glad that the Lithuanians, Latvians and Estonians would again be part of the Soviet State. This meant the expansion of our territory, the augmentation of our population, the fortification of our borders, and the acquisition of an extensive coastal frontier on the Baltic Sea.[3]

Later he argued that this was also a great triumph for the Baltic peoples and furthered Soviet 'progressive aims' in that area. The truth of the argument that they were 'again' becoming part of the Soviet state refers to their acquisition by Imperial Russia in the 18th Century; in 1918, in accordance with Lenin's policy of self-determination, they had declared their independence.

When Kruschev denounced Stalin's crimes in 1956 he also implied that the national question would be dealt with differently. Indeed, at the Twenty-second Party Congress in 1961 he advocated not only a rapprochement of cultures (*sblizhenie*) but also an amalgamation of cultures (*sliyanie*). Essentially Kruschev underestimated the continued force of nationalism. Writing about the national antagonisms between Ukrainians and Russians he could declare bluntly that "the basic goal had already been achieved . . . all knew that only through unity could we be strong".[4] Kruschev's successors did not continue the move towards assimilation at the same pace, and at the Twenty-third Party Congress in 1966 Brezhnev called for respect for the national traditions of the republics which made up the USSR. The consensus in the 1970s was that overall social and economic progress could help overcome tensions between the nationalities Nevertheless, there were still those who argued that the Soviet Union was in fact a single nation by all of Stalin's criteria (see Chapter 4) except that of language. In 1981, Brezhnev declared with some understatement that

> The unity of Soviet nations is now closer than ever. This does not mean, of course, that all questions of nationality relations have been solved already.[5]

Since 1917, Lenin had tried optimism, Stalin had used force, Kruschev had tried destalinization and Brezhnev promoted economic development to deal with the 'national problem'. But the reality of nationalism always proved resistant. As Carrère d'Encausse writes, "all the groups in power were [then] struck by the size of the problem, its permanence, its exceptional importance for the future of the USSR".[6]

What have been the results of Soviet national policy? The first aspect to consider is whether it has diminished the economic differentials between national groups. Post-revolutionary Soviet governments have encouraged industrialization in the previously underdeveloped areas, but at first this resulted in 'Russianization' — importing labour — because the skills were not available locally. Whereas between 1913 and 1935 large-scale industry increased five-fold in the USSR as a whole, it was increased 15 times in the Georgian Soviet Socialist Republic (SSR) and 83 times in the Kirghiz SSR.[7] That the non-Russian republics were starting from a much lower level of economic development may inflate these figures; but the general trend was to deliberately overcome the problems of uneven development. Davis concludes with the restrained judgement that there has been "substantial equalization" in terms of income for workers living in different part of the vast territory of the USSR.[8] More recent evidence, based on Soviet statistical sources as analysed by the CIA, indicates that "ethnic disparities in occupational structure declined rapidly in the 1960s".[9] This applies to blue-collar and white-collar occupations generally, and the trend was maintained into the 1970s, if at a slightly slowed pace. Nevertheless, in the more sluggish economic climate of the late 1970s, the 'affirmative action' policies of the central government appeared to contradict the goals of improved economic performance, and were watered down if not totally discarded. But the overall balance sheet of economic policies *vis-à-vis* the nationalities must still be judged relatively successful by any international standards.

In political terms the USSR is composed of 15 Union Republics, 20 autonomous republics and 8 autonomous regions; but in practice the central government is the key political force. However, political participation by the 177 diverse nationalities which make up the USSR has increased considerably since 1917. The recent survey quoted above concludes that

During the 1960s the increases in relative CPSU [Communist Party of the Soviet Union] participation rates were registered by all titular minorities except the Georgians and Armenians, whose rates [already] exceeded those of the Russians . . . .[10]

Again, these trends continued into the 1970s, if at a slower rate. There was indeed an "over-representation" of the minorities in the political structures of the republics, so much so that Soviet leader Andropov declared against formal quotas for minorities in 1977. A CIA-sponsored report was particularly impressed by the fact that in 1979 half of the republic KGB chairmen were 'natives'.[11] Increased political participation by the minorities does not, however, mean that the 'national problem' has been solved in the USSR. In 1966 a group of intellectuals in the Ukraine were arrested for the heinous crime of 'nationalism'.[12] In 1972, author Ivan Dzuba (cited below) was arrested for his criticism of Soviet cultural policy; he was only released when he recanted. Overall, we must agree with Joseph Rothschild who writes that "the ethno-national problem is currently being managed and contained in the Soviet Union at a level below that of crisis", but that it may well become "incendiary in the coming decade and/or insoluble within the prevailing economic system".[13]

One of the most volatile aspects is culture, despite the increased access for the minorities to higher education and the spreading of bilingualism. Zvi Gitelman, in a suggestive article entitled 'Are Nations Merging in the USSR?', concludes that "the ethnic harmony described by Soviet commentators is more wish than reality".[14] General trends are one thing; but specific grievances can accumulate in particular areas. These may become particularly acute when the national grievance is fused with a general resentment against the Soviet bureaucracy. Democratic participation for the Soviet nationals cannot really exist without a full democracy at all levels of society. Without entering into a debate on the 'nature of the USSR', we can assert, without fear of contradiction, that socialist democracy is far from being realized. The treatment of the Muslim religion is one example of cultural repression. In the early 1930s, the leaders of the faith amongst the Central Asian peoples were imprisoned and the mosques were closed, because Muslim rituals were considered anachronistic in an urban industrial civilization.[15] After Iran, can we not suspect that this is a somewhat dangerous attitude? Perhaps the Soviet invasion of Afghanistan may yet lead to a revival of the Muslim religion in the USSR.

The politics of nationalism in the USSR are highly complex and we must suspect any analysis which sees Russian policy as a model of democracy as much as any which sees it as categorically evil. Rudolf Bahro argues that

Nationalism has an objectively necessary role to play in the destruction of the holy alliance of party apparatuses, in as much as it shows that these have not settled the national question in any productive way . . . .[16]

This is correct, but we must recall, with Davis, that the nationalist agitation within and outside the Soviet borders is not necessarily democratic.[17]

The Samizdat literature in the Soviet Union provides many examples of the potent role of nationalism within the dissident movement generally, from

Solzhenitsyn's reactionary mysticism to the democratic socialism of genuine Bolsheviks. A group of long-standing Latvian communists wrote in 1972 of how the Soviet party

> had deliberately adopted a policy of Great Russian chauvinism and that the forcible assimilation of the small USSR nations had been set as one of the most immediate and important domestic policy goals.[18]

They list economic, political, social and cultural acts of repression or discrimination which point to a situation in which "all expressions of Latvian nationalism are suppressed, that there is a forcible assimilation and no equality among nations, cultures and traditions".[19] The only reply in the Soviet press was that the letter was a forgery and anyway all its contents were false.

More recent accounts from Estonia point to a continuation of these trends into the 1980s. Yrgö Malmilähde points to an openly recognized and "deliberate Russification in the Baltic Republics", evident from the fact that in the national capital Tallin, Estonians are already in a minority.[20] Nationalism has been largely channelled into the cultural domain, although in 1980 there were anti-Russian demonstrations led, apparently, by schoolchildren. Further strikes in late 1981 and in 1982 were not surprisingly dampened by events in Poland and what seemed like an imminent Soviet invasion.

Ukrainians, the largest non-Russian national group in the USSR, have recently pursued a vigorous national cultural opposition. Ivan Dzuba described the brutality with which Stalin cut short the highly positive Ukrainization programme in the 1930s.[21] After the Second World War there was a significant Ukrainian guerrilla movement which included a revolutionary socialist tendency. Dzuba stresses the importance of culture today: "Communism is impossible if we do not foster the enrichment and proliferation of national cultural attainments".[22] He does not call for Ukrainian independence but urges a wider circulation of Lenin's last letters on the national question (see Chapter 4). As one of the speeches at the funeral of Aleksei Kosterin said:

> We will carry on his work — the struggle for the restoration of Leninist national autonomy to the Crimean Tatar and Volga German peoples. The issue is not one of concern only to the unfortunate nationalities — Not at all!! It is everyone's business.[23]

Strictly speaking we are dealing with the Soviet Union; but nationalism has had a profound impact on the socialist states outside its frontiers. The Soviet interventions in Hungary in 1956 and Czechoslovakia in 1968 are part of the popular socialist consciousness throughout the world. There are arguments for seeing COMECON as an instrument of Soviet economic imperialism, which shapes the Eastern European economies to suit a 'socialist' international division of labour.[24] At one time the leaders of the subordinate socialist states accepted their role in good grace. In 1956 the Czechoslovak and East German leaders Novotny and Ulbricht condemned 'national communism' as the worst of all sins, and reiterated that "unshakeable friendship with the USSR is the condition for the victory of socialism in every country".[25] They also gave a warm endorsement to the Soviet military intervention in Hungary. Nationalism was defined as the pursuit of narrow self-interest; true internationalism meant the unconditional support of the Soviet Union, and for their tanks when they rolled into other countries. The widespread debate over the Soviet intervention in Afghanistan in 1981 showed a persistent reluctance amongst Western Marxists to offer an unequivocal condemnation. The hypocrisy of imperialism was no excuse for not taking an unequivocal stand for the right of nations to self-determination. If Lenin's principles were indeed basic democratic rights then they should apply even more under socialism.

In the late 1960s we saw, as Fejtö writes, "from Budapest to Tirana, from Bucharest to Prague, the disintegration of the internationalist myth, [and] the contagious revival of nationalist feelings . . . ."[26] This was probably the natural result of the Stalinist heavy-handedness of Novotny and Ulbricht. National communism had taken root in Yugoslavia, now it was spreading to Hungary, Czechoslovakia, Romania and the other 'people's republics'. Hungarian historians took their stand on Marx and Engels to lament the passing of the Austro-Hungarian Empire in 1848 (see Chapter 1), and revived the ghost of the 'non-historic' peoples. As Fejtö describes,

> the basic tendency of the Eastern Communist parties . . . was to take up the 'bourgeois-nationalist' heritage, to concern themselves with national interest, and turn themselves into genuinely national parties.[27]

Past deviations from the national interest could be blamed on the Communist International and Stalin, who was now everybody's scapegoat. From an extreme, and quite false 'internationalism', it was easy to pass into a nationalist phase which just as effectively denied the true proletarian internationalism proclaimed by the *Communist Manifesto*. The 'internationalism' of Russian tanks had helped revive national chauvinism in Eastern Europe. This has its counterpart in Western Europe where many socialists are coming to believe that the region may survive a nuclear war between the superpowers if only it remains neutral, thus not requiring a transition to democratic socialism.

Yugoslavia: multi-national state

The ability of Tito's communist partisans to harness the different nationalities within Yugoslavia in a common effort was a major factor in their victory. As Tito himself wrote,

> A great deal of perseverance was necessary to convince all nationalities that only a people's liberation struggle, only a struggle against the invaders and domestic and treacherous reactionaries could win national rights and thus create a new Yugoslavia.[28]

In a sense it was the war against the Nazis which forged a Yugoslav sense of nationality. The Nazis had tried to use national divisions to *their* advantage, by such means as creating the so-called Independent State of Croatia. As Fred Singleton comments,

> There is no doubt that many Catholic Croats who were not fascists welcomed the creation of an independent Croat state as a step toward the realisation of the nationhood which had been denied them by Hungary in the nineteenth and by Serbia in the twentieth century.[29]

The ultra-nationalist *ustaša* movement in Croatia was engaged in such brutal actions against the Serbians that the Nazis themselves had to restrain them. Tito's partisans were able to overcome these deep-seated divisions, often through force, and forge a strong popular armed struggle committed to ousting the Nazis and building a socialist republic.

Post-war Yugoslavia was the first of the 'national communist' heresies, excommunicated by the 'internationalist' communist movement. The underlying issue was Tito's refusal to accept a subordinate inclusion within the Soviet Union's 'socialist' international division of labour. The victory over fascism in Yugoslavia was based on a dynamic mass movement, whereas in Eastern Europe the Red Army played a dominant role. Tito was a national leader in Yugoslavia as much, or even more than a communist. Yugoslavia was therefore in a strong position to make the first break with the Stalinist monolith. The positive results of nationalism on the foreign front did not prevent its emergence as a disruptive factor internally.

The first Yugoslav constitution in 1953 described the new state as federal in structure, although its basic mechanisms were undoubtedly centralist. In 1963, Tito was still promoting the notion of an integrated Yugoslav culture, which would overcome internal national divisions. By 1968 the international 'student revolt' had spread to Yugoslavia, where it took the form of nationalist demonstrations. In 1971 there was a major nationalist explosion in the republic of Croatia, which some observers thought might lead to civil war. The Albanian minority in Yugoslavia continues to make the international headlines. The questions raised by the persistence of nationalist rivalries must be approached firstly by a consideration of the regional economic inequalities. Only then can we return to the political dimensions of nationalism in Yugoslavia.

Perhaps the major aim of the post-war Yugoslav government was to reduce the economic inequalities between the regions. There was a deep-rooted division between the industrialized republics of the north-west, Croatia and Slovenia, and the largely agricultural republics of the south-east: Bosnia-Herzegovina, Montenegro and Macedonia. Serbia contains within it prosperous areas such as Vojvodina but also the impoverished autonomous region of Kosovo (ethnically Albanian). In Table 1 we can see how the ranking of the republics in terms of income per capita has remained basically unchanged since the Second World War.

Table 1
Income per head 1947-1973

	1947	*1955*	*1964*	*1973*
Yugoslavia	100	100	100	100
Slovenia	153	175	177	191
Croatia	105	120	118	120
Vojvodina	122	115	121	121
Serbia proper	99	91	100	101
Bosnia-Herzegovina	82	77	65	64
Montenegro	79	71	68	68
Macedonia	69	69	77	73
Kosovo	50	41	36	31

Source: B. Horvat, *The Yugoslav System*, New York, M.E. Sharpe, 1976, p.62.

The gap between the richest area (Slovenia) and the poorest (Kosovo) has actually widened between 1947 and 1973, in spite of consistent policies to narrow regional differentials.

Post-war Yugoslav governments had indeed focused their economic strategy on building up centres of heavy industry in all six republics, precisely to overcome the problems of uneven development. By 1966 the less developed areas were producing a third of the country's electrical power and over half of its steel.[30] A federal fund was set up in 1961 to promote economic development in the underdeveloped areas. Yet absolute and relative differences between the areas deepened. This apparent paradox can be explained in terms of the particular type of socialism adopted in Yugoslavia, i.e. 'market socialism'. Before the economic reforms in Eastern Europe, Yugoslavia had adopted a system which gave a strong role to the market in the central plan. Workers' self-management in the enterprise was matched by capitalist competition between enterprises. The richer areas resented what they saw as 'reverse discrimination' in favour of the less developed areas. So, for example, in Slovenia, private enterprise was promoted vigorously, particularly in the area of tourism, whereas in Montenegro the private sector was discouraged and private hotels were banned by regional assemblies. In Croatia there was great resentment at the fact that the state brought in nearly half the country's hard currency through tourism, export earnings and remittances from workers abroad, and yet retained only 8% of the country's hard currency for investment (this was raised in 1971 so that Croatia retains 20% of its export earnings and 45% of its tourist revenue).

The 1971 economic reform abolished the central investment fund and generally promoted decentralization. Singleton writes that now the "outlines began to emerge of a series of six national economies, based on the republics, each with its own embryonic national bourgeoisie".[31] The 1974 Constitution still paid lip-service to the need to promote regional development; yet by now the logic of the market place was firmly installed. Economic decentralization in

Yugoslavia had never been accompanied by a true devolution of political power to the base. This lack of involvement in political decision-making at a national level could only encourage the development of particularism and the cultivating of regional advantages. Decentralization can only encourage uneven development and the widening of economic differentials between regions. Not surprisingly, it was the republics of Croatia and Slovenia which were in the forefront of the agitation which led to the 1971 economic and political reforms. Market socialism can only strengthen their position. Yugoslavia had come a long way since the immediate post-war period when the communist partisans hoped economic development would resolve the problems of internal nationalist rivalries, in a relatively short historical period. Singleton writes perceptively that

> They are today sadder and wiser men. The phenomenon of nationalism is not cured by proclaiming the legal equality of nations and by affirming the brotherhood and unity of all the Yugoslav peoples.[32]

The nationalist explosion of 1971 was centred on the prosperous region of Croatia. Middle class elements, and students in particular, took to the streets in protest at the central government's perceived milking of the republic's resources. The continued emigration of young Croatians also raised the spectre of a threat to national survival. In Slovenia, similar grievances were raised, if in less strident fashion. This highly industrialized republic was also concerned by the lack of 'biological purity' caused by the one-fifth of 'foreign' (i.e. non-Slovenian) workers in the republic. The regional bureaucracies of Croatia and Slovenia were centrally involved in pushing through the constitutional reforms of 1971. Nevertheless, the agitation continued in defence of national privilege. Davis describes how

> Mass meetings were held at which only Croatian flags and signs were carried, Croatian national songs were sung, and anti-Titoist slogans and signs were carried.[33]

All this could be seen as a healthy reaction against bureaucratic socialism. Some writers have suggested indeed that the nationalist revolt was a confused anti-bureaucratic rebellion by backward sectors of the masses.[34] Yet when the students of Zagreb University went on strike to gain the admission of Croatia to the United Nations, this could perhaps be described as a product of national chauvinism. Uneven development was usually seen by Marxists to lead to nationalist movements in the deprived or oppressed areas; here was a privileged area taking its nationalist stance in defence of its economic advantages.

In other areas of Yugoslavia the nationalist revival took more classical forms. During the Second World War, Tito's partisans had clashed with Albanian separatists in the Kosovo region. The orientation of Enver Hoxha's regime in Albania later made the Yugoslav state suspicious of the loyalties of the people in that area. The Albanians formed nearly three-quarters of the population in Kosovo but accounted for less than half of the communist party members; the provincial government was even more biased against the Albanians.

In 1966 there was a certain relaxation of central control over the province and this opened the floodgate for nationalist demands. Again, intellectuals were in the forefront, and one of the main concessions gained was the 'Albanianization' of the provincial university. The province gained the national trappings of flag and national anthem; popular chauvinism led to the forced eviction of many Serb and Montenegrian families from their homes. The Albanians in Macedonia also began to make cultural demands, in particular for the use of their own language in higher education. In 1959 the Macedonian League of Communists had suggested that the Albanians should simply learn Macedonian; Lazar Kolissevski argued that

> Every nationality in the course of its development transcends the exclusiveness of its own language because that presents an obstacle to its further development and its ability to master the modern achievements of science and culture.[35]

With such insensitivity from the dominant nationality it is not surprising that the Albanian minority reacted and even revived reactionary dreams of a 'Greater Albania'. In 1981 a serious outbreak of rioting in Kosovo was ruthlessly suppressed and led to the breaking of cultural and scientific relations between Yugoslavia and Albania.[36]

Having examined some of the diverse manifestations of nationalism in socialist Yugoslavia, we must turn now to the various explanations advanced to account for its survival and, indeed, recent revival. After interviewing a number of leading communists in 1973, H.B. Davis reported that "they were nearly unanimous in their belief that it was the economic crisis . . . that had caused the revival of nationalism".[37] Indeed, decentralization had produced mass unemployment as constraints on the free operation of market forces were removed. The much vaunted system of self-management was never extended to the political sphere, so that individualistic reactions were bound to appear. Branko Horvat, a promoter of the 'labour-managed' system admits that

> Gradually, a dualistic system developed in which authoritarianism of the political superstructure came into conflict with the self-managed nature of the rest of the system.[38]

This perhaps ignores the level of bureaucratization which has affected plant level workers' control; but the general point is sound. More questionable is his argument that the frustrations between the ideals of the revolution and practice "lead to apathy, apathy to introverted individualization, and from there the road naturally continues to nationalism".[39] The implication is that nationalism exists as some kind of primaeval and universal response to the frustration of socio-economic advancement. In fact, the nationalist manifestations in Yugoslavia were a response to quite distinct situations. In Croatia, nationalism was the banner chosen by a relatively privileged stratum. It expressed frustrations of a discontented political elite, excluded from power and eager to share in the spoils of office. It was in a way an inter-bureaucratic struggle. In Kosovo and elsewhere, national minorities advanced a cultural nationalism which could easily be reconciled by a Leninist policy of self-determination. Repression of both varieties of nationalism by the state tended to tar them with the same brush, and give both a progressive aura in the West. Economic causes may have been at the root of the nationalist revival; but we must not neglect the cultural element.

In 1967, K. Jončić argued that party policy towards the national question had defused it and, indeed, that national diversity was "one of the strongest factors of unification of the Yugoslav peoples".[40] A few years later such illusions were disabused. One Yugoslav writer and political leader, Edvard Kardelj, stands out as someone who gave an early warning of the continued relevance of nationalism. Against a popular conception that socialism, in itself, would overcome nationalism, he argued that it would survive into the foreseeable future.[41] Nations and nationalism were seen by him to spring from the social division of labour characteristic of capitalism. Struggles over the distribution of social surplus would also lead to the cultural assertiveness of the national unit. One could argue that if nationalism is tied to capitalist competition, it persists in Yugoslavia because the economic system adopted there grants a continued role to competition, both by integration into the world capitalist market and, internally, between the theoretically worker-managed enterprises. Nevertheless, Kardelj's point that people always fight for that portion of the globe where their social consciousness is formed, is hard to refute.

Kardelj, in his *Socialism and War* (1970), advances what he considers a post-Leninist theory of nationalism. Kardelj asks whether nationalism would "wither away" after international war or whether revolution has inaugurated a "world socialist system". His answer is that

> vestiges of hegemony, nationalism, inequalities between nations and so forth [would] still [be] lingering on ... [and] ... for a certain time those vestiges would not merely inevitably continue but would in many a case gain in strength.[42]

This may be sobering for international socialists but it is undoubtedly true. Perhaps even more importantly, Kardelj argues that Stalin's 'internationalism' was basically a sham and that no one nation should dictate the form of socialism to be adopted by another. Furthermore, even before the Chinese spoke of "letting a hundred flowers bloom" Kardelj was arguing for a decentralized development of socialism on a world scale, which

> will unfold the less painfully and the more democratically and so much the more rapidly, the more freely every nation is in a position independently to choose the ways and forms of its own socialist development.[43]

In this perspective the struggle against national oppression runs in parallel with the class struggle and is in no way secondary to it.

Indo-China: 'fraternal wars'

When the Socialist Republic of Vietnam invaded neighbouring Democratic Kampuchea in December 1978 and the People's Republic of China then invaded Vietnam, the whole concept of 'proletarian internationalism' was brought into question. Fundamental issues were raised about the principle of national self-determination as it applied to the relations between socialist states. In a sense, these 'fraternal wars' were inscribed in the logic of national communism and the deformation of democratic socialism from Stalin onwards. There was a close parallel with the events of 1948 when Stalin suggested to Yugoslav envoy Milovan Djilas that the "government of the USSR has no pretensions whatsoever concerning Albania. Yugoslavia is free to swallow Albania any time she wants to".[44]. Yugoslavia took no such drastic, and non-socialist, action and the problem of Kosovo (see above) has been handled relatively well between the two states. The question arises whether China today is playing such a manipulative and Machiavellian role in South-east Asia. We must also examine the real roots of the Vietnam-Kampuchea conflict which cannot simply be reduced to 'ancient national rivalry'. After considering the background to the wars we turn to the various explanations produced to account for them.

It is commonplace to say that Hanoi and Peking were played off against each other by Washington; but the conflicts between the two countries were real ones. The border between the two countries was a disputed one and when the Vietnamese gained victory in 1975 it flared up again. The strategically located Spratly and Paracel islands were claimed by both countries and China threatened to use force to dislodge the Vietnamese troops occupying them. The Chinese media asserted that "All islands belonging to China must also return to the fold of the motherland" and that China would "never allow others to invade or occupy our territory, whatever the pretext".[45] The Vietnamese responded with an analysis which traced Chinese foreign policy back to 'Great Han chauvinism', mounting a large-scale propaganda campaign to exalt the four thousand year history of the 'great Vietnamese nation'. Was all this the result of a disputed interpretation of an 1887 treaty between the French colonialists and the Qing court in China, determining the borders between China and Vietnam? This localized conflict can only be understood in terms of the particular path to socialism taken by each country and the relation between them. The role of nationalism in the Chinese revolution (see Chapter 5) continued into the post-revolutionary era. Chinese aid to the Vietnamese revolution was by no means unequivocal or unstinted. The Vietnamese Communist Party was equally, if not more so, a product of its country's nationalist history.[46] Vietnam's desire to remain non-aligned in the Sino-Soviet dispute (for example by not joining COMECON) was frustrated by undoubted Chinese 'hegemonism' in the area. The long-standing Vietnamese project of reviving the Comintern's 1930s proposal for an Indo-Chinese Communist Federation embracing Vietnam, Laos and Cambodia, could only confirm China's hostility. The Chinese invasion of 1979 was significantly accompanied by the accusation that Vietnam would not be permitted to become the "swashbuckling Cuba" of the Orient.

In Vietnam itself there was another source of friction; the one and a quarter million ethnic Chinese or Hoa. Peking had no complaint over Hanoi's policy towards the Hoa in the North; the problems arose after the liberation of the South. One issue was the Vietnamese nationality which the Hoa had been forced to assume by the pre-revolutionary regimes and which the new socialist state saw little sense in revoking. The main Hoa resentment was the compulsory military service which this entailed. The trouble began in earnest when the new regime carried out a vast reform of capitalist trade in 1978 which entailed the expropriation of Hoa traders and their removal to the New Economic Zones as colonists. The end result of this was the 'Boat People' tragedy, prompted in part by China's whipping up of ethnic Chinese nationalism. Vietnam's leadership realized that the anti-capitalist measures they took would be interpreted as anti-Hoa, but, perhaps justifiably, did not stop them. Their suspicions of anti-Vietnamese agitation by the Hoa were not allayed by a conference in 1978 of overseas Chinese which said they were part of the "international united front against hegemonism".[47] As Vietnam was being portrayed as a Soviet lackey the implications were clear. With the border issue and the exodus of the ethnic Chinese escalating, Chinese preparations for war became evident, and Vietnam had less reason to hold back from military action against Kampuchea.

Vietnam's conflict with Kampuchea was rather more complex than that with China.[48] Again, there were border problems, but the area involved was small, and this in itself would probably not have led to war. There were, however, different perceptions as to how to solve the border issue. For Vietnam, it was largely a question of solving the specific irregularities inherited from the French-imposed boundaries. For Kampuchea, on the other hand, negotiations were not a question of give and take, but rather of Vietnam accepting or rejecting the Kampuchean definition of the borders. On the Vietnamese side the border issue was complicated by the presence in the border territories of Khmer and Hoa ethnic communities and various religious groups hostile to the new socialist regime. When border incidents began, as early as 1975, and according to most observers with the Kampucheans as aggressors, Vietnam saw little choice. It would have to fight a defensive war to ensure the gains of the revolution. In doing so, it would have to overthrow the Pol Pot regime which, in the eyes of the world, had become a symbol of Stalinist stone-age type socialism.[49] The Vietnamese and Kampuchean revolutions had been inextricably bound up with one another, and resentments had built up leading to this final conflict.

The Vietnamese Communist Party, with its long historical legacy and powerful international support, was the undoubted leader of the region. The Kampuchean communists had only formed as an autonomous movement in the 1960s, and had developed a highly repressive and autarchic model of socialism. They had certain resentments towards the Vietnamese: they were abandoned at the Geneva conference of 1954, Moscow supported the Lon Nol regime against them in 1960, and in the Paris peace talks of 1973 the Vietnamese tried to impose a coalition with Lon Nol on them again. So, their extreme nationalist and isolationist outlook was not just a pathological aberration. Furthermore, Vietnam had encouraged opposition movements against the new regime from amongst the military and political cadres who had trained in North Vietnam. As Heder notes,

The lessons that the CPK [Communist Party of Kampuchea] learned in the 1960s fit well into the radical nationalist tendencies. A communist Kampuchea would not be part of the socialist bloc; it would be an independent revolutionary Kampuchea.[50]

The Kampucheans saw 'proletarian internationalism' as a cover for Vietnamese imperialist claims over their revolution. Indeed, Vietnam neatly combined the internationalizing of the Indo-Chinese revolution with defence of its own state. Vietnam understandably sought a 'special relation' with its neighbouring socialist state but, as Summers wrote, "in denying rights of sovereignty and independence to the Kampuchean nation, the Vietnamese state has simply lost its revolutionary war".[51] It was a largely futile exercise for Marxists to seek out the 'progressive' side in the 1978-9 wars between Vietnam, Kampuchea and China: all were to blame, and all lost out.

The military operations themselves took on a dynamic of their own once the logic of the conflicts outlined above was played out. Border disputes between China and Vietnam and between the latter and Kampuchea escalated into full-scale war. This was aggravated by the position of the Chinese minority in Vietnam and the latter's difficult ethnic situation along the border with Kampuchea. The superpowers were not likely to take decisive action to prevent the conflict. The USA was pleased to see China 'teach the Vietnamese a lesson'; the USSR was pleased to see the Vietnamese 'take out' a pro-Chinese government in Kampuchea. Underlying the specific conflicts was the quite different understanding of socialism held by Kampuchea/China and Vietnam on the other hand. To apportion 'blame' would be futile. China was the major power in the area so had a greater responsibility for maintaining peace. Kampuchea lost the right to national sovereignty by attacking first. Vietnam was hardly blameless, because the Indo-Chinese Federation was not just a myth. The end result was China's three-week long invasion of northern Vietnam; in the end China withdrew ignominiously while retaining some territory, thus guaranteeing that the conflict would flare up again. Vietnam, on the other hand, became bogged down in Kampuchea in a situation not unlike that of the Soviet Union in Afghanistan. Having overthrown the Pol Pot regime, the Vietnamese found that they had to maintain substantial armed forces in the country to face renewed guerrilla warfare, fought to defend the Kampuchean nation against a foreign aggressor.

The favourite explanation for the 'wars between comrades' shared by bourgeois and socialist commentators alike was nationalism. For the *New York Times* (12 March 1979), the sight of "The Red Brotherhood at War" drew the following comment:

They are singing 'The Internationale' on all sides of the Asian battles as they bury the hopes of the Communist fathers with the bodies of their sons . . . . Ugly nationalism has triumphed once again in the human family.[52]

For this capitalist organ the war demonstrated that no ideology (e.g. Marxism) could counter the innate human tendency towards aggression and chauvinism. This gloomy message also tended to justify retrospectively the long and bloody involvement of US intervention in the area. The West German paper *Der Spiegel* (26 February 1979) also gloated how

> Karl Marx wanted to make his supporters into cosmopolitans. 'The workers have no fatherland'. But when they get into power, the Reds very soon become flaming patriots, mostly at the expense of the neighbouring countries.[53]

National glory was seen as a substitute for the communists' lack of majority support. The 'national idea' is granted some validity for the underdeveloped countries, where it can further state cohesion. The assumption is that the advanced industrialized societies have resolved the problem of national antagonisms and settle their differences through civilized diplomatic means. That the capitalist press should take such a view is not surprising, but the socialist press also condemned nationalism *per se* in a similar fashion.

Ernest Mandel discussed the differences which lay behind the military conflicts in South-east Asia, and concluded that they were "the ultimate fruits of the petty-bourgeois nationalist poison of 'socialism in one country' ".[54] Certainly Stalin's notion of 'socialism in one country' has encouraged a tendency for socialist states not to look beyond the boundaries of their own nation. This has led to what Mandel calls "national-communist messianism": a belief in my country right or wrong. The general interests of the world revolution are replaced by the narrow interests of defending self-privilege. Yet how had this "despicable nationalism" emerged from the "patriotic anti-imperialism" of a few years before? There is an air of unreality running through an analysis which can praise the same phenomenon (nationalism) one year and deride it the next as the cause of all evil. Ultimately 'nationalism' is not a sufficient explanation of the Indo-China wars, any more than it was for the First World War (see Chapter 2). There is no evidence of antagonism at the level of the people between the various nationalities, which after all had a long history of common struggle against colonialism. Mandel's critics have pointed out correctly that

> Insofar as nationalism is a motivation, it is the nationalism not of the masses, but of the governing regimes that conceive of their own interests as those of the entire nation and thus present their policies in a chauvinistic guise.[55]

There is a tendency among socialists towards a certain fatalism about the power of nationalism. Thus Anthony Barnett writes that on inter-socialist state relations, "inevitably, the national movement take priority over the socialist one".[56] It is hard to see anything 'inevitable' about the wars in Indo-China, nor why normal diplomatic negotiations between nations could not prosper. Nor for that matter is socialist internationalism such a weak vessel that it must inevitably be swamped by the tide of nationalism. In fact, it was left to a representative of the bureaucratic caste of Eastern Europe to provide a clear guideline in this case. President Ceausescu of Romania declared when visiting Kampuchea in 1978:

> For the successful development of a new socialist society it is essential to reinforce national independence and sovereignty . . . we are of the view that

relationships of a new kind, based on full equality and respect for the independence of each nation, must be developed among socialist countries and . . . serve as a model of cooperation and friendship among peoples.[57]

The leader of the Romanian Communist Party has good reason to profess these beliefs: he does not want to go the way of Dubcek in Czechoslovakia. This does not make the thrust of his argument any the less relevant. Essentially, he argues that the right of nations to self-determination and sovereignty applies equally, or even more so, under socialism than under capitalism.

This is not the place to offer a full alternative explanation of the China-Vietnam-Kampuchea triangle. Following Evans and Rowley we would argue that the inter-socialist wars have their roots in the differing effects of colonialism on the various societies of the region, and the specific imprint of the cycle of anti-imperialist wars in each country.[58] Ancient historical antagonisms between the Hoa, Viet and Khmer peoples, even if they were shown to exist, cannot be substituted for a full explanation. Nor can we accept some 'inevitable' priority of national self-defence over socialist internationalism. No one country is the bastion of the 'world revolution', and 'national communism' is no reason to reject the right of all nations to self-determination. The legacy of borders left behind by imperialism is one common to the Third World as a whole, and does not necessarily lead to wars. The exacerbation of nationalism in the 'Third' Indo-China war was, finally, not the result of some primaeval instinct, but of the material self-interest of the ruling bureaucracies in each country. Essentially, the argument of this chapter is that the debate on the 'national question' in post-capitalist societies is inseparable from the much wider question of what type of societies they are. That they differ from Marx's version of communism is obvious; so too is the conclusion that they have not practised the international "brotherhood of nations" called for in the *Communist Manifesto*.

Notes

1. H. Carrère d'Encausse, 'The Bolsheviks and the National Question (1903-1929)', in E. Cahm and V. Fišera (eds.), *Socialism and Nationalism*, Vol. 3 (Spokesman, Nottingham, 1978) p.125.

2. Cited in F. Barghoorn, *Soviet Russian Nationalism* (Greenwood Press, Westport, 1976) p.9.

3. *Kruschev Remembers* (Sphere Books, London, 1971) p.131.

4. Ibid., p.202.

5. Cited in Z. Gitelman, 'Are Nations Merging in the USSR?', *Problems of Communism*, Vol. XXXII, No. 5, 1983, p.37.

6. H. Carrère d'Encausse, 'The Bolsheviks and the National Question', p.124.

7. D. Lane, *Politics and Society in the USSR* (Weidenfeld and Nicolson, London, 1972) p.443.

8. H.B. Davis, *Towards a Marxist Theory of Nationalism* (Monthly Review Press, New York, 1978) p.127.

9. E. Jones and F. Grupp, 'Modernisation and Ethnic Equalisation in the USSR', *Soviet Studies*, Vol. XXVI, No. 2, 1984, p.170.

10. Ibid., p.172.

11. Ibid., p.174.

12. H.B. Davis, *Towards a Marxist Theory of Nationalism*, p.116.

13. J. Rothschild, *Ethnopolitics: A Conceptual Framework* (Columbia University Press, New York, 1981) pp.226-7.

14. Z. Gitelman, 'Are Nations Merging in the USSR?', p.46.

15. D. Lane, *Politics and Society in the USSR*, p.444.

16. R. Bahro, *The Alternative in Eastern Europe* (New Left Books, London, 1984), p.333.

17. H.B. Davis, *Towards a Marxist Theory of Nationalism*, p.117.

18. G. Saunders (ed.), *Samizdat: Voices of the Soviet Opposition* (Pathfinder Press, New York, 1977) p.428.

19. Ibid., p.436.

20. Y. Malmilähde, 'An Upsurge of Dissatisfaction in Estonia', *Critique*, No. 16, 1983, p.146.

21. I. Dzuba, *Internationalism or Russification? A Study in the Soviet Nationalities Problem* (Weidenfeld and Nicolson, London, 1968).

22. Ibid., p.23.

23. G. Saunders (ed.), *Samizdat*, p.298.

24. See G. Graziani, 'Dependency Structures in COMECON', *The Review of Radical Political Economics*, Vol. 13, No. 1, 1981.

25. Cited in F. Fejtö, *A History of the People's Democracies* (Penguin, Harmondsworth, 1974) p.127.

26. Ibid., p.271.

27. Ibid., p.280.

28. J.B. Tito, 'Specific Features of the Yugoslav Liberation Struggle', in W. Pomeroy (ed.), *Guerilla Warfare and Marxism* (Lawrence and Wishart, London, 1969) p.147.

29. F. Singleton, *Twentieth Century Yugoslavia* (Columbia University Press, New York, 1976, pp.88-9).

30. Ibid., p.248.

31. Ibid., p.258.

32. Ibid., p.224.

33. H.B. Davis, *Towards a Marxist Theory of Nationalism*, p.152.

34. E.g. C. Samary, 'Yugoslavie: vers le capitalisme ou vers le socialisme', *Critiques de l'Économie Politique*, No. 7/8, 1972, p.267.

35. Cited in F. Singleton, *Twentieth Century Yugoslavia*, p.240.

36. See P. Artisien, 'A Note on Kosovo and the Future of Yugoslav-Albanian Relations: A Balkan Perspective", *Soviet Studies*, Vol. XXVI, No. 2, 1984.

37. H.B. Davis, *Towards a Marxist Theory of Nationalism*, p.158.

38. B. Horvat, *The Yugoslav Economic System: The first labor managed economy in the making* (M.E. Sharpe, New York, 1976) p.38.

39. Ibid.

40. K. Jončić, *The Relations Between the Nationalities in Yugoslavia* (Belgrade, 1967) pp.8-9.

41. E. Kardelj, *Socialism and War: A Survey of Chinese Criticisms of the Policy of Coexistence* (McGraw-Hill, New York, 1960).

42. Ibid., p.180.

43. Ibid., p.193.

44. V. Dedijer, *Tito Speaks* (London, 1953) p.320, cited by A. Barnett, 'Inter-Communist Conflicts and Vietnam', *Bulletin of Concerned Asian Scholars*, Vol. 11, No. 4, 1979, p.2.

45. *Kwangnung Daily*, cited in G. Porter, 'Vietnamese Policy and the Indochina Crisis', in D. Elliott (ed.), *The Third Indochina Conflict* (Westview Press, Boulder Co., 1982) p.81.

46. See P. Rousset, *Le Parti Communiste Vietnamen* (Maspero, Paris, 1975).

47. Cited in G. Porter, 'Vietnamese Policy and the Indochina Crisis', p.86.

48. See S. Heder, 'The Kampuchean Vietnamese Conflict', in D. Elliott (ed.), *The Third Indochina Conflict*.

49. For a balanced view see B. Kiernan and C. Boua, *Peasants and Politics in Kampuchea, 1942-1981* (Zed Press, London, 1982).

50. S. Heder, 'The Kampuchean-Vietnamese Conflict', p.39.

51. L. Summers, 'In Matters of War and Socialism, Anthony Barnett would Shame and Honour Kampuchea too much', *Bulletin of Concerned Asian Scholars*, Vol. 11, No. 4, 1979, p.17.

52. Extracted in *Intercontinental Press*, Vol. 17, No. 9, 1979, p.234.

53. Ibid.

54. E. Mandel, 'Behind Differences on Military Conflicts', *Intercontinental Press*, Vol. 17, No. 3, 1979, p.347.

55. G. Horowitz, 'Mounting Imperialist Pressure on Hanoi', *Intercontinental Press*, Vol. 17, No. 9, 1979, p.231.

56. A. Barnett, 'Inter-Communist Conflicts and Vietnam', p.3.

57. Cited in L. Summers, 'In Matters of War and Socialism', p.16.

58. G. Evans and K. Rowley, *Red Brotherhood at War: Indochina Since the Fall of Saigon* (New Left Books, London, 1984).

8. Contemporary Debates

The revival of interest in the Marxist theory of the state during the 1970s led to renewed interest in the 'national question'. The first point in defining the terrain is to note its diversity; Marx, Lenin, Mao, Cabral and Guevara all faced different national questions. Hussain and Tribe have written that the "agrarian question" is not posed in Marx's *Capital* but is rather a series of political problems faced by the socialist movement. Much the same could be said about the national question. Hussain and Tribe argue that

> The identification of political and economic problems in diverse circumstances makes the 'agrarian question' as much a false unity as 'the peasantry' who are sometimes thought to constitute the problem.[1]

This applies likewise to the 'national question' and 'the nation'. Indeed, Zubaida has gone as far as to argue that "it is not a problem for Marxist theory to define 'a nation' — it is not a theoretical problem, but one of political practice".[2] For this reason Lenin did not develop a full-blown theory of nationalism. Yet contemporary Marxist debates on the national question have been posed on a theoretical terrain. Rather than approaching the 'national question' in the abstract, our discussion of contemporary debates focuses on three key areas: 1) nationalism and development, or how the first is seen as functional for the latter; 2) nation and state, or whether the two terms are inseparable; and 3) nationalism and class, or the issue of whether nationalism represents any particular class interest. No less than for the classics of Marxism, these theoretical debates all have political consequences.

Nationalism and development

Marxist and non-Marxist writers on nationalism tend to agree on the crucial role this ideology plays in the process of economic development or modernization. Thus Ernest Gellner writes that

> Nationalism is *not* the awakening of an old, latent, dormant force, though that is indeed how it presents itself. It is in reality the consequence of a new form of social organization, based on deeply internalized, education-dependent high cultures, each protected by its own state.[3]

For Gellner, 'modern society' is politically centralized, economically specialized, and socially mobile. The industrial society also requires a common language to provide a shared medium of communication. In short, "it is an objective need for homogeneity which for better or for worse manifests itself as nationalism".[4] From the Marxist camp we find similar, if by no means equivalent, perspectives. Thus Tom Nairn compares nationalism to the Roman god Janus, "who stands above gateways with one face looking forward and one backwards. Thus does nationalism stand over the passage to modernity, for human society".[5] Like Gellner, Nairn argues that nationalism looks to the past to gain strength for the process of social and economic development. More recently, Ben Anderson has examined the origin of the idea of nationalism and produced a thesis similar to Gellner's: the interaction between capitalism and printing and the birth of the vernacular languages in early modern Europe, are seen as the major processes that created the 'imagined communities' of nationality.[6]

The general assumption these writers make is that nationalism can be explained by the development process and that there is a 'fit' between the two. From this perspective, as Anthony Smith writes, "nationalism is one of a class of sociopolitical movements whose matrix is the disintegration of traditional structures".[7] With the breakdown of traditional communities a new ideology of integration is required. That is where nationalism emerges as a veritable religion of modernization. Nairn, while relating his version to the process of 'uneven development', admits "the powerful connection that common sense suggests between nationalism and the concept of development or social and economic growth' ".[8] Another way of linking nationalism to development is through the theory of anti-colonialism. For Samir Amin,

> The national question, which in the nineteenth century was primarily that of oppressed European nations, was transferred in the twentieth century to Asia and Africa, where it became the colonial question.[9]

The 'new' national question is thus defined as anti-imperialism. Peter Worsley, likewise, wrote that Afro-Asian nationalism satisfied three basic needs of the population: independence, decolonization and development.[10] Nationalism is seen as the natural response to colonial domination: it resists the impact of capitalist imperialism. Capitalist development, whether in the metropolis or the Third World, is thus seen as a key explanatory variable for the emergence of nationalism, both as ideology and as political movement.

There are several criticisms which can be made about this conception, which is shared, with variations, by such diverse authors. The emphasis is on world-wide processes, be it modernization or imperialism, which leaves little room for historical specificity. Nairn frequently refers to 'world history', the 'world political economy' and the need for Marxism to become an authentic 'world-theory'.[11] Gellner shares with the sociology of modernization a certain teleology which sees the world advancing inexorably to a pre-destined goal: modernity. The advances of communication and education, which he links with nationalism, are idealized trans-historical classless processes. Zubaida has rightly noted the similar structure of Gellner's and Nairn's theories in which

'Nations' seem to be historical super-subjects with attributes of agency and action: they 'mobilize', 'aspire', 'propel themselves forward', 'react' and they even have atavistic, irrational 'ids' seething with traumas which explode periodically.[12]

On the world-wide stage of modernization or imperialism, 'nations' become the main actors. Classes are either idealized — the 'intelligentsia' or 'the peasants' are the motive force of nationalism — or they are quite simply ignored. Indeed, Nairn is even more prone than his non-Marxist counterparts to conceive of 'nations' as unitary entities, thus riding roughshod over their internal history of exploitation and struggle.

Blaut has further argued that "Nairn's concept of progress is completely in the classical tradition of Eurocentric diffusionism".[13] The underlying assumption is that 'civilization' first made its appearance in Europe and then spread throughout the globe. Nairn does indeed refer somewhat uncritically to "the positive or universal aspects of the Enlightenment".[14] He is somewhat over-critical of those who in his view only provide "little more than a more sophisticated justification of romantic nationalism, now transformed into 'Third Worldism' ".[15] Nairn appears somewhat more ironical when referring to "the rhetoric and doctrine of nationalism" as "re-formulated and replenished" by those such as Amílcar Cabral and Che Guevara, than when dealing with the nationalism of Scotland. Essentially, however, Nairn cannot be accused of offering a hymn of praise to the virtues of Western capitalism as provided by Bill Warren.[16] Indeed Nairn stresses the need to broaden Marxism out from its previously limited Eurocentric perspective. The weakness of Nairn's theory is probably most obvious when dealing with Northern Ireland. There he argues that "there is no 'anti-imperialist' struggle going on" in Ireland, and that "as a separate entity Northern Ireland has become quite useless" to Britain.[17] His uncritical endorsement of Protestant nationalism and pious belief that international capitalism is a rational entity, keen to rid itself of such an anachronistic problem, demonstrate a clear lack of Marxist theoretical bearings.

It would be wrong to 'throw out the baby with the bathwater' after criticizing the theories linking nationalism with development. Indeed, Nairn's emphasis on the process of uneven development is an important one. The world-wide expansion of capitalism was not a smooth and even process; it was characterized by a dialectic process of uneven, yet combined development. Nationalism is then seen as a natural response of the disadvantaged regions, much as socialism is for the oppressed classes. In Nairn's words, nationalism was "generated as a compensatory reaction on the periphery".[18] Thus nationalism developed in the 19th Century in the European 'periphery' of Germany and Italy. These countries developed rapidly through a 'revolution from above' and in turn called forth the nationalism of England and France. This second generation nationalism was indeed more powerful and solid than the first, and later remained the underlying basis of imperialism. Some writers have objected that nationalism does not always spring from deprivation: the Basque country (*Euzkadi*) is one of the most industrialized areas of Spain, yet separatism is strongest there; likewise Belgium was one of the most industrialized areas of Europe when it separated from the Netherlands in the 1830s.[19] This does not, however, contradict Nairn's version of uneven development as the motor of nationalism because he argues that this "ideology has always been produced on the periphery (or at least, by people thinking about its dilemmas, whether they are themselves in it or not)".[20] In other words, uneven development can cause nationalism, whether at the poor or rich pole of the process. What we saw of the development of nationalism in Croatia, Yugoslavia's richest area, (see Chapter 7) would seem to confirm this. It could be argued, as Orridge does, that

> More difficult to accommodate within the theory, however, are instances of nationalism not accompanied by any great differences in development levels from their surroundings.[21]

The separation of Norway and Sweden, in 1905, which served as an example of self-determination for Lenin, would be a case in point. There are more substantial objections at a theoretical level: political fragmentation may be explained by uneven development but not why this should take the shape of nations; opposition to imperialist domination may be inevitable but there is no particular reason this should take the form of nationalism. We could argue that 'uneven development' explains the economic basis of national divisions, but as with much of Marxism it tends towards economic reductionism. We should then reincorporate the cultural aspect of nationalism into historical materialism. Finally, we could accept Gellner's provocative statement that "It is nationalism which engenders nations, and not the other way round."[22] Indeed this is what Ben Anderson seems to be doing implicitly when he argues that nationalism is an "imagined community".

When we refer to the nation as "the totality of men [sic] bound together through a common destiny", following Otto Bauer (Chapter 2), we are bound to break with simplistic notions of nationalism as bourgeois ideology pure and simple. For Marxism the capitalist mode of production is characterized fundamentally by the exploitation of the proletariat. The bourgeois nation-state plays a key role in ensuring the stability of that system. Yet concrete social formations (countries) are characterized by a minimal social consensus and sense of community. The nation carries out this process of cultural integration and forging of community. As Michel Freitag argues, if we renounce this last aspect *a priori*, out of dogmatism, it means that in examining the 'national fact' we are denying it any real existence, reducing it to a reflection of reality in the realm of ideology.[23] If the nation is to have some specificity *vis-à-vis* the state (to which we return below) it must, according to Freitag, be thought of as a political community.[24] The national can thus be understood as the concrete historically shaped articulation of two dimensions: the capitalist mode of production and the particular social formation. Nationalist idealism ignores the first aspect; Marxist reductionism would lead us to neglect the second. We should, in short, reject a version of the Marxist theory of nationalism which conceives of the nation as a bourgeois ideology simply masking through a communal pseudo-identity the underlying reality of the class struggle (another theme we will return to).

With a more dialectical conception of nationalism, we can return to the 'nation-building' function it is accorded in the Third World by the theorists of modernization. Ben Anderson refers to how

> In the 'nation-building' policies of the new states one sees both a genuine, popular nationalist enthusiasm and a systematic even Machiavellian, instilling of nationalist ideology . . . .[25]

Leaving aside the questions of why nationalist ideology should be 'Machiavellian', this point confirms what we saw in Chapter 6 about Third World nationalist movements and regimes. Nationalism is indeed both progressive and a stabilizing conservative influence. This is more helpful than trying to categorize nationalism into 'good' and 'bad' variants. The experience of Vietnam was a clear indication of how progressive anti-imperialist patriotism could become something more ambiguous after its victory was ensured. Anderson expands on this theme too in relation to the 19th Century independence movements in South America:

> Out of the American welter came these imagined realities: nation-states, republican institutions, common citizenships, popular sovereignty, national flags and anthems, etc, and the liquidation of their conceptual opposites: dynastic empires, monarchical institutions, absolutisms, subjecthoods, inherited nobilities, serfdoms, ghettoes, and so forth.[26]

In the real history of the South American republics, as distinct from their official ideologies, the latter, less savoury institutions continued to play a role. In North America, this process of re-writing history reached new heights when the history of slavery was replaced by one of pristine democracy from day one.

The classical Marxist-Leninist theory of nationalism (Chapter 4) tended to equate the rise of nationalism with that of capitalism. As Lenin expressed it,

> Throughout the world, the period of the final victory of capitalism over feudalism has been linked up with national movements. For the complete victory of commodity production, the bourgeoisie must capture the home market, and there must be politically united territories whose population speak a single language . . . .[27]

This symbiotic and necessary relationship between the rising bourgeoisie and nationalism is now widely questioned. As Poulantzas writes,

> The modern nation is not the creation of the bourgeoisie, but the outcome of a *relationship* of forces between the 'modern' social classes — one in which the nation is a *stake* for the various classes.[28]

The bourgeoisie was indeed the first world-historical class and Marx's praise for the class was not misplaced; but it did not 'invent' nations. Nations existed before capitalism; their unique combination in Western Europe lead to a "West-centred distortion of the concept of nation", as Amin puts it.[29] The word nation was itself transformed in the course of the French Revolution: the revolutionary democratic ideology which helped overthrow absolutism became the new French nation-state. In South America, from 1810 onwards a similar ideology inspired the *criollo* landowners and merchants in their struggle against Spanish domination.

Nationalism and capitalism (a more appropriate term than development) continued their diverse yet related paths. John Ehrenreich has recently argued that nationalism is the ideological offspring of the contradiction between the world-unifying and world-fragmenting tendencies of capitalism.[30] The first phase of nationalism was based on the primacy of the unifying, homogenizing impact of capitalism over the old order. Later, nationalism emerged in the periphery in response to the fragmenting aspect of capitalism. All social classes in the periphery are affected by expanding capitalism and thus the struggle takes on a national character. Later still nationalism, once the product of resistance to capitalist penetration, becomes institutionalized in the official ideology of the Third World nation-states. Thus, as Ehrenreich writes "Third World nationalism has even become useful and stabilizing to the capitalist world order".[31] Yet if the term nation has a longer trajectory than that of nation-state, so nationalism continues to be contradictory. If in the neo-colonial situation it sometimes acts as a stabilizing force, in Iran, Nicaragua, Ireland and Namibia it motivates a social movement profoundly *destabilizing* for the world capitalist order.

Nation and state

Samir Amin argues that "although state and nation are not identical, the national phenomenon cannot be separated from the analysis of the state".[32] In arguing thus, Amin follows a long tradition going back to Marx's mentor Hegel for whom "Nations may have had a long history before they finally reach their destination — that of forming themselves into states".[33] From this perspective, the real history of a nation begins at the point when it forms its own state. This teleology of the nation-state is similar to that of nationalism-development considered above; similarly it is both true and false.

The nation-state is a comparatively recent phenomenon if we take a broad historical perspective. Hobsbawm writes that nationalism is a dual phenomenon: 1) a mode of confronting social changes (as seen above), and 2) "it consists of a 'civic religion' for the modern territorial centralised state . . . ."[34] This modern state emerged during the transition from feudalism to capitalism and adopted the national form. This state does indeed play a crucial role in forging national unity, in all the ways discussed by Lenin: unifying the home market, constituting a politically united territory, etc. It is important to distinguish, however, between the link established by the rising bourgeoisie and the nation-state and the nation itself. Nationalism may have been created from above, and become the official ideology of the new states; yet this does not mean that nations did not previously exist.

Marxist analysis of the national question has tended towards a certain reductionism which assimilates the national in general with the particular form given it by the bourgeoisie in its nation-states. The nation was never defined theoretically by Lenin, precisely because of this negative definition of the nation as the superstructural reflection of the economic base of capitalism. As the national is assimilated into the bourgeois nation-state, so nation, nationality, nation-state and nationalism become practically synonymous terms. Only Otto Bauer, on the other hand, advanced a positive definition of the nation as a cultural and historical community, which could take a state form. A group of Breton Marxists have also argued recently that

> One must recognise, behind the nation-state, another concept which is largely independent: that of nationality which designates the community of culture of a people, determined by an identical history and material conditions of existence.[35]

Nationality cannot be understood as neutral with regard to the class struggle, but it is relatively independent from class relations. If the national fact is not borne solely by the rising bourgeoisie and its nation-state, it follows that it will not disappear once the capitalist order is overthrown. Nationality in the post-capitalist era will still embrace the economic and cultural aspirations of a people.

Once this distinction between the nation-state and nationality is accepted, the persistence of national problems in the socialist states becomes more understandable. The traditional Marxist position on this issue is presented by Blaut for whom

> Persistence of national conflicts there [i.e. the 'socialist part of the world'] is attributable in the final analysis to external pressure from the capitalist world . . . .[36]

This is seen to lead to the survival of non-socialist ideologies such as demands for autonomy along national cleavage lines. It is also held responsible for "tensions between socialist countries which would not exist in the absence of a capitalist threat . . . ."[37] If nationalism is a creation of the bourgeoisie it follows that when this class is overthrown its ideology would go with it. National problems within the multi-national socialist states such as the Soviet Union and Yugoslavia cannot, however, be blamed so simply on external pressure. Nor can the 1978-9 Indo-China wars be explained by the capitalist threat, as though without this, proletarian internationalism would prevail.

From a non-Marxist perspective Ernest Gellner has also helped clarify the relation between nations and states. He argues that

> Nations, like states, are a contingency, and not a universal necessity. Neither nations nor states exist at all times and in all circumstances. Moreover, nations and states are not the *same* contingency.[38]

150

States have emerged independently from nations and vice versa; their coincidence is contingent on certain historical facts. Poulantzas follows Otto Bauer in stating that "the State cannot entirely encapsulate the nation".[39] Capitalism — as the generalization of commodity exchange — is not an adequate explanation for the national form of the modern bourgeois state. The economism of traditional Marxist theories of nationalism can lead to a reaction against it which falls into a cultural idealism. This was the problem with certain of Bauer's formulations in which the nation seemed to rise above social classes and even nations. Poulantzas, in examining the elements which constitute the nation, argues that "these elements of territory, language and tradition are often understood as transhistorical essences possessing an immutable nature".[40] To accept such a view would be fundamentally alien to the basic principles of historical materialism. Yet it may be necessary for Marxism to recognize that a nation possesses a unique collective subjectivity, structured by language and a common economic history, which is specific to a particular people. To say that a social group has a common history and that it constitutes a particular type of community is by no means to deny the conflict between the social classes which compose it. It is only to recognize that the concept of nation existed before the bourgeoisie created the nation-state, and will probably persist after its demise. It is to break with all mechanical and simplified notions on the national question, which have led to abstract definitions (Stalin) and general political principles which were then ignored (Lenin).

The traditional Marxist conception of the nation-state was by no means devoid of historical insights. Marxist historians such as Pierre Vilar and Eric Hobsbawm have argued persuasively that the most fruitful approach to the national question is a historical one. Vilar states that

> The nation, as a historical category, can only be defined historically, with attention to its psychological, social and ethnic characteristics, which also must be understood historically.[41]

The nation loses its transhistorical irreducibility, its 'natural' characteristics, and becomes another object for historical materialist investigation. Hobsbawm, in a similar vein, argues that

> If nations and nationalism are seen as phenomena which develop within a specific situation and are determined by it, a good many of our difficulties disappear.[42]

These difficulties arise when we seek the eternal 'essence' of nations or of nationalism. This is the case with theories of nationalism which reduce its 'function' to that of modernization or the rise of the bourgeois nation-state. It reduces a complex and multi-faceted phenomenon such as nationalism to the permanent expression of a particular social group, for example the 'intelligentsia' for modernization theories, the "national bourgeoisie" for Marxism.

Nicos Poulantzas has also carried out a powerful restatement of the traditional Marxist theory of the nation-state. He begins by stating that the capitalist state is 'functional' to the nation.[43] But he clarifies this by considering the spatial matrix of the nation (territory) and its temporal matrix and historicity (tradition). His basic conclusion is that national unity "becomes *historicity of a territory and territorialization of a history* — in short, a territorial national tradition concretized in the nation-state".[44] Marxism has neglected this spatial dimension, and Poulantzas does well to remind us of the peculiar relationship between history and territory in the nation-state. Poulantzas also helps to clarify the debate raised above on the distinction between the nation-state and nation *per se*. He states that

> The modern nations, the national state and the bourgeoisie are all constituted on, and have their mutual relations determined by, one and the same terrain.[45]

The relations between nation, state and bourgeoisie take place on the same terrain, but they are not reducible to each other. The nation-state is the site of the struggle between social classes, not necessarily the logical accomplishment of the nation as per Hegel. Finally, Poulantzas points to that as yet unspecified but fundamental point that "the nation does not have the same meaning for the bourgeoisie as it does for the working-class and popular masses".[46] Marxism, in short, must lose its instrumental conception of the nation.

A further reason for distinguishing between the nation-state and nationality lies in the realm of political practice. Hobsbawm has taken Nairn to task for his rather sympathetic analysis of the nationalist revival in the advanced capitalist countries. He echoes Lenin in his warning: "Do not paint nationalism red".[47] This warning is undoubtedly necessary in those situations where Marxists wish to seek a shortcut to socialism by riding the nationalist train. We saw in Chapter 6 some of the fallacies involved in the ideology of Third Worldism and the tendency to smooth over the differences between nationalism and socialism by adopting the term 'revolutionary nationalism'. Yves Person stresses the opposite side of the coin in an article 'Against the Nation-State'.[48] He focuses on the position of national minorities and argues that their revindications put the nation-state of the bourgeoisie into question. It follows that "a socialist project must necessarily place that state into question, taking care not to confuse it with the relatively permanent reality of nationality".[49] Marxists, especially in the dominant nations, have often preached the virtues of an abstract internationalism to the nationalists of small nations or national minorities. Person reminds us that the modern nation-state, instrument of the bourgeoisie, tends to usurp the idea of nation. Marxists, who seek the destruction of the capitalist state, should logically support the revolt of national minorities who seek the same end, even if for their own particular reasons. Kiernan writes that "once harnessed to the state, national feeling was distorted, and its prime function was to obscure class issues . . . ."[50] Nationalism can also act to exacerbate class contradictions, bringing them into the open and questioning them from a generally democratic perspective.

None of this is to deny that the ideology of nationalism can be used just as effectively by the bourgeoisie. President Johnson declared with no embarrassment in 1966, "We are fighting to uphold the principle of self-determination, so that the people of South Vietnam may be free to choose their own future".[51]

Prime Minister Thatcher declared with equal fervour in 1982 that Britain's task force was sailing to the South Atlantic to pursue the 'liberation' of the Falkland islanders and to defend the principles of 'self-determination'.[52]

We turn now to John Breuilly's recent book *Nationalism and the State*, which is a wide-ranging reconsideration of these issues. The distinctive contribution of this book is, the author claims, that "it treats nationalism primarily as a form of politics".[53] Maybe this should be obvious; but Marxism has tended to overlook the fact with its concern for abstract definitions and timeless political formulae. Breuilly seems to doubt that Marxism could be capable of elaborating "some theory of modern politics which will relate nationalism to the pursuit and exercise of state power in the capitalist era".[54] Poulantzas did embark on this mammoth task, and, whether he was successful or not, non-Marxist political scientists have not proved the superiority of their approach. As to the question of the state, Marxists such as Peter Worsley have clearly stated that: "National*ism* refers to movements, to activities and ideologies developed in order to acquire or sustain a state of one's own".[55] If Breuilly's analysis is limited as a critique, its positive contribution to our understanding of nationalism as politics is considerable.

Breuilly begins by denying that nationalism can be linked to any *particular* class interest or economic relationship; it is simply a form of politics. The state is the key factor: it both shapes nationalist politics and provides it with its objective (state power). Marxism would hardly dispute that there is a close relationship between the modern state and nationalism. Nor would contemporary Marxism dispute the critique of a one-to-one relationship between nationalism, capitalism and the bourgeoisie. Breuilly, in his conclusion, seems to slip back into a functionalist explanation of nationalism. Nationalism, for him, has certain functions: 1) it seeks to bind together people in a particular territory in a bid to gain and use state power; 2) it can be seen as a way of making a particular state legitimate in the eyes of those it controls.[56] Almost all writers on nationalism have drawn attention to the first point; but it hardly amounts to a theoretical explanation. The second point about legitimacy is important and, indeed, fits in nicely with the renewed interest in the Gramscian problematic of hegemony. The ideology of nationalism can of course motivate an opposition movement and it can legitimize a bourgeois state. It motivated the Vietnamese victory over US imperialism, and it sanctioned Britain's military adventures in the South Atlantic.

In a sharp observation Breuilly notes that "Nationalism remains distinctive only so long as it is unsuccessful".[57] Its objective is to bridge the gap between the state and society; once accomplished its *raison d'être* disappears. Gellner says something similar: "Nationalism is primarily a political principle, which holds that the political and the national unit should be congruent".[58] For Gellner, again echoing Breuilly, "nationalism is a theory of political legitimacy, which requires that ethnic boundaries should not cut across political ones . . . ."[59] We can see now why the definition of a nation is not really a Marxist problem: that ethnic boundaries should coincide with state borders is not a principle of historical materialism. The only abiding principle is whether this or that nationalist movement is democratic in content and whether it advances the struggle for socialism.

Breuilly provides further examples of what nationalism is not. He argues that "nationalism is a parasitic movement and ideology, shaped by what it opposes".[60] That is why nationalists provide poor histories of nationalist struggles; their ideology is based on few scientific underlying principles. Furthermore, Breuilly's broad historical survey leads him to the conclusion that nationalism "is not the expression of nationality" nor is it "a response to simple oppression".[61] Nationalism becomes an effective form of politics only under certain specific conditions: it neither springs from "the nation" nor is it an automatic response to oppression. We might conclude at this point that having cleared the decks of false conceptions of nationalism we now have a fruitful research agenda for a concrete analysis of nationalism, provided we do not jettison the conceptual arsenal of Marxism: class, state, exploitation, hegemony, ideology, etc.

Nationalism and class

Gellner has written with justifiable irony of "The Wrong Address Theory" of nationalism maintained by Marxism: "The awakening message was intended for *classes*, but by some terrible postal error was delivered to *nations*".[62] Some Marxists do indeed continue to explain how 'really' it is all to do with the class struggle. Others now accept the irreducible specificity of gender, ethnic and national based conflicts.

Ernesto Laclau has made what is probably the boldest attack on what he calls the "class reductionism" of orthodox Marxism.[63] He argues that an ideology such as democracy has no necessary "class belonging" — it is, as it were, neutral until seized upon by a class discourse. On the specific issue of nationalism he asks,

> Is it a feudal, bourgeois or proletarian ideology? Considered in itself it has no class connotation. The latter only derives from the specific articulation with other ideological elements.[64]

The bourgeoisie may seize on nationalism in the fight against feudal particularism, and to mask class conflict by appealing to national unity. Yet, argues Laclau,

> A communist movement can denounce the betrayal by capitalist classes of a nationalist cause and articulate nationalism and socialism in a single ideological discourse — think of Mao, for example.[65]

Nationalism takes on a different meaning in both cases as it is linked to a different ideological domain. It is clearly not the 'necessary' superstructure of any particular social or economic system. The political implications of this approach is that the socialist movement should seek to articulate the popular-national or popular-democratic ideologies of a particular country. For example,

Laclau argues that "a 'socialist populism' is not the most backward form of working class ideology but the most advanced . . . ."[66]

Laclau has effectively criticized a reductionist version of Marxism, but we must question whether an ideology such as nationalism is really so 'free-floating' between the social classes. Laclau seems to have completely obliterated Marx and Lenin's distinction between the nationalism of the oppressed and that of the oppressor. This is similar to recent Marxist treatments of democracy, where previously negative views have been replaced by a theory of its 'political indeterminacy' which supersedes previous clear-cut distinctions between bourgeois and proletarian democracy. Nationalism, or national tasks, are not the sole prerogative of the bourgeoisie; but the working class cannot adopt all the ideological elements of nationalism uncritically. The idea that Hitler's 'national socialism' could have been outflanked by a more vigorous pursuit of German nationalism by the Communist Party is simply ludicrous. A critique of economism and 'class reductionism' can all too easily become a Marxism without the class struggle. Nationalism, like other ideologies, cannot be seen as somehow neutral, totally devoid of class content, as Otto Bauer would have it.

The theoretical basis of Laclau's approach, is of course, Antonio Gramsci's concept of the "national popular". Gramsci considered that Italy lacked a Jacobin force which could organize the "national popular collective will" to found the modern state.[67] It follows that

> The modern Prince [i.e. the revolutionary party] must be and cannot but be the proclaimer and organiser of an intellectual and moral reform, which also means creating the terrain for a subsequent development of the national-popular collective will towards the realisation of a superior, total form of modern civilization.[68]

The revolutionary party is thus seen as the organizer and active expression of the national popular. French culture is considered more strictly "national popular" and therefore better placed to "offer a model of hegemonic ideological construction".[69] The task of the Marxist party is thus seen by Gramsci as one of organizing and expressing the "national popular" in a historic bloc in which the proletariat exercises hegemony. This historic bloc is seen to express the national and popular aspiration in a broad sense. Yet, we must recall with Nowell Smith that the national popular "is a cultural concept, relating to the position of the masses within the culture of a nation, and radically alien to any form of populism or 'national socialism' ".[70] Laclau takes his inspiration from the writings of Togliatti on fascism and the cultural policy of the Italian communists since the war, but Gramsci's own notion of the "national popular" does not necessarily lead to this national reformist type of reading.

The proletariat lives, works and struggles on the national terrain, and is shaped by these "national popular" aspirations. Regis Debray points to an incontrovertible historical fact when he says that

> Every time a socialist regime is imposed against an affirmation of national identity, the former loses out . . . . All modern history demonstrates that

proletarian dictatorships have only taken root where they fused with a national liberation struggle, or where they defended a national identity.[71]

Even the Russian Revolution only achieved stability and national solidity after the wars of intervention in the post-revolutionary period, and most clearly during the 'Great Patriotic War'. Debray argues that communism, if it is to mean anything, must be a national communism. He then goes on to sing the praises of the French nation, concluding: "I can conceive of no hope for Europe save under the hegemony of a revolutionary France . . . ."[72]. His interviewer reminds him that national continuity and tradition may be necessary for a revolutionary party: "But in France the tricolour was also the flag of the Versaillais who crushed the Commune, the flag of bourgeoisie and Empire".[73] The Italian writer Asor Rosa has argued effectively, against a certain reading of Gramsci, that reformism is the inevitable consequence of any attempt to base movements for social reconstruction on the traditions of the nation; a revolutionary consciousness can only be the product of a radical and conscious break with these traditions.[74]

From outside Marxism, Gellner has also confronted the relation between nationalism and class. Not surprisingly he is hostile towards a Marxism which sees only class and ignores vertical divisions of society along other fissure lines. He goes further than this and argues that Marxism should be stood on its head: "Nationalism is not a class conflict which has failed to reach true consciousness. Class conflict is a national one which has failed to take off . . . ."[75] In a provocative phrase Gellner has touched on a weak point of Marxist treatment of nationalism, often seen as a disguised class struggle trying to burst out. What he is saying, with Debray, is that classes have only succeeded in overthrowing the state when they have been able to define themselves nationally. Neither nations nor classes are adequate political catalysts, only 'nation-classes' can fulfil this role.[76] Nation-class was precisely the term used by Amílcar Cabral (Chapter 6) to express the modern version of Marx's leading or national class (Chapter 1). It is worth noting that Gramsci developed a similar category of 'people-nation'.[77] Gramsci believed that the working class was only able to be a truly 'national' class if it could interpret the unique national combination of forces which made up a concrete social formation. To wage the 'people's war' necessary under conditions of advanced capitalism, Gramsci believed that an international class such as the proletariat had to become 'nationalized'.

Marxist orthodoxy has recently been defended by J.M. Blaut who criticizes the tendency of writers such as Poulantzas, Debray, Nairn and Davis to conceive of nationalism as an autonomous force. He believes that Nairn's theory of nationalism, for example, sees national struggle as "unrelated to exploitation, class, struggle, and the working class".[78] H.B. Davis, who wrote *Toward a Marxist Theory of Nationalism*, is criticized for adopting "the traditional conservative thesis that nationalism is a European idea of the early nineteenth century which has diffused to the rest of the world".[79] Some of these criticisms are pertinent, and Marxism can hardly conceive of nationalism as the motor of history, above and independent of the class struggle. Yet with Blaut's conclusion we are back to the old orthodoxy which simply declares that "National struggle is class struggle . . . ."[80] In discussing the national basis of the Cuban revolution, Blaut simply comments that, "In Cuba, as everywhere else, the national struggle is indeed a class struggle".[81] Simply stating this explains nothing. Social classes certainly do participate in national struggles; but this does not mean we can reduce them to the class struggle. In fact, Blaut is denying the specificity of national oppression by turning all national liberation struggles into a mythical class struggle. In the real world, divisions along gender, race, ethnic or national lines have their own dynamic and Marxism, often 'gender-blind', would be equally blind to national oppression if it followed Blaut's uncritical return to Lenin and Stalin.

The Leninist theory of nationalism has to confront certain uncomfortable facts. Tom Nairn phrases some of these doubts eloquently when discussing how the nationalist solution 'worked' in practice:

> Nationalism could only have worked, in this sense, because it actually did provide the masses with something real and important — something that class consciousness could never have furnished, a culture which however deplorable was larger, more accessible, and more relevant to mass realities than the rationalism of our [sic] Enlightenment inheritance.[82]

In short, nationalism cannot be simply reduced to 'false consciousness', as an orthodox Marxism might be tempted to do. It was relevant and it worked when confronted with real historical problems: national unification and national independence. The form of nationalism was largely determined by the class structure of the societies in which it operated; in this sense class was of crucial importance. Uneven development, as it occurred with the world-wide expansion of capitalism, engendered national contradictions. These are no more or less real than the capital/wage-labour relation which lies at the heart of capitalism. Where Nairn is probably mistaken is in seeing the failure of Marxism to deal with the national fact as 'inevitable'. In the Third World in particular, Marxist political leaders have grasped the nationalist nettle firmly, even if they have, to an extent, become nationalists themselves.

To criticize 'class-reductionism', is not to deny the crucial role of social class in understanding nationalism. As Emmanuel Terray notes, Marxism cannot accept a theory of history in which

> The national question becomes the problem of the incarnation of an atemporal entity; posed outside any reference to the existence and the struggle of class.[83]

This course is inevitable if we follow Stalin's empirical procedure of defining a nation, and then according it a permanent and transhistorical role. The problem is *how* the formation of classes determines that of nations. Terray begins by distinguishing the nation as an historical force from the nation as an objective ensemble of social classes. Taking the French Revolution as example, Terray argues that

> The coalition of classes which sustains the French Revolution thinks its unity is
> the idea of Nation; at the same time the Nation, as historical force, draws its
> existence and its capacity for initiative from the existence and capacity for
> initiative of that coalition of classes.[84]

The nation was a political definition, not an ethnic one: the king and the nobles
were not to form part of it, they were excluded, they were 'foreign'. Today's
nationalism, whether in the Third World or in Europe's national minorities,
expresses a quite different class alliance. The nation today is expressing a
coalition of all oppressed strata and excludes the 'comprador' bourgeoisie. As
the national bourgeoisie becomes a comprador bourgeoisie, thoroughly
subordinated to international capital, so it excludes itself, at a real and symbolic
level, from the nation in process of formation. In the conditions of dependency,
characteristic of the Third World, it is not chauvinism to declare that a social
sector is 'foreign' — it is part of the definition of a class alliance. Marxism can in
this way understand nations as historical forces rather than mystical
entities.

The modern nation is a collective entity with a high degree of internal social
cohesion; a cohesion produced by the integrating power of specific social
classes. This leads to a break with economism, and we may agree with Torres
Rivas that the nation in Latin America was formed in the political domain and
not by the consolidation of the internal market.[85] This does not imply a
teleological interpretation in which a social class advances inexorably to its
national goal; rather national development is shaped by the particular
constellation of classes in a given territory and the relations established
between them. Torres Rivas writes succintly that

> In the problem class-nation, the pertinent question is not to seek the
> determination of one over the other, but to find the relations which are
> established between classes for the determination of the nation.[86]

The distinct forms of national development can thus be understood as the result
of the class struggle. This is not to say simplistically that the national struggle
'is' a class struggle.

We began this chapter by saying that the main concern of Marxism with
nationalism was not with definitions but with political strategies. We have
argued that nationalism cannot be seen as a simple epiphenomenon of the
capitalist mode of production. Nor can it be reduced to the obvious ideology of
the bourgeoisie. The category of the 'nation-class' opens up a whole area of
political debate, where nationalist deviations are possible. With Jenkins and
Minnerup we must ask whether national struggles are legitimate decentralizing
and democratizing struggles within the nation, or inevitably chauvinist and
reactionary.[87] There are strong parallels here with the recent Marxist debates
on democracy, and the possibility of forging a genuinely 'popular-democratic'
movement.[88] Marxism once characterized democracy as a bourgeois sham
designed to dupe the working class into submission. Now Marxists are more
likely to stress how much democratic socialism and bourgeois democracy have

in common. Nationalism also has two sides: it does indeed mask class contradictions but it also can represent the first stirrings of a more general resistance against oppression. Whatever political strategy is adopted, Marxists operate within the framework of specific nation-states, workers feel their particular nationality as something real, and nationalism has immense power as a historical force. In short, it is incumbent on Marxism to take nationalism seriously if the debilitating 'fraternal wars' of Indo-China are not to become a regular feature in the future.

Notes

1. A. Hussain and K. Tribe, *Marxism and the Agrarian Question* (Macmillan, London, 1983) p.296.

2. S. Zubaida, 'Theories of Nationalism', in G. Littlejohn *et al.*, (eds.), *Power and the State* (Croom Helm, London, 1978) p.65.

3. E. Gellner, *Nations and Nationalism* (Basil Blackwell, Oxford, 1983) p.48.

4. E. Gellner, 'Nationalism', *Theory and Society*, No. 10, 1981, p.767.

5. T. Nairn, 'The Modern Janus', *New Left Review*, No. 94, 1975, p.18.

6. B. Anderson, *Imagined Communities: Reflections on the Origins and Spread of Nationalism* (New Left Books, London, 1983).

7. A. Smith, *Theories of Nationalism* (Duckworth, London, 1983) p.41.

8. T. Nairn, 'The Modern Janus', p.7.

9. S. Amin, *Class and Nation: Historically and in the Current Crisis* (Heinemann, London, 1980) p.173.

10. P. Worsley, *The Third World* (Weidenfeld and Nicolson, London, 1964) pp.83-4.

11. T. Nairn, 'The Modern Janus', pp.5, 21, 27.

12. S. Zubaida, 'Theories of Nationalism' p.69.

13. J. Blaut, 'Nairn on Nationalism', *Antipode*, Vol. 12, No. 2, 1981, p.2.

14. T. Nairn, 'The Modern Janus', p.21.

15. Ibid., p.13.

16. Cf. B. Warren, *Imperialism: Pioneer of Capitalism* (New Left Books, London, 1980).

17. T. Nairn, *The Break-up of Britain* (New Left Books, London, 1977) pp.232, 236.

18. T. Nairn, 'The Modern Janus', p.14.

19. A.W. Orridge, 'Uneven Development and Nationalism: 2', *Political Studies*, Vol. XXIX, No. 2, 1982, p.182.

20. T. Nairn, 'The Modern Janus', p.14.

21. A.W. Orridge, 'Uneven Development and Nationalism: 2', p.182.

22. E. Gellner, *Nations and Nationalism*, p.55.

23. M. Freitag, 'Theorie marxiste et realité nationale: autopsie d'un malentendu', *Pluriel*, No. 26, 1981, p.34.

24. Ibid., p.37.

25. B. Anderson, *Imagined Communities*, p.104.

26. Ibid., p.78.

27. V.I. Lenin, *On the National Question and Proletarian Internationalism* (Novosti Press, Moscow, 1970), p.7.

28. N. Poulantzas, *State, Power, Socialism* (New Left Books, London, 1978) p.115.

29. S. Amin, *Class and Nation*, p.20.

30. J. Ehrenreich, 'Socialism, Nationalism and Capitalist Development', *Review of Radical Political Economics*, Vol. XV, No. 1, 1983, p.9.

31. Ibid., p.27.

32. S. Amin, *Class and Nation*, pp.19-20.

33. G. Hegel, *Lectures on the Philosophy of World History* (Cambridge, 1975), p.134, cited in E. Gellner, *Nations and Nationalism*, p.148.

34. E. Hobsbawn, 'Some Reflection on Nationalism', in T. Nossiter *et al.*, (eds.), *Imagination and Precision in the Social Sciences* (Faber and Faber, London, 1972) p.404.

35. Commission Bretagne LCR-Brest, 'Marxisme revolutionnaire et minorites nationales', *Critique Communiste No 10: Marxisme et Question Nationale*, 1976, p.25.

36. J. Blaut, 'Nationalism as an Autonomous Force', *Science and Society*, Vol. XLVI, No. 1, 1982, p.18.

37. Ibid.

38. E. Gellner, *Nations and Nationalism*, p.6.

39. N. Poulantzas, *State, Power, Socialism*, p.94.

40. Ibid., p.96

41. P. Vilar, 'Nationalism', *Marxist Perspectives*, No. 5, 1979, p.11.

42. E. Hobsbawm, 'Some Reflections on Nationalism', p.386.

43. N. Poulantzas, *State, Power, Socialism*, p.99.

44. Ibid., p.114.

45. Ibid., p.117.

46. Ibid.

47. E. Hobsbawm, 'Some Reflections on "The Break-up of Britain" ', *New Left Review*, No. 105, 1977, p.23.

48. Y. Person, 'Contre l'Etat Nation', *Pluriel*, No. 8, 1976.

49. Ibid., p.65.

50. V. Kiernan, 'Nationalist Movements and Social Classes', in A. Smith (ed.), *Nationalist Movements* (Macmillan, London, 1976) p.125.

51. A. Schlesinger, *The Bitter Heritage* (Boston, 1967), p.108, cited in Lowy, M., 'Marxists and the National Question', *New Left Review*, No. 96, 1976, p.99.

52. See A. Barnett, 'Iron Britannia', *New Left Review*, No. 134, 1983.

53. J. Breuilly, *Nationalism and the State* (Manchester University Press, 1982) p.1.

54. Ibid., p.24.

55. P. Worsley, *The Three Worlds* (Weidenfeld and Nicholson, London, 1984) p.248.

56. J. Breuilly, *Nationalism and the State*, pp.365, 371.

57. Ibid., p.374.

58. E. Gellner, *Nations and Nationalism*, p.1.

59. Ibid.

60. J. Breuilly, *Nationalism and the State*, p.380.

61. Ibid., p.382.

62. E. Gellner, *Nations and Nationalism*, p.129.

63. E. Laclau, *Politics and Ideology in Marxist Theory* (New Left Books, London, 1977).

64. Ibid., p.160.

65. Ibid.

66. Ibid., p.174.

67. Q. Hoare and G. Nowell Smith (eds.), *Selections from the Prison Notebooks of Antonio Gramsci* (Lawrence and Wishart, London, 1971), p.131.

68. Ibid., pp.132-3.

69. Ibid., p.421.

70. Ibid., p.421, fn. 65, cf. the analysis in D. Forgas, 'National-Popular: Genealogy of a Concept', *Formations of Nations and People* (Routledge and Kegan Paul, London, 1984).

71. R. Debray, 'Marxism and the National Question', *New Left Review*, No. 105, 1977, p.33.

72. Ibid., p.41.

73. Ibid., p.40.

74. A. Rosa, *Scritori e Popolo*, (Rome, 1965).

75. E. Gellner, 'Nationalism', p.772.

76. E. Gellner, *Nations and Nationalism*', p.121.

77. Q. Hoare and G. Nowell Smith (eds.), *Selections from the Prison Notebooks*, p.418.

78. J. Blaut, 'Nationalism as an Autonomous Force', p.15.

79. Ibid., p.16.

80. Ibid., p.22.

81. Ibid., p.20.

82. T. Nairn, 'The Modern Janus', p.22.

83. E. Terray, 'L'idée de nation et les transformations du capitalisme', *Les Temps Modernes*, Vol. 2, 1973, p.495.

84. Ibid., p.497.

85. E. Torres Rivas, 'La Nación: Prolemas Teóricos e Históricos', in N. Lechner (ed.), *Estado y Politica en America Latina* (Siglo XXI, Mexico, 1981), p.120.

86. Ibid., p.103.

87. B. Jenkins and G. Minnerup, *Citizens and Comrades: Socialism in a World of Nation States* (Pluto Press, London, 1984).

88. See S. Hall, 'Popular-Democratic vs Authoritarian Populism: Two Ways of "Taking Democracy Seriously" ', in A. Hunt (ed.), *Marxism and Democracy* (Lawrence and Wishart, London, 1980).

9. By Way of Conclusion

In the pages above we have seen that Marxism and nationalism have sometimes fused in an explosive encounter, but more often the relation between them can only be described as a misencounter. The founders of Marxism left a contradictory legacy for the movement which followed them: partly through lack of interest in the issue, but even more because of their inconsistency in recognizing national independence as a basic democratic demand. Lenin made a clean break in the Marxist discourse by enshrining the principle of the right of nations to self-determination. The Second International, on the other hand, practised a form of social imperialism in the colonies and Rosa Luxemburg refused to admit any common ground between Marxism and nationalism. The Third International led to the extension of Marxism beyond the boundaries of the advanced industrial societies and the confrontation of a new nationalism in the colonies. This area of the globe, known as the Third World, created a closer relationship between Marxism and nationalism, but questioned the nature of Marxism as an essentially European ideology. Finally, those countries which had ostensibly achieved the transition to socialism predicted by Marxism have shown that nationalism is a sturdier phenomenon than it would have been if it were the simple transient expression of the capitalist mode of production.

Of models and history

To understand Marxism's relationship with nationalism it is well to start with the origins of Marxism itself. Lenin provides a commonly accepted version:

> It is the legitimate successor to the best that man produced in the nineteenth century, as represented by German philosophy, English political economy and French socialism.[1]

These three sources of Marxism provided it with all that is radical and progressive in the doctrine, but also led to certain 'deviations' which shaped Marxism's understanding of the national question.

The 'German philosophy' which lay behind the doctrine of Marxism was, above all, Hegelian. Though Marx 'inverted' Hegel, traces of the latter's idealism still permeated the Marxist discourse on nationalism. In Hegel's system of thought, states, nations and individuals follow pre-determined stages of development set by the "Idea of the world mind". For Hegel, "The nation whose life embodies this moment secures the good fortune and fame, and its deeds are brought to fruition".[2] As for those less fortunate in the world historical process determined by the mystical idea: "the minds of the other nations are without rights, and they . . . count no longer in world history".[3] Many of the more reactionary formulations on nations by Marx and especially Engels (see Chapter 1), spring directly from these obscure pages in Hegel's *Philosophy of Right*. It was a legacy not fully overcome until Third World Marxism came into its own.

Hegel was not only responsible for the untenable early Marxist distinction between "historic" and "non-historic" nations. He also set the terms of Marxism's evolutionary paradigm in which development is seen as a pre-determined process. On the one hand, "the nation to which is ascribed a moment of the Idea . . . is entrusted with giving complete effect to it in the advance of the self-developing self-consciousness of the world mind".[4] This dominant nation moves inexorably towards the freedom embodied in the constitution of a state. Hegel refers to "the right of heroes to found states".[5] However,

> The same consideration justifies civilized nations in regarding and treating as barbarians those who lag behind them in institutions which are the essential moments of the state.[6]

This is the distilled essence of the modern sociology of development which has also permeated much of the Marxist discourse on 'underdevelopment'. Marx and Engels took over from Hegel a certain evolutionary schema. It would be difficult to develop a concept of the rights of nations to self-determination in this contextual framework. Hegel's view on this question was unequivocal: "The civilized nation is conscious that the rights of barbarians are unequal to its own and treats their autonomy as only a formality".[7]

The effect of 'English political economy' was fundamental in shaping the thought of Karl Marx; but it is sometimes forgotten that Marx was forging a "critique of political economy". By accepting that Marxism is a simple continuation of bourgeois political economy there is the danger of falling into the trap of economism. For authors such as Chantal Mouffe it is this economism and reductionism within Marxism which has led to a "lack of true understanding of the nature of politics, and which has fettered the expansive capacity of Marxism".[8] The nation was one concept to suffer from this 'epiphenomenalism', in which politics and ideology are denied any effect and reduced to a pale reflection of the economic base. Lenin, for example, stated bluntly that "political institutions are a superstructure on the economic foundation".[9] The 'modern nation' was thus for classical Marxism a historical phenomenon bound up exclusively with the rise of the bourgeoisie as an economic force. In so far as it was 'progressive' — i.e. led to the development of the forces of production — this trend was to be supported. It also led to Marxist approval for the larger and more centralized nation-states and a continuous suspicion of smaller units apparently outside the flow of capital's mission. As Nimni remarks, "Nationalist movements and national communities are always defined in terms of their position in the capitalist system".[10]

The tendency towards economism results in an undue assimilation within the Marxist discourse of the nation, the nation-state and the bourgeoisie (see Chapter 8). The history of capitalism in England became a universal model; as Marx wrote in *Capital*, "The country that is more developed industrially only shows, to the less developed, the image of its own future".[11] There was a Hegelian inexorability to this process whereby history was reduced to the implacable advance of the bourgeoisie. Small and frail national groupings would inevitably be trampled underfoot by the capitalist juggernaut. If a nation was not 'viable' in economic terms it should, according to Marx and Engels, simply be assimilated by a larger neighbour. When Lenin granted the right of self-determination to the component nationalities of the Soviet states he assumed that economic necessity would compel them to remain part of the centralized state. It took an unorthodox figure such as Sultan Galiev (see Chapter 4) to question the 'one-sidedness' of the Soviet leadership's focus on the industrialized West as a revolutionary arena with, on the other hand, "the lack of knowledge of the East . . . and the fear of it called forth by this".[12] Indeed, the long-standing Marxist emphasis on the economic preconditions for socialist revolution led to a certain amount of surprise when revolutions broke out in 'underdeveloped' countries. The Russian Revolution should have cured Marxism of its economism; but it did so only partially.

The third component of Marxism discerned by Lenin was "French socialism". Indeed, as we have already mentioned, it was the French Revolution which served as the model, or paradigm, of the democratic revolution for Marx and his successors. In the consolidation of the French nation-state we see the classical pattern of centralization and language standardization. Yet this was by no means a 'natural' product of the revolutionary upsurge: the 'French' language was spoken mainly by the court of Versailles whereas in the rest of the territory various dialects were used. Not surprisingly the oppressed nationalities became the focus for counter-revolutionary agitation. Administrative centralization was no more natural in its logic: present nationalist agitation in Brittany and other areas of the French state, not to mention Corsica, could simply not have been envisaged by Marx and Engels. The 'French model' did not even apply in the rest of Europe: England, Germany and Italy all followed quite distinct paths. By reducing the nation to the nation-state, Marx and Engels could not comprehend either the cultural or ethnic dimension of nationalism in Eastern Europe. When it came to the area now known as the Third World the French paradigm was even more inappropriate, as is, for example, shown in Marx's singular inability to understand the process of national formation in South America (see Chapter 1).

Marxism is very much a European ideology and a product of the Enlightenment period. Palestinian author El Kodsky argues that

Once, however, we leave the field of European history, we discover that the concepts on which Stalin's theory of the nation was based are no longer adequate to reality.[13]

Basque author Ortzi writes in a similar vein that "Lenin's schemas on the national question, valid for a certain phase of the national struggles, in a certain zone of Europe, are no longer valid".[14] In the era of monopoly capitalism the struggle of the national minorities — like that of the colonies earlier — has become part of the world socialist revolution. The nationalism of the small oppressed nationalities is no longer in contradiction with the global interests of the working class, but flows along similar lines: the enemy is not another nationality but the centralist bourgeois state. Outside of Europe the inadequacy of classical models is even more evident. To assume that the nation is a product of capitalism — where the bourgeoisie unifies the nation, rules it and generates its ideology — is to deny the existence of nations beyond the pale of the advanced industrial societies. As El Kodsky asks, "What, then, are we to call those social realities of the pre-capitalist world where an old tradition of state unity coincides with the real linguistic and cultural unity?"[15]

Marxism, like any other theoretical perspective, would only be transformed by a practical failure. In this context No Sizwe forcefully argues that

> The anti-colonial and anti-imperialist struggles conducted, especially since the end of the second world war, in Asia, Africa and Latin America, have thrown this [Marxist-Leninist] originally Eurocentric theory of nationality into a crisis.[16]

Even the Soviet experts on nationalism were forced to recognize that Stalin's definition of the nation was based on exclusively European historical experiences. This was important because the early attempts made by South African Marxists to deal with the national question were, for No Sizwe, "hamstrung by Soviet theories formulated in a different historical context and elevated to the pedestal of a dogma".[17] To deploy concepts such as nationality, national minority or national group to the quite specific context of South Africa was simple dogmatism. The key difference between the colonial and the European context, was, of course, imperialism. The development of capitalism in its original environment took an organic form quite distinct from its cataclysmic effect in Africa and other areas of colonial expansion. In that context, as Cabral and others argued and demonstrated, the nation would consist of all the people struggling to overthrow imperialism and the yoke of racial oppression. In many ways the struggle against imperialism could produce a new nation which could overcome the natural and artificial barriers of caste, religion and language.

The three sources of Marxism have each in their turn produced a model of nationalism which tends towards evolutionism (Hegel), economism (political economy) and Europeanism (French model). We must, in short, reject all Marxist theories of nationalism which see it as reducible to some underlying cause, or a simple epiphenomenon of economic processes, or indeed, which reduce it to any mono-causal explanation. Nationalism is a complex political phenomenon which is irreducible and must be understood in its own terms. We cannot, therefore, accept the view of the Institute of Marxism-Leninism for which

> Though the national question is very important, it is not, in the view of Marxist-Leninists, an independent and self-sufficient issue. It is entirely subordinate to the class problems in the development of society.[18]

In Chapter 8 we argued that national and class issues are inseparable; but it is not the same to argue that one is "entirely subordinate" to another. To understand nationalism it cannot simply be viewed through the Marxist grid in an instrumentalist fashion but must be seen as a political movement in its own right. Above all, nationalism cannot be reduced to models: it must be conceived historically.

Nationalism is not a timeless transhistorical essence, which is not amenable to scientific analysis. We can locate the origins of nationalism quite precisely at the point where European feudalism went through an economic, political and social regeneration which culminated in the modern capitalist nation-states. But that was not the only form of nationalism. If we understand nationalism as a historical phenomenon then we are in a better position to unravel its diverse political effects. This is a more fruitful approach than attempting to seek the eternal essence of a nation or the ultimate causes and functions of nationalism. We must distinguish the 'classical' nationalism of the bourgeois democratic revolution from the Third World variant; and both of these are different from the nationalism of the socialist states (Poland) and the 'neo-nationalism' of Western Europe (the Basques). There are quite specific relations between each of these movements and the constituent social classes of each society. The political implications of each variant of nationalism are also quite different in each case. Jenkins and Minnerup are quite correct to indicate that

> Nationalism as a political programme to fill the void left by capitalist conservatism and proletarian socialism is the common denominator . . . in all three sectors of the contemporary world.[19]

Whether in the capitalist West, the socialist East or the dependent South, nationalism responds to deeply rooted popular aspirations for socio-economic, political and cultural liberation. When these do not take a socialist form this is largely because of the failure of Marxism to understand nationalism and articulate its progressive elements. Nationalism is a political movement akin to the regimes of Bonapartism: it ostensibly stands above social classes and it emerges when there is an equilibrium between the fundamental social classes.

If nationalism is a product of history it is also a cultural artifact, an "imagined community" as Anderson terms it: it is not a natural product or something mystical. Nationalism is, indeed, an "invented tradition" as Hobsbawm has recently argued; the nation, nationalism and associated phenomena "all rest on exercises in social engineering which are often deliberate and always innovative".[20] We saw above how the French Revolution 'created' the French nation but indeed most nationalisms have to forge a 'national history' which is part fact and part fantasy. For Hobsbawm nationalism as we know it emerged in Europe between 1870 and 1914 and it "became a substitute for social cohesion through a national church, a royal family or other cohesive traditions, or collective group self-representations, a new secular religion . . . ."[21] This admirable analysis can also, however, be applied to Marxism itself. Marxism is not the 'natural' ideology of the proletariat, nor is socialism the inevitable result of capitalist crisis. Marxism has its iconography too, and in many ways it is also a secular religion. It is by any standard an 'invented tradition', albeit a more scientific one than religion or belief in a hereditary monarchy. It is well to remember such things, as Marxists are prone to dissect and dismiss nationalism from the lofty heights of the dialectical materialist citadel of science and reason.

Politics in command

Having established that nationalism cannot be conceived as a simple reflection of economic processes, we must now deepen our political reading of nationalism. Lenin broke with economism when he asserted categorically that nationalism pertained to the arena of political democracy. The attitude of Marxists towards particular nationalist expressions would be dictated fundamentally by the criteria of whether they strengthened democracy or not. Jenkins and Minnerup refer to Marxism's "inability to recognise the democratic impulse that lies at the heart of nationalism . . . ."[22] To accept this statement we need to take two further steps. Firstly, we must decide what to call that British ideology mobilized by the Thatcher government to recover the Falkland-Malvinas islands in the name of democracy and the right of self-determination. Is it just a sham, a clever ploy to dupe the proletariat? To label it 'chauvinism' cannot really detract from it as a manifestation of nationalism, just as Hitler was a product of a certain German nationalism. So, nationalism is not intrinsically democratic. The national question can take revolutionary forms (the colonial revolution) or be amenable to reformist solutions (the socialist states), or be a manifestation of imperialist expansionism (Reagan's "Make America Great"). The second issue raised by the Jenkins and Minnerup statement is Marxism's own relation to democracy.

Marxists have traditionally taken a somewhat pragmatic attitude towards democracy, refusing to recognize that the self-determination of women and of nations (to name but two) are essential to socialism. In the Marxist tradition, nationalism has been a 'problem' to be examined only so as to overcome it. For Marx, Irish nationalism was positive because it could further the British workers' cause; for Luxemburg nationalism was simply an encumbrance. Marx and Engels were quite happy to deride democratic national demands if they were seen to conflict with the interests of the world revolution as they saw it. For Lenin the right to self-determination was far from automatic once the socialist revolution had been victorious. The socialists who did attempt to come to grips with nationalism, attempting a serious analysis which went beyond a simple instrumentalism, were derided for their unorthodox approach. Otto Bauer was painted as a crass reformist and "national opportunist", Ber Borochov was simply ignored because of his Zionism, and James Connolly became a simple Irish nationalist. It is now necessary to forge some kind of coherent Marxist approach to nationalism on the basis of these writers and also Gramsci who was preoccupied by the national question in Italy.

To the Marxist categories of the forces and relations of production, Borochov added the conditions of production, which referred to the different geographic, historic and even anthropological contexts in which production took place. Workers are interested in the social and historic environment in which they exist because "no class in a society is outside the conditions of production of that society".[23] The genuine nationalism of the progressive class (the proletariat) is embodied in "demands to assure the nation normal conditions of production, and to assure the proletariat a normal base for its labour and class struggle".[24] For workers the national territory is seen as a place of employment, but there are other related cultural interests, those of education, language and literature. Genuine nationalism, as Borochov terms it, does not in any way obscure class consciousness. Even the struggle of the oppressed nationalities which may take a cultural form, and where national solidarity may mollify the class antagonisms, will create "in a new and clear form a healthy class structure and a sound class struggle".[25] Nationalism cannot be reduced to the ideology of the rising bourgeoisie or the pathology of late or declining capitalism: it results from a form of struggle which is relatively independent of class conflict and its resolution is the precondition for a 'normal' or healthy class struggle.

Otto Bauer goes even further in providing a non-reductionist theory of nationalism. Bauer was less interested in a definition of the nation than its derivation from the integrated process of economic development, changes in the social structure and the articulation of classes within society. The nation is a historical phenomenon "since the living national character which operates in every one of its members is the residue of a historical development".[26] For him, "the task of the International can and should be, not the levelling of national particularities, but the engendering of international unity in national multiplicity".[27] Under socialism, the cultural history of the nation, hitherto the history of the ruling classes, would henceforth be appropriated by the masses who could give free rein to their national characteristics. Here Bauer was opposing Lenin's position that there were two cultures in every nation: that of the bourgeoisie and that of the proletariat. For Bauer, the cultural domain was rather a site of struggle between the classes. This conflicted with the crass economism of Luxemburg's follower Joseph Strasser who argued that "any cultural question is in the last instance an economic question".[28] Bauer dubbed this a "shopkeeper's perspective" and argued that Marxism was an ideology of liberation which transcended simple economic advancement. Implicitly, Bauer was advancing a political strategy which Gramsci later developed around the concept of 'hegemony', based on the idea of the working class contesting the rule of the bourgeoisie at the broader cultural/ideological level.

Another of Bauer's strengths was his analysis of how national and class struggles were interrelated. He wrote that "nationalist hatred is a transformed class hatred".[29] He was referring specifically to the petty bourgeoisie of the oppressed nation affected by the shifts in population and other convulsions engendered by capitalism; but the point is a more general one. Bauer bids us seek "the social roots of national struggles" on the one hand and "the national content of the class struggle" on the other.[30] The ruling classes are well able to mask the class struggle with nationalist rhetoric; but the working class must also struggle for national self-determination. Bauer preached the need for working class autonomy in the realm of political democracy as the best means and base for seizing power. National autonomy was also, however, an indispensable revindication for the working class, especially when different nationalities coexisted within a given nation-state. Finally, in the age of imperialism, the 'principle of nationality' or the right of nations to self-determination is betrayed by the bourgeoisie and becomes the banner of the working class. The struggle against imperialism becomes a class struggle even though at first in the oppressed nation "all the social contradictions of the country appear as national ones".[31] As to the workers of the advanced industrial societies, their internationalism only gains relevance through the struggle against imperialism.

After Bauer it was Antonio Gramsci who paid most attention to the cultural element of the working class struggle. In particular he developed the category of the "national popular" which implies a radically different political practice than that of orthodox Marxism-Leninism. In spite of its cultural origins (see Chapter 8) the term "national popular" has now taken on a clear political meaning. Essentially, it involves the recognition that ideologies have no necessary class connotations and that popular democratic struggles must be included within the socialist project. National oppression would be one such form of domination which cannot be subsumed under the economic-class rubric. In the specific context of Italy, Gramsci pointed to a separation of 'nation' and 'people' which he compared to France where

> The meaning of 'national' already includes a more politically elaborated notion of 'popular' because it is related to the concept of 'sovereignty': national sovereignty and popular sovereignty have, or had, the same value.[32]

Leaving aside the repeated myths of the 'French model', Gramsci's analysis leads to certain political conclusions. The reason it is not a purely cultural analysis is because, as Forgas notes, " 'Culture' in Gramsci is the sphere in which ideologies are diffused and organized, in which hegemony is constructed and can be broken and reconstructed".[33] And one way in which proletarian hegemony is constructed is precisely through a global contestation of the bourgeois domain and a co-option of national-popular traditions, compatible with the democratic socialist project. According to Gramsci, "It is no longer the bourgeoisie today that has unified interests in economics and politics . . . . Today, the only 'national' class is the proletariat . . . ."[34] Gramsci recognized that the working class lived and fought on a specific national terrain. To become the 'national' class entailed assuming the mantle of intellectual, political and moral leadership which Gramsci termed hegemony. For Gramsci, finally,

The internal relations of any nation are the result of a combination which is 'original' and (in a certain sense) unique: these relations must be understood and conceived in their originality and uniqueness if one wishes to dominate and direct them.[35]

As we have already seen, the great African revolutionary Amilcar Cabral also developed a conception of the 'national popular' and stressed the importance of the cultural domain (see Chapter 6). Cabral pointed to "the close, dependent and reciprocal connexion existing between the *cultural factor* and the *economic* (and political) *factor* in the behaviour of human societies".[36] Imperialist domination has to practise cultural oppression to maintain its rule, so the struggle for national liberation necessarily has a cultural component. Even further, as Cabral argues, "Study of the history of liberation struggles shows that they have generally been preceeded by an upsurge of cultural manifestations . . . ."[37] As to the 'nation class', this is a debatable category; but it correctly denotes the interaction of the national and class struggles in a situation of imperialist domination. The legacy of Cabral is, like that of Gramsci, fragmented and in parts contradictory; but it is rich in hints on how to pursue the national question within Marxism.

We can note in this context, following Cedric Robinson, the historian of *Black Marxism*, that

> The dismissal of culture, that is a transmitted historical consciousness, as an aspect of class consciousness, did not equip the Marxian movement for the political forces which would not only erupt in Europe over the Third World but within the movement itself.[38]

Whereas the Russian Revolution did go some way towards recognizing the crucial importance of the national question in political practice, it did not lead to the necessary theoretical breakthrough. An example of Marxism's failure in this respect was its economic/rational view of capitalism which, rather, is permeated by its racist and patriarchal features. Consciousness is moulded by all these elements and not simply by the economic exploitation of wage-labour, so that revolutions are inevitably shaped by their particular national context. Robinson points out that, because of their emphasis on the economic and European aspects of capitalism,

> Marxists have often argued that national liberation movements in the Third World are secondary to the interests of the industrial proletariat in the capitalist metropolis, or that they need to be understood only as the social efflux of world capitalism.[39]

It is no longer acceptable to view the national question as derivative of some deeper underlying and determinative historical process. National oppression, like that based on gender or race, is an independent phenomenon and requires an independent solution.

To return to the theme of this section we must again 'place politics in command'. Nationalism motivates political movements throughout the modern world and Marxists must inevitably adopt political positions towards them.

Lenin provided guidelines which are still pertinent to those living in the imperialist heartlands: support the nationalism of the oppressed, oppose that of the oppressor nation. Yet it was the Irish socialist James Connolly who in theory and in practice best exemplified the Marxist attitude towards nationalism in what we would today call dependent societies. Connolly condemned the abstract internationalism of those who would deny the historical impact of imperialism over their nation and neglect the national tasks of the proletarian revolution. He could not understand how any socialist could claim to be opposed to all oppression yet not support the struggle for national independence. For Connolly the 'cause of labour' was inseparable from the broader aim of achieving an independent Ireland. Yet the other side of the coin was a profound mistrust in the ability of the nationalists to carry through the revolution to its avowed democratic ends. For this reason Connolly warned the Citizen Army before the 1916 Rising:

> In the event of victory, hold on to your rifles, as those with whom we are fighting may stop before our goal is reached. We are out for economic as well as political liberty.[40]

In other words, Marxism has a common interest with revolutionary nationalism in 'liberty' but defines this in social and economic terms as well as political.

The attitude that socialists in the advanced countries take towards imperialism is the very touchstone of their politics. McCann argues quite bluntly for the Irish case that, "there is no such thing as an anti-imperialist who does not support the Provos [Provisional IRA] and no such thing as a socialist who is not anti-imperialist".[41] There are, of course, socialists in Ireland, as elsewhere, who believe that imperialism is progressive and nationalism a simple superstition; but McCann expresses the Leninist position with admirable clarity. From outside Marxism, Dudley Seers has come to recognize the great importance of nationalism on the Third World. Starting from a liberal cosmopolitan view on the evils of nationalism, Seers developed a conception of Third World nationalism as a necessary defence against both major superpowers, the USA and the USSR:

> Nationalism is, of course, inconvenient for the superpowers, as it once was for Britain. Their ideologists treat it as anathema and their governments try to suppress it — at least in *other* countries.[42]

Nationalism stands in the way of economic dependence, cultural imperialism and military subjection which the large powers attempt to impose on the Third World. In this context, argues Seers, "internationalism, is not only naive but also hypocritical, merely a vehicle for propaganda that suits one of the superpowers".[43] For Marxists, of course, internationalism lies at the very heart of the socialist project; but it is hard to deny the validity of Seer's accusation.

And internationalism?

The Basque writer Ortzi argues that "a Basque socialist not only can but must be *abertzale* [a patriot] at the same time as internationalist".[44] If patriotism means fighting for the national liberation of Euzkadi, internationalism entails

> never oppressing or disdaining any country, strengthening the links of fraternity with all peoples, especially those who fight their own fight against the state of the oligarchy and the monopolies.[45]

The Basque *abertzale*, in short, also wants to see socialism in all the countries of the world. This nationalism is light-years away from that of the dictator Franco who preached the national virtues of the Spanish state and oppressed its various national components. Internationalism cannot be conceived as the simple polar opposite of nationalism. Yet there is also a difference between the professed internationalism of the Basque militant and that of the International Brigades who flocked to Spain during the Civil War to fight against Franco and for democracy. In a similar way there was a split in the ranks of Irish republicanism in the 1930s between those, such as Frank Ryan, who saw Spain as the nerve-centre of the international revolution and joined the International Brigades, and those who saw the main priority as carrying on the old struggle for national liberation from Britain.

Marxism has, since its origins, preached the virtues of 'proletarian internationalism', even though at times it became a somewhat empty abstract slogan. Yet it was not without reason that al-Husri, founder of Arab nationalism, referred to this doctrine as "a new and very dangerous enemy".[46] One of the main tasks of patriotism was to combat this new variant of cosmopolitanism, but al-Husri takes some comfort from the fact that "now patriotism has been victorious over internationalism in Soviet Russia".[47] It is indeed a common mistake to confuse internationalism with cosmopolitanism, in spite of the explicit disclaimers by Marx and Engels (see Chapter 1). A further distinction needs to be drawn between internationalism and simple co-operation between nation-states. Anthony Smith argues, for example, that "cosmopolitanism is the real enemy of nationalism; internationalism is simply the mutual recognition and legitimation of other people's nationalisms, institutionalised in a global framework".[48] Following this criteria, the United Nations, NATO and the Warsaw Pact would all be examples of internationalism. In the pages below we will restrict the term internationalism to the contacts and actions of the labour and socialist movements across national frontiers. This also entails a healthy dose of scepticism towards the official 'proletarian internationalism' professed by most socialist states but rarely practised by them.

The modern history of internationalism began with the formation of the First International in 1864. The London Trades Council had turned towards international organization to answer the threatened use of foreign strikebreakers by the city's building trade employers in the late 1850s. The new international body achieved its successes fundamentally in the area of trade union activity, in spite of the attempt by Marx to 'politicize' it over Poland, Ireland and other international issues. Between 1867 and 1869 there were international demonstrations of support for, amongst others, the Lyon silk-spinners, the Leipzig typesetters, the Waldenburg miners and the Geneva building-workers. Yet a cold analysis of these actions shows a motivation no different from that of national trade union organizations, namely to protect that unionized workforce from low-paid, unorganized workers elsewhere. In a paean to internationalism, Novack admits that "the International called upon the workers to support in their own interests the struggle of their foreign comrades".[49] In a similar way, Marx was to argue that English workers should support the right of the Irish people to self-determination "in their own interests", rather than as a democratic right in itself. The International virtually collapsed after the English trade unions began to withdraw in the 1870s and industrial relations in Britain gradually became institutionalized on a more stable basis.

The Second International formed in 1889 also had economic motivations as one of its main objectives, in this case the establishment of uniform national labour legislation. However, as Logue notes,

> Through their activity in defense of narrow economic aims, the Internationals began to create a sense of international working class solidarity that transcended the narrow economic dimensions of the international actions.[50]

Even though the trade unions and socialist movements had become internationalized out of self-interest, an international proletarian solidarity was beginning to take shape. In 1890, May Day was designated a day for labour in which simultaneous one-day strikes and demonstrations for the eight-hour day would be held in all countries. The social democratic leader Victor Adler proclaimed that

> The knowledge that at a given hour, on the same day, wherever capitalist power prevails, the workers were filled with *one* ideal, gives a deeper and more genuinely revolutionary content to the occasion than mere preoccupation with labour legislation.[51]

However, the period from 1890 to the First World War was one of relative capitalist stability, rising incomes and few practical manifestations of trade union internationalism. By the eve of the world war the now deeply reformist leaders of social democracy were unable to prevent the outbreak of chauvinism on a mass scale (see Chapter 2) and the demise of internationalism for a whole generation.

The Third, or Communist, International arose out of the embers of the second in 1919 and immediately placed nationalism at the centre of its concerns. In its long history down to 1943 (see Chapter 5) the new International firmly established solidarity with the colonial peoples as a prerequisite for genuine socialism in the advanced industrial societies. It also set up a trade union international, the Red International of Labour Unions, which gained affiliates in many countries and practised a genuinely revolutionary trade unionism. Whereas the Second International had turned its back on the struggles of the colonial peoples, the new International practised solidarity within the terms of reference set by the new Soviet state. The trade union affiliates of the International were also expected to serve the interests of their respective communist parties, themselves subject to the dictates of the 'centre'. Internationalism was gradually redefined to mean an uncritical defence of the Soviet Union. When it came to dissolving the International in the interests of the Soviet Union's foreign policy, Stalin justified it in terms far removed from proletarian internationalism:

> It facilitates the work of the patriots in the freedom-loving countries for uniting the progressive forces of their respective countries, regardless of party or religious faith, into a single camp of national liberation.[52]

Thus the Third International was disbanded in 1943 in circumstances every bit as negative for internationalism as the collapse of the Second International in 1914.

A new wave of labour internationalism began in the late 1960s as a result of the growing contacts established by workers employed by the multinational corporations in various countries. For some, the increasingly international organization of production led, almost inexorably, to an increase in proletarian internationalism. Thus Ernest Mandel argues that "the higher the level of internationalisation of capital and of the productive forces, the more the class struggle itself becomes international".[53] This perspective can lead to a somewhat fantastic analysis of the 'world revolution', which sees a miners' strike in Britain, a riot in South Africa and a new dissident manifesto from Poland as all part of the same 'rise in the class struggle' and advance for the forces of revolution. The class struggle still has a predominantly national base tied to particular histories, and it is an idealistic abstraction to speak of 'world classes'. None of this is to deny the very real advance made in terms of international contacts by grass-roots workers' organizations. It is well known that workers in many transnational industries, particularly the motor industry, have through their shop stewards built up contacts which transcend national frontiers.[54] Even sporadic examples of international strike action can be advanced to demonstrate the relevance of internationalism for the contemporary labour movement. It is necessary, however, to set this incipient level of internationalism in its proper context.

We should recognize, along with Haworth and Ramsay, that "there is no necessary reason for labour to reproduce the internationalisation shown by capital".[55] Capital has an international mobility and capacity for action which labour simply does not possess. The labour movement is grounded in a national reality and needs to develop a political strategy to confront and deal with its own nation-state. Furthermore, "syndicalist internationalism" as Olle and Schoeller call it, "can only reproduce the competition between nationally different conditions of production in the form of a latent national fractionalisation within the trade-union movement".[56] A purely trade-union based internationalism based on economic criteria — wage differences between countries — can only be a fragile one. It is indeed possible to find a less than altruistic reason behind the solidarity of the trade unions in the advanced industrialized societies, namely, preventing the low wages of the Third World from drawing work away from their members. Trade unions' internationalism can, in short, be a type of labour cartel rather than a harbinger of a socialist future. There is finally the sobering thought of Logue's that "The stronger the national trade union movement, the less likely it is to be internationalistic".[57] In the USA the unions are openly nationalistic and protectionist; but at a more general level we can ask why the new trade union internationalism had to wait for a period of generalized capitalist recession to come on the scene.

There is also, of course, a tradition of political internationalism stretching back to the International Brigades of the Spanish Civil War. Even earlier, workers in the West carried out a blockade of weapons shipments to Poland in 1920, with British workers even threatening a general strike if their country had intervened. In Spain itself between 1936 and 1939, some 50,000 foreign volunteers came to fight against fascism, and in the battle 2,000 lost their lives. For a later generation it was the anti-imperialist struggle in Vietnam which symbolized the need for proletarian internationalism. Ernesto 'Che' Guevara was one of the few who called for international brigades to be sent to Vietnam; but many more prosaic examples of internationalism played a not inconsiderable role in that struggle. Guevara was uncompromising in his call:

> Let us develop a true proletarian internationalism, with international proletarian armies; the flag under which we fight would be the sacred cause of redeeming humanity. To die under the flag of Vietnam, of Venezuela, of Guatemala, of Laos, of Guinea, of Colombia, of Bolivia, of Brazil — to name only a few scenes of today's armed struggle — would be equally glorious and desirable for an American, an Asian, an African, even [sic] a European.[58]

From these stirring words and Guevara's own undoubted example of internationalism we must turn to the more sober reality of 'proletarian internationalism' today.

For the major socialist powers 'proletarian internationalism' is largely a symbolic and rather hollow phase, used to describe acts of the most diverse sort. Even in the case of Cuba, the armies of 'internationalists' working throughout the Third World play a complicated role. On the one hand, as in Angola, they may help save a revolutionary nationalist regime from the onslaught of imperialism. On the other hand, as in Ethiopia, they may directly or indirectly repress a genuine national liberation movement. In Latin America itself, the 1960s period of 'exporting revolution' has given way to a more stable system of inter-state relations. The aid to revolutionary Nicaragua is conditioned, inevitably one might add, by the needs of the Cuban state itself. The situation can even be extended to Nicaragua in turn, where the revolution saw a considerable internationalist contribution, but which now must limit its aid for the guerrilla movement in El Salvador to placate the United States. For Mandel the cause of this complex set of processes is simple: "The bitter fruits of 'national communism' are . . . increased nationalism and national suspicion among nations even after the overthrow of capitalism".[59] However, to call for a new revolutionary international to replace the communist one, will not of itself overcome the very difficult dilemmas to be faced by any victorious socialist revolution, which will inevitably, for a whole historical period, be based on particular nation-states.

We can conclude that for Marxism nationalism and internationalism are not incompatible, if both are informed by a genuine democratic dynamic. The struggle for socialism does operate on the national terrain and a Marxist movement which cannot make much headway in its own nation-state will not be able to practise a credible internationalism. Engels had long ago made it clear that proletarian internationalism was only possible among free peoples and that national nihilism was alien to Marxism.[60] Lenin was even more specific:

> The proletariat must demand freedom of political separation for the colonies and nations oppressed by 'their own' nation. Otherwise, the internationalism of the proletariat would be nothing but empty words . . . .[61]

Class solidarity would be impossible while one nation still oppressed another. Internationalism cannot thus be counterposed as the automatic response to 'narrow and parochial' nationalism, listed along with the other sources of division within the working class such as racism and sexism. One conclusion from our analysis of the interaction between Marxism and nationalism is that the latter is a complex, and even contradictory phenomenon. The two main criteria for determining its nature are its relation to democracy — does it favour its development or not? — and imperialism — does it oppose it unequivocally or not? For internationalism to become a viable alternative it is not sufficient to appeal to economic self-interest: Marxism must forge the socialist morality required to guide its mission of liberating humankind.

Notes

1. V.I. Lenin, 'The Three Sources and Three Component Parts of Marxism', in *Selected Works*, Vol. 1 (Progress Publishers, Moscow, 1970) p.66.

2. G.W.F. Hegel, *The Philosophy of Right* (Encyclopaedia Britannica, Chicago, 1971) p.111.

3. Ibid.

4. Ibid.

5. Ibid., p.112.

6. Ibid.

7. Ibid.

8. C. Mouffe, 'Hegemony and the Integral State in Gramsci: Towards A New Concept of Politics', in G. Bridges and R. Brunt (eds.), *Silver Linings, Some Strategies for the Eighties* (Lawrence and Wishart, London, 1981) p.182.

10. E. Nimni, 'Marxism and Nationalism', *Capital and Class*, No. 25, 1985, p.63.

11. K. Marx, *Capital*, Vol. 1 (Penguin, London, 1976) p.91.

12. M. Sultan Galiev, 'The Social Revolution and the East', *Review*, IV 1, 1982, p.7.

13. A. El Kodsky, 'Nationalism and Class Struggles in the Arab World', *Monthly Review*, Vol. 22, No. 3, 1970, p.2.

14. Ortzi, *Historia de Euzkadi: El nacionalismo vasco y ETA* (Ruedo Ibérico, Paris, 1975) p.422.

15. El Kodsky, 'Nationalism and Class Struggles in the Arab World', p.2.

16. No Sizwe, *One Azania, One Nation: The National Question in South Africa* (Zed Books, London, 1979), p.166.

17. Ibid., p.127.

18. Institute of Marxism-Leninism, *Leninism and the National Question* (Progress Publishers, Moscow, 1977) p.57.

19. B. Jenkins and G. Minnerup, *Citizens and Comrades: Socialism in a World of Nation States* (Pluto Press, London, 1984) p.59.

20. E. Hobsbawm, 'Introduction: Inventing Traditions', in E. Hobsbawm and T. Ranger (eds.), *The Introduction of Tradition* (Cambridge University Press, 1984) p.13.

21. E. Hobsbawm, 'Mass-Producing Traditions: Europe, 1870-1914', in E. Hobsbawm and T. Ranger (eds.), *The Invention of Tradition*, p.303.

22. B. Jenkins and G. Minnerup, *Citizens and Comrades*, pp.9-10.

23. B. Borochov, *Nationalism and the Class Struggle: A Marxian Approach to the Jewish Problem* (Greenwood Press, Westport, 1973) p.157.

24. Ibid., p.166.

25. Ibid.

26. O. Bauer, *La Cuestión de las Nacionalidades y la Socialdemocracia* (Siglo XXI, Mexico, 1979) p.144.

27. Ibid., p.21.

28. R. Calwer, *et al.*, *La Segunda Internacional y el Problema Nacional y Colonial (segunda parte)* Cuadernos de Pasado y Presente (Siglo XXI, Mexico, 1978) p.239.

29. O. Bauer, *La Cuestión de las Nacionalidades y la Socialdemocracia*, p.259.

30. Ibid., p.549.

31. Ibid., p.228.

32. Cited in D. Forgas, ' "National-Popular": Genealogy of a Concept', *Formations: of Nations and People* (Routledge and Kegan Paul, London, 1984) p.91.

33. Ibid.

34. Cited in C. Buci-Glucksmann, *Gramsci and the State* (Lawrence and Wishart, London, 1980) p.144.

35. Q. Hoare and G. Nowell Smith (eds.), *Selections from the Prison Notebooks of Antonio Gramsci* (Lawrence and Wishart, London, 1971) p.240.

36. A. Cabral, *Unity and Struggle* (Heinemann, London, 1980), p.141.

37. Ibid., p.142.

38. C. Robinson, *Black Marxism: The Making of the Black Radical Tradition* (Zed Books, London, 1983) p.78.

39. Ibid., p.84.

40. Cited in R. Dudley Edwards, *James Connolly* (Gill and Macmillan, Dublin, 1981) p.145.

41. E. McCann, *War and an Irish Town* (Pluto Press, London, 1980) p.176.

42. D. Seers, *The Political Economy of Nationalism* (Oxford University Press, 1983) p.12.

43. Ibid., p.12.

44. Ortzi, *Historia de Euzkadi*, p.422.

45. Ibid., p.422.

46. Cited in B. Tibi, *Arab Nationalism: A Critical Enquiry* (Macmillan, London, 1981) p.129.

47. Ibid.

48. A. Smith, *Nationalism in the Twentieth Century* (Martin Robertson, Oxford, 1979) p.192.

49. G. Novack *et al., The First Three Internationals* (Pathfinder Press, New York, 1974) p.39.

50. J. Logue, *Toward a Theory of Trade Union Internationalism* (Kent Popular Press, Kent, 1980), p.34.

51. Cited, ibid., p.35.

52. Cited in G. Novack *et al., The First Three Internationals*, p.21.

53. E. Mandel and J. Ross, 'The Need for a Revolutionary International', *International Marxist Review*, Vol. 1, No. 1, 1982, p.29.

54. See, for example, 'Raising the Curtain; the new shopfloor internationalism emerging in the auto industry', *TIE-Europe*, No. 16, 1983.

55. N. Haworth and H. Ramsay, 'Grasping the Nettle: Problems with the Theory of International Trade Union Solidarity', in P. Waterman (ed.), *For a New Labor Internationalism* (ILERI, The Hague, 1984) p.71.

56. W. Olle and W. Schoeller, 'World Market Competition and Restrictions upon International Trade-Union Policies', in P. Waterman (ed.), *For a New Labor Internationalism*, pp.53-4.

57. J. Logue, *Toward a Theory of Trade Union Internationalism*, p.11.

58. J. Gerassi (ed.), *Venceremos! The speeches and writings of Che Guevara* (Panther, London, 1969) p.581.

59. E. Mandel and J. Ross, 'The Need for a Revolutionary International', p.39.

60. See F. Engels, 'The Festival of Nations in London', in K. Marx and F. Engels, *Collected Works*, Vol. 6 (Lawrence and Wishart, London, 1976).

61. V.I. Lenin, *Collected Works*, Vol. 22 (Progress Publishers, Moscow, 1964) p.147.

Bibliography

Abdel-Malek, A. (1981), *Nation and Revolution*, Vol.2, Macmillan, London.

Amin, S. (1978), *The Arab Nation: Nationalism and Class Struggles*, Zed Books, London.

———— (1980), *Class and Nation*, Heinemann, London.

Anderson, B. (1983), *Imagined Communities: Reflections on the Origin and Spread of Nationalism*, New Left Books, London.

Avineri, S. (ed.), (1969), *Karl Marx on Colonialism and Modernisation*, Anchor Books, New York.

Beresford, Ellis P. (ed.), (1973), *James Connolly: Selected Writings*, Penguin, Harmondsworth.

Bloom, S. (1967), *The World of Nations: A Study of the National Implications in the Work of Karl Marx*, AMS Press, New York.

Boersner, D. (1982), *The Bolsheviks and the National and Colonial Question (1917-1928)*, Hyperion Press, Connecticut.

Borochov, B. (1973), *Nationalism and Class Struggle: A Marxian Approach to the Jewish Problem*, Greenwood Press, Connecticut.

Breuilly, J. (1982), *Nationalism and the State*, Manchester University Press.

Cahm, E. and Fisera, V.C. (eds.), (1978), *Socialism and Nationalism*, Spokesman, Nottingham.

Carr, E.H. (1945), *Nationalism and After*, Macmillan, London.

———— (1982), *The Twilight of Comintern 1930-1935*, Macmillan, London.

Chun, L. (1966), *The National Question and Class Struggle*, Foreign Language Publications, Peking.

Carrère d'Encausse, H. and S. Schram (eds.), (1969), *Marxism and Asia*, Allen Lane The Penguin Press, London.

Connor, W. (1984), *The National Question in Marxist-Leninist Theory and Strategy*, Princeton University Press.

Cummings, I. (1980) *Marx, Engels and National Movements*, Croom Helm, London.

Davis, H.B. (1967), *Nationalism and Socialism: Marxist and Labor Theories of Nationalism to 1917*, Monthly Review Press, New York.

———— (1978), *Toward a Marxist Theory of Nationalism*, Monthly Review Press, New York.

Evans, G. and Rowley, K. (1984), *Red Brotherhood at War: Indochina Since the Fall of Saigon*, New Left Books, London.

Gellner, E. (1983), *Nations and Nationalism*, Basil Blackwell, Oxford.

Haupt, G. (1972), *Socialism and the Great War: The Collapse of the Second*

International, Clarendon Press, Oxford.

Herod, C. (1976), *The Nation in the History of Marxian Thought*, Martinus Nijhoff, The Hague.

Jayawardena, K. (1986), *Feminism and Nationalism in the Third World*, Zed Books, London.

Jenkins, B. and Minnerup, G. (1984), *Citizens and Comrades: Socialism in a World of Nation States*, Pluto Press, London.

Lenin, V.I. (1974), *Critical Remarks on the National Question: The Right of Nations to Self-Determination*, Progress Publishers, Moscow.

Logue, J. (1980), *Towards a Theory of Trade Union Internationalism*, Kent Popular Press, Kent, Ohio.

Low, A. (1951), *Lenin on the Question of Nationality*, International Publishers, New York.

Luxemburg, R. (1976), *The National Question: Selected Writings* (ed. by H.B. Davis), Monthly Review Press, New York.

Macfarlane, S.N. (1984), *Superpower Rivalry and Third World Radicalism*, Croom Helm, London.

Marx, K. and Engels, F. (1971), *Ireland and the Irish Question*, Progress Publishers, Moscow.

Nairn, T. (1977), *The Break-up of Britain: Crisis and Neo-Nationalism*, New Left Books, London.

Pipes, R. (1954), *The Formation of the Soviet Union: Communism and Nationalism, 1917-1923*, Harvard University Press, Cambridge, Mass.

Ponnambalam, S. (1984), *Sri Lanka: The National Question and the Tamil Liberation Struggle*, Zed Books, London.

Sathyamurthy, T.V. (1984), *Nationalism in the Contemporary World*, Frances Pinter, London.

Seers, D. (1983), *The Political Economy of Nationalism*, Oxford University Press.

Shaheen, S. (1956), *The Communist (Bolshevik) Theory of National Self-Determination*, W. Van Hoeve, The Hague.

Shoup, P. (1968), *Communism and the Yugoslav National Question*, Columbia University Press, New York.

Sizwe, No (1979), *One Azania, One Nation: The National Question in South Africa*, Zed Books, London.

Smith, A. (1983) *State and Nation in the Third World*, Wheatsheaf Books, Brighton.

Stalin, J. (1971), *Marxism and the National Question*, Progress Publishers, Moscow.

Tibi, B. (1981), *Arab Nationalism: A Critical Enquiry*, Macmillan Press, London.

Trotsky, L. (1971), *The War and the International*, Wesley Press, Wellawalle.

Waterman, P. (ed.), (1984), *For a New Labour Internationalism*, ILERI, The Hague.

Zwick, P. (1983), *National Communism*, Westview Press, Boulder, CO.

Articles

Arrighi, G. and Saul, J. (1973), 'Nationalism and Revolution in Sub-Saharan Africa', in their *Essays on the Political Economy of Africa*, Monthly Review Press, New York.

Bauer, O. (1978), 'The Concept of the "Nation" ' in T. Bottomore and P. Goode (eds.), *Austro-Marxism*, Clarendon Press, Oxford.

Blaut, J. (1981), 'Nairn on Nationalism', *Antipode*, Vol. 12, No. 2.

——— (1982), 'Nationalism as an Autonomous Force', *Science and Society*, Vol. XLVI, No. 1.

Carr, E.H. (1971), 'The Bolshevik Doctrine of Self-Determination', in his *The Bolshevik Revolution 1917-1923: 1*, Penguin, Harmondsworth.

Carrère d'Encausse, H. (1971), 'Unité proletarienne et diversité nationale: Lenin et la théorie de l'autodétermination', *Revue Francaise de Science Politique*, Vol. 1, No. 2.

Critique Communiste (1976), *Marxisme et Question Nationale*, special issue No. 10.

Deutscher, I. (1971), 'On internationals and internationalism', in his *Marxism in Our Time*, Ramparts Press, Berkeley.

Ehrenreich, J. (1983), 'Socialism, Nationalism and Capitalist Development', *Review of Radical Political Economics*, Vol. XV, No. 1.

El Kodsky, A. (1970), 'Nationalism and Class Struggles in the Arab World', *Monthly Review*, Vol. 33, No. 2.

Forgas, D. (1984), 'National-Popular: Genealogy of a Concept', *Formations: Of Nations and People*, Routledge and Kegan Paul, London.

Freitag, M. (1981), 'Theorie marxiste et realité nationale: autopsie d'un malentendu', *Pluriel*, No. 26.

Gellner, E. (1981), 'Nationalism', *Theory and Society*, No. 10.

Gilbert, A. (1978), 'Marx on Internationalism and War', *Philosophy and Public Affairs*, Vol. 7, No. 4.

Gomez-Quiñones, J. (1982), 'Critique of the national question: self-determination and nationalism', *Latin American Perspectives*, Vol. IX, No. 2.

Gorter, H. (1978), 'The Origins of Nationalism in the Proletariat', in D. Smart (ed.), *Pannekoek and Gorter's Marxism*, Pluto Press, London.

Haupt, G. (1977), 'Dynamisme et conservatisme de ideologie: Rosa Luxemburg a l'oree de la recherche marxiste dans le domain nationale', *Pluriel*, No. 11.

Hobsbawm, E. (1972), 'Some Reflections on Nationalism', in T. Nossiter *et al.*, (eds.), *Imagination and Precision in the Social Sciences*, Faber and Faber, London.

——— (1977), 'Some Reflections on "The Break-up of Britain" ', *New Left Review*, No. 105.

Howard, P. (1967), 'The Definition of a Nation: A Discussion in Voprosy Istrioni', *Central Asian Review*, Vol. XV, No. 1.

Kiernan, V. (1976), 'Nationalist Movements and Social Classes', in A. Smith (ed.), *Nationalist Movements*, Macmillan, London.

Löwy, M. (1976), 'Marxists and the National Question, *New Left Review*, No. 96.

Maldonado-Denis, M. (1976), 'Prospects for Latin American Nationalism: the case of Puerto Rico', *Latin American Perspectives*, Vol. 111, No. 3.

Mariategui, J.C. (1977), 'The Anti-Imperialist Perspective', *New Left Review*, No. 70.

Matossian, M. (1957), 'Two Marxist Approaches to Nationalism', *The American Slavic and East European Review*, No. 4.

Nairn, T. (1975), 'The Modern Janus', *New Left Review*, No. 94.

Nimni, E. (1985), 'Marxism and Nationalism', *Capital and Class*, No. 25.

Mann, M. (1983), 'Nationalism and Internationalism', in J. Griffith (ed.), *Socialism in a Cold Climate*, Allen and Unwin, London.

Orridge, A.W. (1982), 'Uneven Development and Nationalism', Part 1 and 2, *Political Studies*, Vol. XXIX, No. 1 and No. 2.

Pannekoek, A. (1978), 'Class Struggle and the Nation', in D. Smart (ed.), *Pannekoek and Gorter's Marxism*, Pluto Press, London.

Partisans (1971), *Le Domaine Nationale* (1), special issue No. 59-60.

Petrus, J.A., 'Marx and Engels on the national question', *Journal of Politics*, No. 33.

————— (1971), 'The Theory and Practice of Internationalism: Rosa Luxemburg's Solution to the National Question', *East European Quarterly*, Vol. IV, No. 4.

Person, Y. (1976), 'Contre l'Etat Nation', *Pluriel*, No. 8.

Poulantzas, N. (1978), 'The Nation', in his *State, Power and Socialism*, New Left Books, London.

Rodinson, M. (1968), 'Le Marxisme et la Nation', *L'Homme et la Societé*, January-March.

Rosdolsky, R. (1965), ' "Worker and Fatherland": A Note on a Passage in The Communist Manifesto', *Science and Society*, Vol. XXIX, No. 3.

Terray, E. (1973), 'L'ideé de nation et les transformations du capitalisme', *Les Temps Modernes*, Vol. 2.

Vilar, P. (1979), 'Nationalism', *Marxist Perspectives*, No. 51.

Wallerstein, E. (1984), 'Nationalism and the world transition to socialism: is there a crisis?', in his *The Politics of the World Economy*, Cambridge University Press.

Wright, A.W. (1981), 'Socialism and Nationalism' in L. Tivey (ed.), *The Nation-State*, Martin Robertson, Oxford.

Zubaida, S. (1978), 'Theories of Nationalism', in G. Littlejohn *et al.*, *Power and the State*, Croom Helm, London.

Index